MULTICULTURAL EDUCATION SERIES

James A. Banks, *Series Editor*

(continued)

Black Male(d)

Peril and Promise in the Education of African American Males

Tyrone C. Howard

Foreword by Pedro A. Noguera

Teachers College, Columbia University
New York and London

Published by Teachers College Press, 1234 Amsterdam Avenue, New York, NY 10027

Library of Congress Cataloging-in-Publication Data

Howard, Tyrone C. (Tyrone Caldwell)
Black male(d) : peril and promise in the education of African American males / Tyrone C. Howard ; foreword by Pedro Noguera.
  pages cm. – (Multicultural education series)
Includes bibliographical references and index.
ISBN 978-0-8077-5490-0 (pbk. : alk. paper)
ISBN 978-0-8077-5491-7 (hardcover : alk. paper)
ISBN 978-0-8077-7245-4 (ebook)
   1. African American boys–Education. 2. African American young men–Education. 3. Academic achievement–United States. 4. Educational equalization–United States. I. Title.
LC2731.H68 2014
371.829'96073–dc23   2013032553

ISBN 978-0-8077-5490-0 (paper)
ISBN 978-0-8077-5491-7 (hardcover)
eISBN 978-0-8077-7245-4 (ebook)

Printed on acid-free paper
Manufactured in the United States of America

21 20 19 18 17 16 15 14   8 7 6 5 4 3 2 1

Dedicated to
Jabari, Jaleel, & Jahlani, three young men who defy stereotypes every day

Contents

Series Foreword

The popular media as well as a litany of scholarly publications describe the enormous and intractable problems that African American males experience in schools and in society writ large. One of the earliest publications in this genre has this evocative title, *Young, Black, and Male in America: An Endangered Species* (Taylor Gibbs, 1988). This seminal and trenchant book by Tyrone Howard turns the deficit perspective from which the schooling experiences of Africans Americans is frequently viewed on its head by describing the resilience of Black male youth, providing profiles of their academic success, and enabling readers to view their experiences from a critical theory perspective. Howard calls for a paradigm shift in the ways in which Black male students are viewed and taught in school. He also describes practical interventions and strategies that educators can implement to improve the academic achievement and social development of Black male students.

The description of student voices in *Black Male(d)* is a valuable and pioneering contribution to the literature because it provides student perspectives on their experiences in school and society, which have been largely neglected in the educational literature. Howard—similar to other visionary scholars such as Lund (2003), Nieto (1994), and Osler (2010)—skillfully uses student voices to reveal important insights and understandings about the lives of students in schools and how they interpret their experiences. The students' descriptions of their school, home, and community experiences in this book are astute, introspective, and revealing. Some of the most perceptive and troubling observations made by the students describe ways in which they are silenced and victimized by teachers and how they are sometimes complicit in their own victimization. The voices of the students are occasionally poignant and troubling, but are often empowering and encouraging because they reveal the tenacity of the human spirit and the resilience of individual students who succeed against tremendous odds.

Another salient, significant, and timely contribution of this well-crafted, engaging, and heartfelt book is the way in which Howard problematizes and explains the complexity and diversity of the experiences of Black males in American society. African American males are too often perceived and responded to as a monolithic group, which often leads to stereotyped conceptions and responses to them. Howard describes the enormous diversity that exists among African American males, which includes differences in social class, attitudes toward achievement, family background, degree of community support, and level of resilience and persistence.

This informative and incisive book will help teachers and other educational practitioners to acquire knowledge and insights needed to better understand the experiences of African Americans males and to creative educational interventions that will enable them to experience more academic success in school and to acquire the knowledge, skills, and attitudes required to become effective participants in the nation's mainstream cultural and civic communities. Reforming the structure of schools to make them more empowering and effective for Black males and more culturally empowering will greatly benefit students from other marginalized and diverse groups who are rapidly increasing in the nation's schools because of immigration.

American classrooms are experiencing the largest influx of immigrant students since the beginning of the 20th century. Almost 14 million new immigrants—documented and undocumented—settled in the United States in the years from 2000 to 2010. Less than 10% came from nations in Europe. Most came from Mexico, nations in Asia, and nations in Latin America, the Caribbean, and Central America (Comarota, 2011). A large but undetermined number of undocumented immigrants enter the United States each year. The U.S. Department of Homeland Security (2010) estimated that in January 2010 10.8 million undocumented immigrants were living in the United States, which was a decrease from the estimated 11.8 million that resided in the United States in January 2007. In 2007, approximately 3.2 million children and young adults were among the 11.8 million undocumented immigrants in the United States, most of whom grew up in the this country (Perez, 2011). The influence of an increasingly ethnically diverse population in U.S. schools, colleges, and universities is and will continue to be enormous.

Schools in the United States are more diverse today than they have been since the early 1900s when a multitude of immigrants entered the U.S. from Southern, Central, and Eastern Europe. In the 20-year period between 1989 and 2009, the percentage of students of color in U.S. public schools increased from 32% to 45% (Aud, Hussar, Kena, Blanco, Frohlich, Kemp, & Tahan, 2011). If current trends continue, students of color will equal or exceed the percentage of White students in U.S. public schools within 1 or 2 decades. In 2010–2011, students of color exceeded the number of Whites students in the District of Columbia and in 13 states (listed in descending order of the percentage of ethnic minority students therein): Hawaii, California, New Mexico, Texas, Nevada, Arizona, Florida, Maryland, Mississippi, Georgia, Louisiana, Delaware, and New York (Aud, Hussar, Johnson, Kena, Roth, Manning, Wang, & Zhang, 2012). In 2009, children of undocumented immigrants made up 6.8% of students in kindergarten through grade 12 (Perez, 2011).

Language and religious diversity is also increasing in the U.S. student population. The 2010 American Community Survey indicates that approximately 19.8% of the school-age population spoke a language at home other than English that year (U.S. Census Bureau, 2010). The Progressive Policy Institute (2008) estimated that 50 million Americans (out of 300 million) spoke a language at home other than English in 2008. Harvard professor Diana L. Eck (2001) calls the United States the "most religiously diverse nation on earth" (p. 4). Islam is now the fastest-growing religion in the United States, as well as in several European nations such as France, the United Kingdom, and the Netherlands (Banks, 2009; Cesari, 2004). Most teachers now in the classroom and in teacher education programs are likely to have students from diverse ethnic, racial, linguistic, and religious groups in their classrooms during their careers. This is true for both inner-city and suburban teachers in the United States, as well as in many other Western nations such as Canada, Australia, and the United Kingdom (Banks, 2009).

The major purpose of the Multicultural Education Series is to provide preservice educators, practicing educators, graduate students, scholars, and policymakers with an interrelated and comprehensive set of books that summarizes and analyzes important research, theory, and practice related to the education of ethnic, racial, cultural, and linguistic groups in the United States and the education of mainstream students about diversity. The dimensions of multicultural education, developed by Banks (2004) and described in the *Handbook of Research on Multicultural Education* and in the *Encyclopedia of Diversity in Education* (Banks, 2012), provide the conceptual framework for the development of the publications in the Series. They are content integration, the knowledge construction process, prejudice reduction, an equity pedagogy, and an empowering institutional culture and social structure.

The books in the Series provide research, theoretical, and practical knowledge about the behaviors and learning characteristics of students of color, language minority students, low-income students, and other minoritized population groups. They also provide knowledge about ways to improve academic achievement and race relations in educational settings. Multicultural education is consequently as important for middle-class White suburban students as it is for students of color who live in the inner city. Multicultural education fosters the public good and the overarching goals of the commonwealth.

This insightful, needed, empowering, and inspiring book makes a number of significant, original, and timely contributions to the literature on diversity and the education of marginalized youth. Although Tyrone Howard focuses on the plight, potential, and resilience of African American male students, the insights, findings, and analyses in this well conceptualized and discerning book have significant implications for improving the education of all students who are victimized by pernicious stereotypes and marginalization within schools and society. I hope that researchers and practicing educators will give this book the serious attention, deliberation, and reflection that it deserves and appreciate the need to improve the education of all of the nation's students.

–James A. Banks

REFERENCES

Aud, S., Hussar, W., Johnson, F., Kena, G., Roth, E., Manning, E., Wang, X., & Zhang, J. (2012). *The condition of education 2012* (NCES 2012-045). Washington, DC: U.S. Department of Education, National Center for Education Statistics. Available at from http://nces.ed.gov/pubsearch

Aud, S., Hussar, W., Kena, G., Bianco, K., Frohlich, L., Kemp, J., & Tahan, K. (2011). *The condition of education 2011* (NCES 2011-033). U.S. Department of Education, National Center for Education Statistics. Washington, DC: U.S. Department of Education, National Center for Education Statistics. Available at http://nces.ed.gov/programs/coe/pdf/coe_1er.pdf

Banks, J. A. (2004). Multicultural education: Historical development, dimensions, and practice. In J.A. Banks & C.A.M. Banks (Eds.), *Handbook of research on multicultural education* (2nd ed., pp. 3–29). San Francisco, CA: Jossey-Bass.

Banks, J. A. (2012). Multicultural education: Dimensions of. In J.A. Banks (Ed.), *Encyclopedia of diversity in education* (vol. 3, pp. 1538–1547). Thousand Oaks, CA: Sage Publications.

Camarota, S. A. (2011, October). *A record-setting decade of immigration: 2000 to 2010*. Washingtton, DC: Center for Immigration Studies. Available at http://cis.org/2000-2010-record-setting-decade-of-immigration

Cesari, J. (2004). *When Islam and democracy meet: Muslims in Europe and the United States*. New York, NY: Palgrave Macmillan.

Eck, D. L. (2001). *A new religious America: How a "Christian country" has become the world's most religiously diverse nation*. San Francisco, CA: HarperSanFrancisco.

Lund, D. E. (2003). Facing the challenges: Student antiracist activists counter backlash and stereotyping. *Teaching Education Journal, 14*, 265–278.

Nieto, S. (1994). Lessons from students on creating a chance to dream. *Harvard Educational Review, 64*(4), 392–426.

Osler, A. (2010). *Students' perspectives on schooling*. New York, NY: McGraw-Hill.

Perez, W. (2011). *Americans by heart: Undocumented Latino students and the promise of higher education*. New York, NY: Teachers College Press.

Progressive Policy Institute. (2008). *50 million Americans speak languages other than English at home*. Available at http://www.ppionline.org/ppi_ci.cfm?knlgAreaID=108&subsecID=900003&contentID=254619

Roberts, S. (2008, August 14). A generation away, minorities may become the majority in U.S. *The New York Times*, vol. CLVII [175] (no. 54,402), pp. A1 & A18.

Taylor Gibbs, J. (Ed.). (1988). *Young, Black, and male in America: An endangered species*. Westport, CT: Auburn House.

U.S. Census Bureau. (2008, August 14). *Statistical abstract of the United States*. Available at http://www.census.gov/prod/2006pubs/07statab/pop.pdf

U.S. Census Bureau. (2010). *2010 American community survey*. Available at http://factfinder2.census.gov/faces/tableservices/jsf/pages/productview.xhtml?pid=ACS_10_1YR_S1603&prodType=table

U.S. Department of Homeland Security. (2010, February). *Estimates of the unauthorized immigrant population residing in the United States: January 2010*. Available at http://www.dhs.gov/files/statistics/immigration.shtm

Foreword

...if we want humanity to advance a step farther, if we want to bring it up to a different level than that which Europe has shown it, then we must invent and we must make discoveries. . . .

    For Europe, for ourselves and for humanity, comrades, we must turn over a new leaf, we must work out new concepts, and try to set afoot a *new man.*

—Franz Fanon, *Black Skin, White Mask*

The Martiniquan psychologist Franz Fanon made his call for a new man during the 1960s, as territories throughout Africa and Asia were emerging as new nations, freed from the yoke of colonialism. Fanon understood that in order for independence and decolonization to mean more than merely a change in flags, it would require a transformation that was far more profound; a change in the very notion of what it meant to be human. The "old man" (or woman for that matter) Fanon sought to do away with was a cultural product of a colonial system, and he understood more than most that colonialism was more than merely a system of economic exploitation. For Fanon, colonialism was most significantly a system of psychological oppression and ideological control, premised on the notion of the inherent inferiority of the colonial subjects. He recognized that until the colonized subject was able to reject the distorted image of self that had been imposed through the colonial experience, it would be impossible to construct a new personhood or new society, free from the damaging psychological bonds of colonialism (Fanon, 1967).

    Like Fanon, Tyrone Howard has set out to construct a new way of seeing and understanding Black males in American society. Yet, unlike others who have embraced the need to "save" Black males, he seeks to do much more than raise achievement and increase graduation rates. Howard is more ambitious. He seeks to initiate a paradigm shift in the way Black men and boys are seen and understood, recognizing like Fanon, that without such a shift, a genuine change in outcomes and circumstances will not be possible. He has undertaken this Herculean task because he understands that the current image of the Black male—as an underachiever, a thug, a criminal, a sexual deviant and predator, a shiftless father, and brainless athlete—is literally destroying Black men and boys.

Unlike Fanon who tied the liberation of the colonized subject to the demise of colonialism, Howard casts his gaze upon schools and calls for them to play a different role than they have historically in educating, socializing, and nurturing Black boys. Though Howard's chosen path to Black male salvation might seem less arduous and perhaps even less ambitious than the one called for by Fanon, those who are familiar with the Black male experience in American schools today will understand the parallels between the two struggles. Like colonized subjects whose ability to realize freedom and equality is limited by their inferior status and their subordinate relationship to the colonizer, Black males in American schools are more often than not trapped in categories associated with hardship and failure. As a group, they are distinguished by their pervasive and persistent clustering in all categories associated with academic pathology—most likely to be behind academically, to be in need of remediation, to be held back, to drop out, to be missing from indicators associated with success and disproportionately present in those associated with failure, or to be punished. Subject to a broad array of structural and psychological barriers that thwart and constrain their ability to thrive, schools have too often become the place where the hopes and dreams of Blacks males are crushed, and ironically the place where their love of learning is destroyed.

Thankfully, Howard is not content with merely indicting the educational system. As a committed scholar, a dedicated practitioner and a loving father to three Black males himself, he understands that he has a responsibility to offer concrete recommendations for what can be done to transform schools so that they can become a source of support for those they too often fail. He does this with clarity and a keen awareness of the challenges present within school systems where negative stereotypes are pervasive and the failure of Black males has been normalized. Howard offers his readers much more than a critique; he provides concrete ideas and strategies for how to beyond the dismal reality of the present.

He is also aware that the obstacles to Black male success don't lie exclusively within schools. He understands that formidable barriers are present outside of school: in families that are in crisis; in communities mired in poverty, unemployment, and despair; in media images that promote athleticism over intellectualism, and in the large numbers of Black men wallowing behind bars in prisons and jails, subject to America's unofficial policy of mass incarceration (Alexander, 2010). Howard puts forth his recommendations for school change ever conscious that we cannot wait until the external barriers fade. He understands that too many lives are being lost every day, and we cannot afford to wait.

Like Fanon, Howard is more than a reformer. He seeks to dismantle a system that stifles dreams, devours hopes, and destroys opportunities. In its place he wants to help schools become places where Black men and boys can grow, learn, and develop their human potential without the encumbrances of constrained opportunities and lowered expectations. He offers us a road map for how to do this and an invitation to join him in this venture. Let us hope that more than a few of those who read this book will enthusiastically accept his offer and join him in this important work.

–Pedro A. Noguera

REFERENCES

Alexander, M. (2010). *The New Jim Crow*. New York, NY: The New Press.
Fanon, F. (1967). *Black Skin, White Mask*. New York, NY: Grove Press.

Acknowledgments

A project such as this one is a labor of love. However, this book would not come to fruition without the support of many people. I would like to acknowledge Jim Banks for his ongoing support and mentorship. I would like to thank Brian Ellerbeck with Teachers College Press, as well as Jennifer Baker who both provided valuable feedback on this project. I also want to acknowledge the staff I work with at the UCLA Black Male Institute. Samarah Blackmon, Terry Flennaugh, LaMont Terry, Rachel Thomas, Devon Minor, and Brian Woodward all are dedicated and committed to the study and improvement of the plight of Black males, and I want to thank each of them. I also would like to acknowledge Tr'Vel Lyons for his work with the BMI, and his gathering of data and graph and chart development. You are a brilliant young man! I also would like to thank Laura Cervantes and Justin McClinton for their research on this project. I want to thank Maisah Howard for her editing, feedback, support and encouragement on this book. I also want to thank Jameelah Howard for her support and interest in all of my work. My parents Beverly Sisnett, Caldwell, and Johonna Howard are always a source of tremendous support. Thanks for believing. I also want to acknowledge Rich Milner for the ongoing conversations about this work, and staying on me about getting it done. Finally, I would like to thank each of the young men who provided their insights, stories, recommendations, and concerns about improving schools. Their intellect was incredible, and I am indebted to you all!

And a special thanks to Debbie Allen for her design of the book development.

Introduction

This book addresses the concerns of Black males in schools, and the ramifications that current school outcomes have for them in society writ large. This work is unapologetic in its focus on Black males because of the myriad concerns affecting this population. Many of the dismal realities facing Black males will be identified, analyzed, and discussed in this book. I have been moved to address this population for a number of reasons both professional and personal. On a professional level, I have traveled across the country and worked with countless numbers of school districts: urban, rural, and suburban; Midwest, southwest, east and west coasts. I have been fortunate enough to work in traditional public, public charter, small private, Catholic, and independent schools. When I ask the person who has invited me to participate in working with the district what some of the most pressing issues facing the particular school or district are, without exception the most common response I hear is, "Can you help us with our Black boys?" This constant plea has left me flummoxed, confused, curious, sad, and angered. In particular, I am often curious as to why schools ask me for help in this area. I recognize my role as a practitioner and scholar who has researched and written about this population. But I also wonder whether my being Black and male has something to do with it. Yet colleagues who are not male and not Black have told me that they are often presented with a similar plea: "Can you help us with our Black males?" I am often curious as to why Black boys are frequently the group that most schools struggle to educate. I am also saddened as to why Black boys are the group most frequently described as being "in crisis" or "in need of intervention," whether they are in small numbers in a school district like Des Moines, Iowa, or a large urban district like Chicago or New York.

On a personal level I am often motivated by this work because I am a Black male who grew up in a predominately Black community (Compton, California) in the 1970s and 1980s, and witnessed firsthand the unlimited amounts of human potential in Black males that, for a variety of reasons, never reaches its zenith. Most of my closest friends when I was growing up were Black males, and I wonder how and why in many instances our paths have differed. Some might suggest that I am a university professor because of choices, determination, hard work, and home environment. I do not discount

1

those factors—they do matter—but I would respond that those same factors applied to many of the Black males I grew up with, yet they did not have the same outcomes as I. In fact, some of their outcomes have been tragic and disheartening, to say the least. Disparate outcomes for Black males have left me asking why and disappointed in how young men growing up in the same communities and similar family structures can have such different educational outcomes and life trajectories. Finally, I am concerned about this topic because as the father of three Black males, I have witnessed their journeys through schools, and the multitude of obstacles that they encounter academically, socially, and culturally. Currently, one of my sons is in college, and the other two are in high school. One would think that their positionality would allow them to escape many of the ailments that afflict many Black males. Yet, in many instances, it has not. Their success often has been questioned. On occasion they have been profiled. And in many ways they still have to negotiate the murky terrain that comes with being a Black male in a predominately White society. They are being raised in a two-parent household, by college-educated parents. All of my sons (and my daughter) attend what many would consider to be "good schools," with highly acclaimed teachers, yet they each have faced unique challenges in their educational journey.

I do not negate, dismiss, or ignore the fact that many of the issues that will be discussed in this book are happening to many other student groups, namely, males of color, and more specifically Latino and Southeast Asian males. I applaud the scholars who have been deliberate in their research investigating those groups (Baldridge, Hill, & Davis, 2011; Conchas & Vigil, 2012; Noguera, 2008). I frequently am asked why only focus on Black males when so many other groups encounter similar challenges. While this position is well taken and holds merit, my contention is that many Black males' severely, intensely, and persistently negative experience with schools requires a laser-type focus and analysis solely on them to seek viable interventions and solutions. The sheer litany of data that I will detail in this book provides overwhelming evidence that suggests Black males experience schools in a different way—sometimes a vastly different way—from any other population. Furthermore, if schools take the required steps to improve the experiences and outcomes of Black males, undoubtedly all other groups will become direct and indirect beneficiaries. I believe strongly in the idiom that "a rising tide lifts all boats." I also am reminded of a statement one of my mentors would frequently quip, "When you help those at the bottom, everyone gains." The other argument that I hear, as I speak about this work, comes from those who contend that there is a need for a more structural analysis and critique of capitalism, and that many students, not just Blacks and males, are victims of capitalism. Again, I recognize the effects of structural inequality and how myriad groups have been affected by limited access to resources and opportunities. Hence, many of these claims are steeped in Marxist, or class-based critique (Massey & Denton, 1993; McLaren, 2006). My rebuttal to this claim is that when one looks at individual groups that have been most severely affected by structural arrangements, Black males arguably have been most damaged by them. In many ways, the outcomes that are witnessed by Black men and boys are a by-product of the historical legacy of slavery, economic and educational exclusion, and political disenfranchisement. I seek to be clear that it is not my intent to engage in a quest to show that Black males have suffered more than any other group. Engaging in such a conversation borders on an "Oppression Olympics" discourse, which would be counterproductive at best, and divisive and destructive at worst. To the contrary, the remnants of racism, sexism, homophobia, xenophobia, and economic exploitation have affected countless groups. However, it is not the focus of this work to examine the multiple types of oppression that afflict various groups. They, too, experience extreme challenges in navigating the academic pathway. This work also recognizes the challenges that Black girls experience in schools and society at large (see Winn, 2011). This population frequently is overlooked because Black girls fare better in schools than Black males; however, an analysis of their outcomes shows that they perform far below their White, Asian, and Latina counterparts. I am pleased to note that the number of works on Black girls is increasing, and there is important scholarship on this group and their experiences (R. N. Brown, 2009; Evans-Winters, 2005; Gurian, 2001).

In this book, "Black males" is used in a broad sense. This book does not focus only on those young men who identify as African American, although they represent a large section of the group being discussed. I want to acknowledge that Black males born outside of the United States experience many of the issues that will be discussed in this work. Black males who are biracial or multiracial are often marginalized in schools as well. It is also important to state from the outset that this work attempts to move beyond monolithic accounts of Black males. One of the limitations with many of the previous works on Black males has been the manner in which they have sought to capture "the Black male experience." This book challenges the notion of a unitary experience for Black males. Moreover, in this book I attempt to create a more dynamic and comprehensive account of Black males. Much of this work seeks to capture voices of high-, middle-, and low-achieving Black males, as well as Black males who attend inner-city and suburban schools. I also have sought to incorporate the voices of non-gender-conforming males, heterosexual and homosexual males, and athletes as well as non-athletes, in addition to capturing the schooling experiences of Black males from different regions of the country. One of the more disturbing trends that was uncovered in this work is the increasing numbers of Black males in foster care. What we know is that Black males are one of the largest subgroups in foster care in this country and are the group least likely to be adopted (Ryan, Testa, & Zhai, 2008). So the intent of this work is fourfold; (1) to identify trends and realities in the state of education for Black males, (2) to discuss theoretical tenets involved in how to improve the schooling experiences and outcomes of Black males, (3) to hear directly from Black males about how they perceive schools, and (4) to identify useful ideas, effective community-based and programmatic interventions, as well as impactful recommendations, cautions, and concerns for future work on Black males.

This book draws from several studies that I have been involved in, or conducted, with Black males over the past 5 years. I have been fortunate to work with a number of school districts, social service agencies, community-based organizations, university-related projects, and national initiatives that focus on Black males. In each of these works we have conducted either surveys, formal interviews, focus groups, or a number of informal conversations with young men about their realities in schools and beyond. I also have drawn heavily on my experiences with my own sons as they have navigated their schooling process. I have queried them for countless hours about their experiences, what issues they encounter as young Black males, and how they develop coping mechanisms to deal with the challenges from school personnel and peers. I have gained new insights from all of the young men I have been able to interact with over the years. I am grateful to each of these young men for sharing their thoughts and impressions. Without them, this work would not be as insightful.

Throughout each of these works, common themes have emerged; one of them is that many Black males succeed in spite of schools and not because of them. Most of these young men demonstrate an uncanny resilience that allows them to persevere in the face of adversity, and at times in uncaring schools. Sadly, many have fallen prey to the circumstances in schools. Some blame themselves for not taking school more seriously, working hard enough, or being more focused, while others have expressed a penetrating and well-informed critique of schools and have questioned whether their failure is by design. Another theme that emerges is that identifying support structures, whether family, peers, or school personnel, is a fundamental variable for those who have positive experiences and outcomes with schools. A number of these young men talked about how they would not have gotten as far as they did, or would not have struggled, without the support of important people along the pathway. Finally, another theme that emerges is around hope: those who are hopeful and those who are on the verge of hopelessness. Many young men believe that their life chances are limitless, and are taking steps to recognize those ambitions. Conversely, there is a segment of this population that is angry, disengaged, and unclear about many things in life, and school is chief among them. The social, emotional, and psychological spirit of many of these young men seems to be damaged beyond repair in some cases, and this is what concerns me most.

ORGANIZATION OF THE BOOK

This book is divided into seven chapters. In the first chapter, I will provide an overview of the educational status of African American males in U.S. schools. This chapter will include current trends and data on the location of African American males in cities across the country, achievement and dropout data, college-going rates, and suspension and expulsion statistics. These data will be examined in an attempt to provide a comprehensive account of African American males, as well as to examine general directions in achievement over the past several decades. Explicating data from multiple sources, such as the U.S. Department of Education and the National Center for Education Statistics, this chapter will seek to provide a foundation that helps to make the case that there is a pressing need to offer authentic interventions to disrupt the current state of affairs for African American males.

In Chapter 2, I will address African American male images from an historical and contemporary perspective. Many of the portrayals of African American males historically have been centered within an anti-intellectual framework that portrays them as culturally and socially deviant, criminal minded, academically inept, and morally bankrupt. Over the past 4 decades a number of works have sought to disrupt these accounts of African American males and create an image that offers a more affirming and humanizing depiction of them in schools and society. Despite these efforts, African American males continue to be undereducated, over-incarcerated, socially and culturally misunderstood, and in pursuit of an identity that allows them to be viewed as intellectually adept and worthy of inclusion in the American dream. The goal of this chapter will be to explore the historical role that social imagery may have on the current state of educational and social outcomes for African American males. This chapter offers an account of how researchers and practitioners can conduct their work in a manner that rejects pathological identities for African American males in pre-K–12 schools and develop a more comprehensive and complex account of them that recognizes their academic promise and multifaceted identities.

In Chapter 3, I use a critical race theory framework to ask the question "Who Really Cares?" about the educational aspirations of African American males. The chapter includes qualitative data from a study of African American males who offer counterstorytelling accounts of their schooling experiences. This chapter also explores the utility and appropriateness of critical race theory as a methodological tool to examine and disrupt the disenfranchisement of African American males in U.S. public schools.

In Chapter 4, I will discuss the lure of sports for African American males. While there has been chronic underperformance of African American males in schools across the country, they continue to be overrepresented in the field of athletics. A litany of works has documented the African American male experience with sports over the past century (C. Harrison, 2007; Harrison & Lawrence, 2003). However, in this chapter I raise the question about the utility of athletics for African American males at a time when sports often are given much more time and attention than academic pursuit and excellence. The academic/athletic paradigm is examined in light of the growing numbers of young men who pursue athletic stardom often at the expense of pursuing academic prowess. The chapter will look at the role of sports in many African American communities and how males often are expected to use athletic talents to salvage financial freedoms for friends and family. This chapter will include interview data from young men, and their parents, about the importance of sports in their lives, the role of academics, and how the two complement or contradict each other.

Chapter 5 will focus specifically on the voices and perspectives of African American males and how they define success in schools, the issues that they believe most influence their schooling experiences, and, more important, what they believe are viable approaches to disrupt the chronic underperformance of many African American males. Drawing from a series of focus groups, survey data, and individual interviews, this chapter examines African American male voices in an authentic and unedited fashion. The purpose is to hear from African American males in urban and suburban communities, from high-achieving and low-achieving African American males, from those who are in elementary, middle, and high school. The goal is to show the complexity and diversity in the experiences and perspectives of African American males. This chapter also highlights the ways in which many share some of the same experiences despite their ages, the communities where they reside, and their experiences in schools.

Chapter 6 will center on cases of African American male success. The goal of this chapter is to make a paradigmatic and conceptual shift away from viewing African American males as being uneducable and academically inferior, to examining research, schools, and programs in which African American males experience academic and social success. An examination of the research and theory on African American male success will provide a much-needed movement away from much of the current literature. It will make a needed contribution toward the development of a more comprehensive and robust picture of the African American male experience in schools–– not one situated in deficit-laden accounts of African American male achievement, but one dedicated to the development of an ideological transformation of the African American male identity in schools.

Finally, Chapter 7, which is titled "The Obama Paradox," examines research on African American males in what some are attempting to label the first U.S. "post-racial" era. In this final chapter, I problematize the term *post-racial* and any suggestion that the United States is beyond race and that race no longer matters in U.S. life, law, policy, and educational experiences. The chapter concludes with an appeal for researchers and practitioners to be mindful of important cautions, concerns, and considerations as they engage in scholarly inquiry on African American males.

It is my hope that this book will offer insight for practitioners, school leaders, researchers, theorists, parents, youth, community-based organizations, family members, as well as concerned citizens in general. I have sought to write this book in a manner that I hope will be accessible to anyone concerned about the challenges that Black males face. For school outcomes and life experiences of Black males to be transformed, I believe requires a collaborative effort across various spectrums working in concert to achieve what some may think is the unthinkable—Black male success in every facet of public and private life. I hold on to eternal hope that each and every young Black male ultimately will fulfill his life destiny and future potential.

CHAPTER 1

Black Male Students

An Overview

Despite a multitude of school reform efforts, increased standardization in schools, the influx of charter schools nationwide, incessant high-stakes testing, the purported promise of educational policies such as No Child Left Behind and Race to the Top, the surge of districts being taken over by states, and the growing corporate presence to oversee schools, there still remains a large segment of students attending U.S. schools who fail to gain access to a high-quality education (Darling-Hammond, 2006, 2010; Delpit, 1995; Howard, 2010). These trends are most disturbing at a time when increasing globalization and the need for highly skilled individuals may lead to countless numbers of students who find themselves on the academic margins today and most certainly on the economic and social fringes tomorrow. Although this academic and social exclusion undoubtedly will affect students across all racial, ethnic, gender, and socioeconomic groups, there are persistent data showing that certain student groups are more severely and disproportionately affected than others by school failures. One of those groups, Black males, is the focus of this book. Black males continue to be one of the more academically and socially marginalized students in U.S. schools (E. Anderson, 2008; Fergus & Noguera, 2010; Gill, 1992; Noguera, 2008; Terry, 2010; Toldson, 2008). School outcomes, in many ways, mirror Black males' condition in the larger society (Coakley, 2004; Polite & Davis, 1999; White & Cones, 1999; Wilson, 1987, 2008). This book seeks to shed light on some of the challenges that exist for Black males in their pursuit of academic success.

A close examination of a number of political, social, and economic indicators reveals the ongoing challenges of what it means to be Black and male in the United States. Many of these challenges begin at birth (E. Anderson, 2008) and persist over the life span of Black males. Like many other individuals reared in economically depressed areas, Black males face disproportionately high infant mortality rates, chronic poverty, and overrepresentation in underfunded schools. What is perplexing is the intensity and persistence of the deleterious effect of these social ills on Black males and how they carry this stigma well into adulthood in ways that do not affect other populations (Children's Defense Fund, 2011). These social ills are apparent when we look at data that reveal the manner in which Black males are undereducated, have chronically high unemployment, are over-incarcerated, have disparate health conditions, and ultimately have lower life expectations than any of the other large racial/ethnic groups in the United States (U.S. Department of Commerce, 2009). The complex, yet complicated, picture of life for Black males in the United States remains a topic of study and analysis across a multitude of disciplines, and while many have described the depth and breadth of the problem from a research, policy, and practice standpoint, minimal change has occurred on a large scale (U.S. Census Bureau, 2011). There is more to be studied, analyzed, and learned if viable solutions are to be identified and implemented. Therefore, the focus of this chapter is twofold: (1) to provide an overview of some of the important educational indicators and to see how Black males fare in them, and (2) to provide a selected synthesis of the research on, about, or concerned with Black males within the context of education.

The accounts for Black males are disturbing, alarming, and almost mind numbing. A little less than half of Black males do not earn high school diplomas in 4 years (Allensworth & Easton, 2001; Swanson, Cunningham, & Spencer, 2003). School dropout levels for Black males are heavily concentrated and most severe in large cities such as Los Angeles, New York, Detroit, and Chicago, which fail to graduate between half and three-quarters of their Black males (Schott Foundation for Public Education, 2010). This graduation gap is the result of a multitude of factors, but is due primarily to the high concentration of poor and minority students in low-performing high schools located in urban centers across the country (Darling-Hammond, 2010; Delpit, 2012). The consequences of not graduating from high school have enormous ramifications on multiple levels. In an economy where living wage employment increasingly requires a college degree or significant postsecondary training, dropping out of high school has disastrous individual, economic, and social consequences.

Twenty years ago, almost 90% of high school dropouts could find regular work. In the 21st century only one-third to one-half of dropouts find full-time employment and only 11% of those jobs offer more than poverty wages (Anyon, 2005). Lack of education is more strongly correlated not only with high unemployment but with welfare dependency and criminal activity that tends to accompany the desperation of poverty (Alexander, 2010). High school dropouts make up half of the heads of households on welfare and three-fourths of the prison population. Overall, it is estimated that the dropout problem costs the country more than $200 billion in lost earnings, unrealized tax revenue, and expended social services (Hale & Canter, 1998). Thus, from this standpoint, the need to address educational equity for Black males has national economic consequences. There is an increasing correlation between Black males who perform poorly in schools, many of whom ultimately drop out, and subsequent involvement in the penal system. According to 2005 Bureau of Justice statistics, Black males outnumber all other ethnic groups in the prison population and have a rate of incarceration that is five times higher than the rate of White males. Moreover, one in eight Black men in their 20s and 30s were behind bars in 2010 (Petit, 2012), and Department of Justice statisticians project that based on current demographics one in every three Black men can expect to spend time in prison, on probation, or on parole during his lifetime. In short, to better understand some of the predictive factors that are associated with larger life challenges for Black males, it is imperative to examine one of the foundational pillars where many of the challenges begin, which is education.

THE LANDSCAPE OF BLACK MALES IN U.S. SCHOOLS

Black males constitute close to 4 million, or 7% of the U.S. student population (U.S. Department of Education, 2011). Like any other subgroup, Black males possess a number of overlapping identities and diverse experiences. Thus, to characterize the group in monolithic terms would be problematic. It is not the goal of this chapter to unpack the complexity and multiple layers of Black male identity. The intersectionality of Black male identity will be examined further in Chapter 2, and it has been discussed in other works (Howard & Reynolds, 2012; McCready, 2004). In this chapter, I attempt to paint a picture that reflects many of the educational challenges (and the contributing factors) facing this population in a variety of ways that often cuts across the multiple identity markers that Black males possess. It has been well established in the professional literature that Black males face a myriad of challenges in the nation's schools and colleges (Harper & Davis, 2012; U.S. Department of Education, NCES, 2012; Jackson, 2007). The academic achievement of Black males in pre-K–12 and postsecondary schools has been the subject of a number of scholarly works over the past 3 decades (Brown & Davis, 2000; J. E. Davis, 2003; C. W. Franklin, 1991; Gibbs, 1988; Gordon, Gordon, & Gordon-Nembhard, 1994; Hopkins, 1997; Howard, 2013; Madhubuti, 1990; Noguera, 1996; Polite, 1993a, 1993b, 1994; Polite & Davis, 1999; Price, 2000; Toldson, 2008). Many of the challenges that Black males encounter are not dramatically different from those encountered by other males of color, namely, Latino, Southeast Asian, and Native American males (Castagno, Brayboy, & McK, 2008; Conchas & Vigil, 2012; Fergus & Noguera, 2010; Noguera, 1996, 2008). Educational research often has fallen short in examining race, class, and gender intersections in schools, and how they influence the schooling experiences of various populations. Ladson-Billings and Tate (1995) contend that race has been, and continues to be, undertheorized. While previous works have documented some of the challenges that Black males encounter in schools, there is a pressing need to examine the larger body of research on Black males and to develop a comprehensive account of what we know about this population and what general trends exist in the literature about them, to identify some of the strengths and problems with the current literature base, and to be able to offer some recommendations for future research, theory, and practice concerning this population.

"HOW DOES IT FEEL TO BE A PROBLEM?"

In his groundbreaking work, *The Souls of Black Folks*, W.E.B. Du Bois (1903) begins his chapter "Of our spiritual strivings" with a provocative question, one that has important relevance for Black males attending U.S. schools today: "How does it feel to be a problem?" Du Bois frames this question within the context of how Blacks, striving for social, economic, and political inclusion at the turn of the 20th century, were persistently seen as a "problem" for the country. In the years before and after Du Bois's work, a number of works in the professional literature characterized Blacks in problematic terms, and a litany of works and their titles over the 20th century illustrated how the population was perceived in troublesome ways. A perusal of these works would reveal titles such as "The Negro Problem: Abraham Lincoln's Solution" (Pickett, 1969), "What Shall We Do with the Negro?" (Escott, 2009), "The American Dilemma: The Negro Problem" (Myrdal, 1944), "The Negro: The Southerners' Problem" (Page, 1904), and "The White Man's Burden" (Riley, 1910), to name a few. The manner in which this issue of Blacks being viewed as "problems" was framed in many academic circles might best have been stated by noted Harvard scientist and prolific writer Nathaniel Southgate Shaler, who in 1884 contended that no other "civilized" world had as difficult a challenge as America's "Negro problem." His assertion was that "there can be no sort of doubt that, judged by the light of all experiences, these people are a danger to America greater and more insuperable than any of those that menace the other great civilized states of the world" (p. 701).

In many ways, Du Bois's question precisely speaks to the manner in which Black males at the turn of the 21st century might feel if they were to peruse much of the social science literature, popular press, mainstream media, and even the academic discourse about their academic performance and overall potential. A read-through of a majority of the literature on Black males would reveal a number of disturbing classifications. In my research for this work, the terms that frequently came up relating to Black males included "at-risk," "endangered," "remedial," "in crisis," "uneducable," "extinct," and "left behind." These terms shed light into the way in which much of the literature has fallen short in providing a more holistic, positive, and affirming account of Black males in schools.

CURRENT STATE OF AFFAIRS FOR BLACK MALES

The educational status of Black males presents a complex picture, with much to be said about the manner in which schools, communities, and homes best meet their needs. The picture, from multiple sources, paints a disturbing account of the overall manner in which many schools are falling woefully short in meeting the needs of Black males. However, what is crucial to note is that the monolithic picture that often is painted is not sufficient to capture the full set of experiences of Black males. One of the aims of this book is to offer an anti-deficit view of Black males' performance in schools. However, there is a need to offer a snapshot of some of the discouraging data that exist on how Black males experience schools. The data offered here on Black male performance are not intended to offer the usual account of how Black males have academic deficiencies. Moreover, in an attempt to redirect explanations for Black males' experiences and outcomes in U.S. schools, these data are laid out in a manner that suggests that the deficits may lie in the structures, policies, practices, curricula, ideologies, teacher attitudes, and programs that exist in schools that Black males attend. Thus, the focus is not centered on how to *fix* Black males; rather, the suggestion is that these data may lead us to question how we can *fix* schools and practices that serve Black males. Accordingly, a cursory view of the statistics will be given to reflect the voluminous data that demonstrate how schools have fallen woefully short in engaging Black males academically and providing the appropriate structures to foster their maximum performance. An examination of national data reveals that approximately 52% of Black males graduated within 4 years from U.S. high schools in 2008, compared with 58% for Latino males and 78% for White males. See Figure 1.1 (Schott Foundation for Public Education, 2010).

There are a number of factors that lead to dismal dropout rates. However, from a subject matter standpoint, perhaps no other subject area is as critical to overall academic success as reading and literacy (Lesnick, Goerge, Smithgall, & Gwynne, 2010). Although reading scores of Black males in grades 4 and 8 have increased over the past decade, they still trail behind those of White, Latino, and Asian males, and a large majority fall short of grade-level proficiency (see Figure 1.2) (U.S. Department of Education, NCES, 2012b). In a number of large urban districts across the country, Black males *without disabilities* had lower reading scores in grades 4, 8, and 12, and lower grade-level proficiency, than White males *with disabilities* (U.S. Department of Education, NCES, 2012). In many large urban districts across the country, the reading achievement scores for 8th-grade Black males are consistent with the reading scores for 4th-grade Asian American and White males (U.S. Department of Education, 2009).

It also has been prevalent for some time in the professional literature that Black males often are seen as one of the most problematic groups of students

Figure 1.1. National Black, White, and Latino Graduation Rates

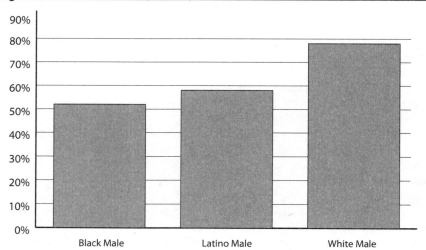

Source: Schott Foundation, Blackboysreport.org (2012).

in schools (Ferguson, 2003). The lack of a solid academic foundation, with proficiency in reading, writing, and math skills, undoubtedly plays a role in their efforts to thrive in schools and contributes to their being viewed as "problematic." Without core academic skills in place, there is an increased likelihood for behavioral challenges to become more commonplace. This reality has led to a significant number of Black males being placed in special education classrooms, where they have been represented at levels higher than any other subgroup (see Figure 1.3). A number of scholars have documented the ongoing correlation between race and gender when it comes to special education disparities and made the argument that Black males are the most severely affected by policies such as zero-tolerance, with some suggesting that implicit racial bias may be a contributing factor in this process (Artiles, Trent, & Palmer, 2004; Harry & Klingner, 2006; Losen & Orfield, 2002; Losen & Skiba, 2010; Skiba et al., 2008).

The disproportionate number of Black males who find themselves in special education often leads to less access to high quality instruction and academic enrichment than would be ideal for students who often are already behind academically. In many instances, special education classrooms and programs across the country become dumping grounds for students (mainly Black and male) who are seen as behavior problems, as unable to be educated, or as problems in general (Noguera, 2008). As one elementary teacher in Chicago once shared with me, "Many teachers export their problems to someone else, and that is why there are so many Black boys in special education." With growing numbers of Black males finding themselves in situations where they are victims of educational neglect and

Figure 1.2. Reading Proficiency Scores

4th-grade reading proficiency among males

Race/Ethnicity	Below Basic	Above Basic	Proficient	Advanced
Black	57%	43%	13%	2%
Latino	52%	48%	17%	9%
White	24%	76%	40%	9%
Asian	23%	77%	46%	15%

8th-grade reading proficiency among males

Race/Ethnicity	Below Basic	Above Basic	Proficient	Advanced
Black	47%	53%	11%	< 0%
Latino	40%	60%	16%	1%
White	19%	81%	37%	3%
Asian	20%	80%	42%	5%

12th-grade reading proficiency among males

Race/Ethnicity	Below Basic	Above Basic	Proficient	Advanced
Black	51%	49%	12%	1%
Latino	45%	55%	18%	1%
White	24%	76%	40%	5%
Asian	22%	78%	45%	8%

Source: U.S. Department of Education, National Center for Education Statistics (2012b).

underperformance, it is not a stretch to understand why their behavior becomes more problematic. This contributes to larger numbers of students who ultimately are "pushed out," suspended, or expelled from schools. Data from the U.S. Department of Education show that Black male students are the group most likely to be suspended from schools (see Figure 1.4).

Each of these educational factors contributes to the troubling state of affairs for Black male students. These factors become even more distressing when examined in greater detail as a comparison across different groups. Despite progress over the past decade, math proficiency scores of Black males continue to significantly trail behind those of their White, Latino, and Asian male counterparts (U.S. Department of Education, Institute of Education Sciences, 2009). While reading is considered the gateway to overall school success, many contend that math proficiency, in particular 8th-grade algebra, is the gateway to college. Unfortunately, far too many Black males fail to pass through this important passage way. In 2009, Black males in grades 4 through 8, *who were not eligible* for free and

Figure 1.3. Percentage of Black, Latino, White, and Asian Males in Special Education

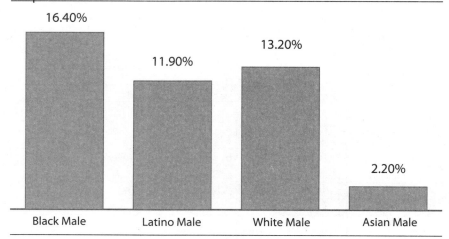

Source: U.S. Department of Education, National Center for Education Statistics (2012e).

Figure 1.4. Percentage of Black, Latino, White, and Asian Males Suspended Once in K–12: 2011

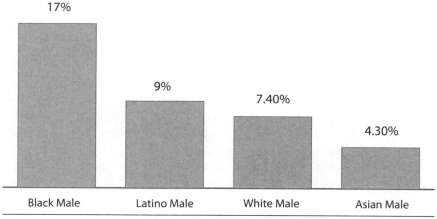

Source: U.S. Department Education, National Center for Education Statistics (2012).

reduced lunch, had lower math scores than White males *who were eligible* to receive free or reduced lunch (National Center for Education Statistics, 2009). At the high school level, Black males are among the subgroups least likely to take and pass AP courses and exams (College Board, 2012). Over the past 3 decades, the SAT scores of Black males were significantly lower than those of their White, Latino, and Asian counterparts (U.S. Department of Education, NCES, 2012d), as shown in Figure 1.5. Black males are the subgroup of students most likely to be retained during their K–8 education (Aud, Fox, & KewalRamani, 2010) and are three times more likely than Latino and Asian males to be suspended from elementary and secondary schools (Aud, Fox, & KewalRamani, 2010; Gregory, Skiba, & Noguera, 2010).

While the above-referenced data highlight a breadth of areas where schooling conditions have not served Black males adequately, it is important to note that the larger body of literature on Black males does present explanations that are tied to historical, community, and home factors that present a multitude of challenges that Black males encounter before they even enter schools (E. Anderson, 2008; Coley, 2011; Wilson, 2008). There is an extensive database that shows that Black children have higher infant mortality rates than Whites (Murphy, Xu, & Kochanek, 2012). Black children are more likely to be born into poverty and to have less access to adequate health care compared with White, Asian, and Latino children (Brookings Institute, 2011). Data on Black males show that they are more likely to live in crime-plagued neighborhoods, become victims of homicide, and become susceptible to many of the challenges that affect low-income communities where many Black males reside (Centers for Disease Control, 2011; Truman & Rand, 2010). It is important to note some of these realities, because they reflect serious challenges that exist in many communities where Black males may reside. E. Anderson (2008) uncovers many of these realities and makes a sociological analysis of how and why institutions

Figure 1.5. Black, Latino, and White Males 2011 SAT Scores

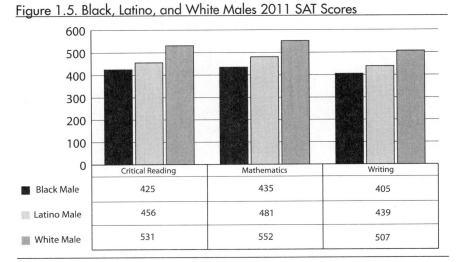

	Critical Reading	Mathematics	Writing
■ Black Male	425	435	405
Latino Male	456	481	439
White Male	531	552	507

Source: U.S. Department of Education, National Center for Education Statistics (2012d).

and public and social policy have fallen short in providing Black males a realistic chance for life success. Some have gone further by stating that the state of affairs for Black males is more of a public health issue than previous research has suggested (Hilfiker, 2002). Because the literature on these variables has been expanded further in other works, they are not given extensive attention and analysis here. Undoubtedly, historical, economic, sociological, psychological, and epidemiological factors all influence the manner in which populations of young people enter, experience, and perform in schools (Ladson-Billings, 2006). Thus, the purpose is to not ignore those factors, but to acknowledge them, although they will not be a major focus of this work. Rather, the unit of analysis in this work is deliberately tied to school factors, and more specifically to school structures and classroom instruction.

One of the problems with the current literature on Black males is an almost exclusive focus on them as being poor and residing in urban communities, and on the challenges that are present in such environments. Many of the challenges that confront Black males in education go beyond their communities and their social class status, and are directly located in classrooms, the lack of racial awareness and cultural ignorance among school personnel, apathetic teacher attitudes, and the poor-quality instruction they receive, whether in urban, rural, or suburban schools (Howard, 2008; Martin, 2007, 2009; Milner, 2007a, 2008; Murrell, 1999). The monolithic portrayal of Black males in poor urban communities fails to consider the increasing social class diversity among Black males. B. Gordon (2012) asserts that today approximately one-third of Black families live in suburban communities and send their children to middle-class schools where they still underperform compared with their White peers. Even the so-called privileges that accompany social and economic mobility do not seem to thwart the presence of race and racism when it comes to the schooling experiences of Black males. Understanding the challenges of race and gender for Black males is crucial to any thorough examination of their schooling experiences. The intersectionality of race, class, and gender, and other identity markers, is fundamentally critical in research concerned with young Black males, as in the case of any subgroup (Crenshaw, 1989, 1995). Each marker, in its own way, profoundly influences identity construction, self-concept, interactions with the world, and meaning-making. Black males possess multiple identities that are profoundly shaped by race, socioeconomic status, and gender in all of their complex manifestations.

PARADIGM SHIFT

One of the goals of this book is to reframe the knowledge base on how Black males experience schools. To that end, I call for a paradigm shift in how Black males are taught, studied, and discussed. A paradigmatic shift suggests casting a new light, or offering a new frame, to analyze a group or a phenomenon. Kuhn's (1970) work on scientific knowledge is appropriate here. According to Kuhn, "A paradigm is what members of a scientific community, and they alone, share" (p. 150). A shift in a paradigm therefore seeks to move to a new set of views, understandings, and types of knowledge constructed. A paradigm shift also attempts to change the basic assumptions or norms within the ruling theory of science and leads to new understandings of concepts, ideas, and knowledge. Banks (1993) contends that the "knowledge construction process describes the procedure by which social, behavioral, and natural scientists create knowledge and how the implicit cultural assumptions, frames of references, perspectives, and biases within a discipline influence the ways that knowledge is constructed within it" (p. 5). In constructing new knowledge about Black males, researchers need to be cognizant of the frames used to engage in the research, the questions that are posed, and the methods used to examine the subjects' experiences. Conceptual and theoretical frames that are centered on a discourse of Black males being endangered, extinct, or at risk lend themselves to identifying problems with the students, without any institutional or structural critique. This shift calls for researchers to dismiss deficit-laden frames and to move toward a more asset-based approach, which recognizes the strengths, promise, and potential of students, and can lead to opening up research approaches that delve into a more comprehensive, nuanced, complex, and authentic account of them.

It is essential for social scientists and practitioners concerned with Black male achievement and experiences in schools to engage in a paradigm shift in how Black males are viewed, studied, taught, and understood. The next sections of the chapter attempt to move the unit of analysis from Black male failure to Black male success, and to highlight empirical works that examine the increasing number of works that offer a different portrayal of Black males in schools. Although these works are not as plentiful as the deficit-based work on Black males, they are works that demonstrate a level of persistence, resilience, and intellectual giftedness in Black males. It is also worthy of mention that this review reveals many more works offering successful interventions than in research prior to 2000, so in some ways the paradigm shift may already be occurring. This work seeks to continue moving the field in this direction, if this is truly the direction that work on Black males is moving. The reality that is frequently absent from the discourse on Black males is that not all of them are suffering and dropping out of schools, most of them are not imprisoned, many of them do experience varying degrees of academic success and social adjustment in schools, and many are hardworking and disciplined. Yet their accounts are frequently absent from the narrative on Black males' educational experiences and realities. In many ways, the normalized depiction of Black males as academic failures has become so enmeshed in the educational fabric of many schools and districts that it almost becomes alarming and inexplicable when Black male success, outside of the athletic domain, occurs (Taylor, 1999). This shift is crucial in order to uncover how certain school cultures and pedagogical practices are able to engage these young men in the learning process in a manner that many practitioners and researchers do not believe is possible or is an aberration when it takes place. Furthermore, when discussing best practices, the question must be posed: *best practices for whom?* Not best practices for teachers who engage in a pedagogy of poverty (Haberman, 1991), which fails to challenge Black males intellectually. Rather, the discussion on best practices here centers on ones that enrich students' academic experiences, enhance their cognitive capacities, build on their sociocultural knowledge and realities, and ultimately prepare them for postsecondary pursuits. These best practices foster the development of knowledge, skills, and dispositions that will allow them to fully participate in a democratic society as capable and contributing members to the nation-state and the global community.

From a theoretical and methodological stance, one of the tools that may be used to combat age-old and narrow constructions of Black male experiences, and can be useful in the paradigm shift, is to center the students as the authors of their experiences. An increasing number of scholars have made the call for narrative inquiry and counterstorytelling that has the potential to relocate and resituate the experiences of marginalized populations in a more accurate context (Posner, 1997). It can be helpful to acknowledge the permanence of storytelling from the dominant paradigm when it comes to ideas such as meritocracy, democracy, and equality, which are ideas and concepts that many citizens in this country believe are just that—ideas and concepts, not realized ways of life. Thus, in constructing the new paradigm on Black male experiences and outcomes, new voices must be centered in the analysis, voices that often are overlooked, ignored, or outright dismissed—and those are the voices of Black males themselves. Sleeter and Delgado Bernal (2004) state, "At issue is the question of what counts as truth and who gets to decide" (p. 249). bell hooks (1990) talks about the dangers of White interpretations of the Black experience and the mainstream's suspicion of the Black experience as told by Black people. Far too often everyone other than Black males has offered commentary, analysis, and narrative of their experience. Black males' accounts of their own school experiences have registered only a minor blip on the radar of social science research because it is assumed that they are unable or unwilling to accurately tell their story. The critics also contest how representative these accounts are of all members of the group, or what Rosen (1996) refers to as "vulgar racial essentialism." In other words, there are those who would challenge the authenticity of these accounts to the point where depictions are represented in grossly overgeneralized ways. While it is important to avoid essentializing of any group, one must resist the propensity to question the veracity of Black male voices, when so many others have not been questioned in a similar fashion. The need for alternative voices and diverse viewpoints is important, and a paradigmatic shift requires the fluidity and multifaceted nature of identity for all individuals, and does not attempt to create monolithic constructions or experiences of any group. All theoretical frameworks have their share of strengths and weaknesses, and narrative theorists recognize that the framework is not a panacea for all that ails children of color in U.S. schools and that it will be subject to various critiques. However, these critiques should not prevent a much-needed examination of student voices and perspectives in education. More important, future research concerned with Black males and their educational experiences can directly address these critiques conceptually and empirically, which will only strengthen the paradigm as it continues to emerge in educational research.

LITERATURE ON BLACK MALES: EXPLANATIONS FOR THE CURRENT CONDITION

The literature on Black male academic performance and experiences, and explanations for it, has been outlined in a number of works over the past 3 decades. Gordon et al. (1994) called for scholars to move away from genetic and cultural explanations of Black male underachievement, and to examine for structural explanations. Using the lens of institutional racism and discrimination, they suggested that drugs, crime, violence, inferior schooling, and economic instability provided more reliable insights into why Black males struggled to adapt in schools. Some scholars have suggested that Black male underperformance is a result of oppositional identities to mainstream cultural norms and practices, and that this has resulted in some Black students refusing to become academically engaged because they run the risk of being ostracized by their peers (Fordham & Ogbu, 1986; Ogbu, 1987b). Subsequent to this work, Ogbu (2003) further contended that the failure of many middle-class Black students to engage was due to community forces that inform Black student school success. He defines community forces as "the ways minorities interpret and respond to schooling . . . the beliefs and behaviors within the minority community regarding education that minority students bring to school" (pp. vii, xiii).

Ogbu's (1987b) work often has been critiqued for its failure to locate the impact of racism and discrimination in the schooling experiences of Black students, their beliefs and actions, and the manifestation of low expectations and differential teacher–student relations. Other scholars, when examining the schooling outcomes of Black males, adopt a structuralist perspective, which attributes negative school experiences and outcomes (underperformance and overall disenfranchisement) to structural factors such as class structures and arrangements (Massey & Denton, 1993; Wilson, 1978, 1987). Stinson (2010) tested Ogbu's oppositional theory and the concept of "acting White," and examined the "voices" of four academically successful Black male students as they responded, in retrospect, to the theoretical concept of the burden of "acting White." He found that the concept did not have much of an effect on the way that the young men saw their academic prospects. These young men saw their identities as complex, multilayered, and still evolving. While they acknowledged some of the stereotypes that existed about them, they did not internalize notions of sacrificing racial or cultural integrity in the pursuit of academic excellence. Stinson states that "although each acknowledged that the burden potentially existed, it was not so much understood as a burden of acting White in regards to school . . . but rather as a burden of somehow molding oneself into the [White] hegemonic images of success" (p. 58).

Wilson (2008) reinforces the structural argument when he states that Black males suffer disproportionately from what he terms the "new urban poverty" (p. 56), wherein poor, racially segregated neighborhoods have a substantial majority of their residents either unemployed or completely withdrawn from the labor force. His analysis shows that the unemployment levels of Black males surpass those of every other subgroup and exclude them from active participation in the political economy, which continues to be dependent upon a highly skilled labor force and adequate levels of education, which many Black males are frequently lacking. One can infer from these findings the trickle-down effect on Black males in K–12 schools, and, in many ways, the genesis of life challenges may lie here as well.

On the other side of the structuralist debate are those who subscribe to a cultural perspective, which would attribute these same experiences and outcomes to factors such as the moral codes that govern families and communities. While there are many who strongly support one viewpoint or the other, some scholars are dissatisfied with the determinism of the structuralist viewpoint, which renders individuals as passive objects of larger forces, and similarly dissatisfied with the "blame the victim" perspective of the culturalists, which views individuals as hopelessly trapped within a particular social–cultural milieu (Ryan, 1976).

Noguera (2001) contends that there are both structural and cultural factors that play out in detrimental ways for Black males, and that these factors must be further analyzed and addressed if changes are to disrupt patterns of school underperformance of Black males. It is essential for educators to understand further investigation of how Black male identity is shaped within school contexts—taking into consideration race, gender, class, and location—–if they are to effectively engage Black males in the learning process. Noguera's work challenges the work of Fordham and Ogbu (1986) by claiming evidence showing that many Black males deliberately challenge racial stereotypes and redefine their racial identities to demonstrate that it is possible to do well in school and still maintain racial pride and cultural integrity. Works such as Noguera's are critical because they offer a counternarrative to the account that repeatedly has been offered on Black males, wherein they are essentially doomed to academic failure because of oppositional behavior and are unable to overcome the myriad of obstacles in their path to academic success. The research on high-achieving Black males consistently shows a level of resilience, persistence, and determination to overcome racialized stereotypes about them (Conchas & Noguera, 2004; Howard, 2008; Price, 2000). Particularly, Noguera (2008) states that investigations into the academic orientations for Black males "must focus on the ways in which subjective and objective dimensions of identity related to race and gender are constructed within schools and how these influence academic performance" (p. 27).

From the perspective of critical race theory (CRT), the plight of Black males in schools is an expression of racism that is endemic to North American society (Bell, 1992, 1995; Crenshaw, Gotanda, Peller, & Thomas, 1995; Delgado, 1995; Howard, 2008; Ladson-Billings & Tate, 1995; Matsuda, 1989). Critical race theorists argue that because racism is such an integral part of society in the United States, it is embedded in practices, norms, ideologies, and values that have become symptomatic of the more explicit and formal manifestations of racialized power (Crenshaw et al., 1995). Scholars such as Duncan (2002) contend that the discourses about and on Black males are embedded in practices and values that normalize racism in the United States and create "conditions that marginalize adolescent black males, placing them *beyond love* in schools and in the broader society" (p. 131, emphasis added). Duncan's work on the manner in which adolescent Black boys experience schools is an example of the type of work that positions their voices at the heart of the analysis, and, in it, the participants shed light on how racial discrimination is a staple of their schooling experiences.

Although not as critical on racism as CRT scholars, Claude Steele (1992) also has suggested that race plays a role in the educational experiences of Black students in ways that many educators may not realize. Contending that racial stigma is an unrecognized component of underachievement among students of color, he argued:

> Doing well in school requires a belief that school achievement can be a promising basis of self-esteem and that belief needs constant reaffirmation even for advantaged students. Tragically, I believe the lives of Black Americans are still haunted by a specter that threatens this belief and the identification that derives from it at every level of schooling. (p. 72)

While most of Steele's work that has examined the effects of stereotype threat has been with students in higher education, an increasing amount of the research has begun to look at the potential effect of the concept on K–12 students. Osborne (1997) tested Steele's hypothesis regarding identity formation and found that as Black males move through high school, the correlation between their academic performance and measures of their self-esteem declined consistently and dramatically, a pattern not observed in other groups. His findings suggest that many Black males believe that their fate has been determined and that failure is inevitable.

An area that has received more attention in the study of Black males has been the expanding definition and conceptualization of masculinity. In an attempt to problematize traditional ways that masculinity is defined, and how these narrow notions impact Black males, some scholars assert that studying gender identity among Black males is crucial to understanding the totality of their experiences (Staples, 1978). McCready (2004) suggests that many Black males experience troubling social experiences in schools because of diverse masculinities, which may affect their academic outcomes. He contends that researchers need to take into account multiple categories of difference and forms of oppression in order to understand and suggest interventions for gay, bisexual, and non-gender-conforming Black male students in urban schools. Therefore, a more complete analysis of how Black males experience schools is needed to create and sustain a discourse about how masculinity often is narrowly defined within Black cultural contexts, thus making it difficult for many Black males to display alternative forms of masculinity. This work is vital because of hyper-masculine and heteronormative ideologies and practices that are pervasive in many Black communities and the larger society. These ideologies and practices characterize what it means to be male and Black in some disturbing ways that are not consistent with how countless numbers of Black males display their own identities.

SCHOOL AND CLASSROOM FACTORS

While some scholars examine cultural, structural, racial, and identity variables in evaluating how Black males see schools, others contend that local-level classroom experiences, in particular, teacher attitudes and perceptions, play a much larger role than is reflected in the literature. In a closer examination of how teacher perceptions and attitudes influence Black males' experiences in schools, Rong's (1996) study showed that teachers' perceptions of student social behavior are a result of complex interactions of students' and teachers' race and gender. The study found that female teachers perceived female students more positively than male students regardless of the teachers' race. In general, White female teachers perceived White students more positively than Black students. Black female teachers, in contrast, made no distinction among race for students. These findings raise important questions about how teacher attitude and perception influence Black male educational outcomes.

Rong's work was not the first to examine the effects of teacher attitudes and perceptions on students and their school experiences and outcomes. Rosenthal and Jacobson's (1968) work was among the first extensive studies to suggest that teacher expectations may influence the academic performance of school-age children. This practice, known as the *Pygmalion effect*, is cited as one of the reasons that many Black students in general, and Black males in particular, are disengaged from schools. Rist's (1970) study further highlighted how the Pygmalion effect can happen as early as kindergarten and subsequently become a self-fulfilling prophecy when teachers' attitudes become internalized by students, affecting academic experiences, performances, and outcomes. A number of other scholars have documented the manner in which teacher perceptions tend to have more of a negative effect on Black males than any other group (Howard, 2008; Milner, 2007a; Reynolds, 2010; Rios, 2011). Much of this work shows that they often are viewed more as having characteristics consistent with academic disengagement (lazy, non-thinkers, hostile in class, discipline problems) than as showing behavior congruent with academic success (Hall, 2001; Wood, Kaplan, & McLoyd, 2007).

More recently, empirical work has demonstrated the manner in which teacher expectations can have an important influence on student outcomes. McKown and Weinstein (2008) examined the relationship between child ethnicity and teacher expectations, and discovered high levels of teacher preference for White and Asian students over Black and Latino students. Moreover, their findings suggest that the teachers' expectation levels contributed in a major way to the academic disparities that existed among racial groups. What this work reinforces is the salience that race continues to play in schools. Despite claims of being in a post-racial era, schools in many instances appear to be a primary location where students, at the earliest of ages, have significant advantages or disadvantages based on racial/ethnic orientation. Moreover, meaningful efforts directed at improving the outcomes of Black males, must pay explicit and careful attention to the intersectionality of race and gender. However, broad characterizations of Black males that do not take intersectionality into account fail to analyze the manner in which being Black, male, middle-class, or poor can profoundly shape educational experiences and outcomes.

Hargrove and Seay (2011) investigated teachers' beliefs and perceptions about the low representation of Black males in gifted education. Their survey research discovered different explanations between teachers of color and White teachers. White teachers were more likely than teachers of color to see non-school factors as explanations (e.g., home/parents/community). White teachers also placed little attention on their instruction and beliefs as a reason that Black males were less likely than any other group to be referred to gifted education. Furthermore, teachers of color did not see in ways that White teachers did, the use of non-standard English as a barrier to school success (Gay & Howard,

2001). Their research documents the salience of teacher attitudes and beliefs to the perception of Black males, in situations where deficit thinking about Black males' potential and promise was quite prevalent. They recommend engaging public school teachers in a more explicit and direct dialogue about the under-representation of Black males in gifted programs.

Reynolds (2010) examined the role that parenting played in school outcomes for Black males. Using a qualitative case study approach with a critical race theory and phenomenological lens for analysis, she interviewed Black middle-class parents about their experiences in public secondary schools. She documented the manner in which Black parents believed that school officials frequently excluded them from access to information that could aid them and their students. Moreover, the parents discussed how their sons, in particular, were victims of lowered expectations and deficit thinking, and were subject to racial micro-aggressions by teachers and school administrators. She recommends that schools move toward seeing Black parents as full partners in a manner that will dispel myths about Black males. She suggests that future research should examine the manner in which Black males and their parents are frequently targets of explicit and implicit forms of racism and discrimination.

Lynn, Bacon, Totten, Bridges, and Jennings (2010) examined teachers and administrators' perspectives and opinions on the persistent failure of Black male high school students in a low-performing, yet affluent, area termed Summerfield County. Their focus group and individual interviews revealed persistent apathy among school personnel, and a permanence of low expectations in an overall environment that stifled teacher care and creativity, which in turn stifled the academic and personal/social development of Black males.

Lewis, Butler, Bonner, and Jourber (2010) examined the impact of disciplinary patterns and school district responses regarding Black academic achievement in a Midwest school. There were four key goals in this work: (1) to investigate all behavior occurrences among Black males in comparison to their peers during the 2005–2006 academic school year; (2) to detail the discipline responses recommended by the school district for these offenses; (3) to calculate the total amount of class time missed as a result of school district–prescribed resolutions; and (4) to provide a connection to performance on standardized test reporting for the larger Black student population in this urban school district. Their findings revealed that Black male students were disciplined at a rate of three to one compared with other student groups, and had the highest level of disciplinary referral of any group. Lewis et al. recommend several steps to address these inequities and to reduce the disproportionate number of Black males who are disciplined in schools: (1) implement culturally relevant professional development (CRPD) for classroom management; (2) establish a discipline advisory committee; (3) enforce a three-strike rule for violent offenses; and (4) refer students for counseling/therapy.

These works represent a consistent stream of ideologies, theories, and narratives about Black male potential that dominate many schools. In her work on what she terms the "institutional narrative" on children, intersectionality, and academic outcomes, Ferguson (2003) writes:

> According to the statistics, the worse-behaved children in the school are black and male, and when they take tests they score way below their grade level. They eat candy, refuse to work, fight, gamble, chase, hit, instigate, cut class, cut school, cut hair. They are defiant, disruptive, disrespectful, and profane. These black males fondle girls, draw obscene pictures, make lewd comments, intimidate others, and call teachers names. They are banished from the classroom to the hall, to the discipline office, to the suspension room, to the streets so that others can learn. (p. 46)

She goes on to state:

> In the range of normalizing judgments, there is a group of Black boys identified by school personnel as, in the words of a teacher, "unsalvageable." This term and the condition it speaks to is specifically about masculinity. School personnel argue over whether these unsalvageable boys should be given access even to the special programs designed for those who are failing in school. Should resources defined as scarce, be wasted on these boys for whom there is no hope? (p. 96)

It is my intent to lay out a compelling case for why there is a need to pay particular attention to Black males. The subsequent chapters attempt to move into a more granular analysis of this challenge, which identifies theories, ideas, concepts, and firsthand accounts from young men about their realities. My goal in this book is to walk a careful line between theory and practice, as both are integral to an understanding of how to disrupt the challenges for Black males in schools. Often practitioners fall short in recognizing the values of theory and research in order to better understand classroom practice and ways that it might be improved. Conversely, researchers and theorists often fail to acknowledge the richness and complexities of everyday practice that practitioners engage and observe. Hence, the goal is to weave a narrative pertaining to Black males that speaks to the needs and concerns of practitioners and scholars who possess deep-seated concerns about the current state of affairs and future life prospects of this population, and to rethink their works in a manner that can contribute to new knowledge, improved schooling experiences, and subsequently better life chances.

CHAPTER 2

Black Males

An Historical Overview and a Need for a Paradigm Shift

One of the aims of this book is to disrupt the age-old, deficit-based depictions of Black males. The hope is that by identifying and theorizing some of the challenges Black males face, and by locating their voices at the center of the analysis for ideas, recommendations, insights, and answers, the likelihood for improved school outcomes and life chances may increase. One of my biggest frustrations in doing work in schools across the country is to hear the manner in which teachers, counselors, and school administrators discuss Black males. The level of carelessness, dispassion, fear, and overall acceptance of the failure of Black males expressed by individuals who have accepted the task of educating them is alarming and is one of the primary culprits in their marginalization in schools. There is much to be said about how much any group of students can be expected to learn when they are viewed in such a negative light, as are countless numbers of Black males. As stated in Chapter 1, a primary goal of this book is to conduct a *paradigm shift,* or an attempt to make a conceptual and theoretical move away from viewing Black males as uneducable and academically inferior, to one where they are seen as individuals who possess unlimited potential and promise that can be recognized when they are situated in a caring and supportive learning environment. The paradigm shift called for here also seeks to move away from singular or essentialized constructions of Black males.

Researchers and practitioners will not be able to effectively address the educational and social issues affecting Black males if they are all seen as the same. Thus, there is a need to think deeply about the diversity that exists within the group. Before the case for a paradigm shift is made, it is helpful to understand the historical context from which many of our contemporary understandings of Black males derive. It is my belief that through identifying some of the root causes of the construction of Black males as being problems, we can begin to engage in scholarship, theory, and practice that challenge these ideas, and then seek to reconceptualize them. In other words, the objective would be to move the pendulum from dehumanizing Black males, to humanizing them, and seeing them in a more dynamic and diverse context wherein they are worthy of love, care, concern, and respect. To that end, in this chapter, I aim to accomplish three goals. Initially I will identify and discuss some of the historical narratives, which still remain today, that have contributed to the depiction of Black males. Second, I call for disrupting the deficit accounts of Black males by challenging singular notions of Black males, and making the case for a more nuanced, complex, and multifaceted framework for viewing Black males. Finally, I seek to move to a space where research is identified that highlights Black male success, and where Black male voices are the focal point. This move is done deliberately to shine the spotlight on those works that have not fallen prey to reporting only the problems, or "what's wrong" with Black males. It is my hope that by reframing, redefining, and reconceptualizing what it means to be Black and male, the contemporary narrative around Black male identity will become one based on diversity, assets, and intellectual prowess, and not one based on deficit and deviance.

FIVE WAYS OF DEFINING A BLACK MALE

The challenges that exist for Black males have been well documented (E. Anderson, 2008; Balfanz & Legters, 2004; Ferguson, 2003; Gibbs, 1988; Gordon et al., 1994; Hopkins, 1997; Howard, 2008; Madhubuti, 1990; Milner, 2013; Mincy, 2006; Noguera, 2001; Polite, 1993a; Polite & Davis, 1999; Staples, 1982). The view of Black males, who are frequently labeled as problems and prone to violence, invoking fear in many, and deemed as undesirable in certain circles, is diverse and extreme on many levels. Loathed in various environments, applauded in others, perhaps no other group of young people is emulated yet despised simultaneously to the extent that Black males are today. However, the paradoxical perception of Black males within the larger society remains puzzling. There are ongoing elements of mainstream and popular culture that have been developed, sustained, and made into multibillion-dollar industries based on the talents, creative genius, intellect, and identities of Black males (Hill, 2009; Kitwana, 2002). Thus in many ways, we have developed a love–hate affair with Black males. We love them if they are seen as nonthreatening, profitable, and entertaining, yet they are reviled if they are viewed as hostile, intelligent, nonconforming, independent, or strong-willed. This love–hate affair represents the illogicality of the way in which many Black males are viewed within mainstream society, and in particular in schools. Ladson-Billings (2011) discusses "the love–hate relationship with Black males" (p. 8). She asserts:

> We see Black males as "problems" that our society must find ways to eradicate. We regularly determine them to be the root cause of most problems in school and society. We seem to hate their dress, their language and their effect. We hate that they challenge authority and command so much social power. While the society

apparently loves them in narrow niches and specific slots—music, basketball, football, track—we seem less comfortable with them than in places like the National Honor Society, the debate team, or the computer club. (p. 9)

In an attempt to develop a complete account of how Black males are viewed contemporarily and to contribute to a paradigm shift, it is essential to take an historical account of how Black boys and men have been viewed in the larger society, and how the remnants of these constructions continue to have an influence on their current-day realities. Many of the contemporary portrayals of Black males have their roots in slavery and age-old racism that limited Black men's mobility and depicted them as subhuman, criminals, absent-minded, and buffoons (Polite & Davis, 1999). Also prevalent during slavery, the dominant caricatures of Black men as coons and toms usually portrayed them as ignorant, docile, and groveling. These caricatures were performed in minstrel shows that often spoke to many of the deep psychic needs of White audiences to see Blacks as inferior (Bogle, 2002; Booker, 2000; Boskin, 1986; Elkins, 1968). For Blacks, this ridicule forged psychic chains such as a bag of rice for Uncle Ben, a box for Aunt Jemima, a cabin in the sky for Uncle Tom. Such images positioned White men within the institution of slavery as the paternalistic caretakers of slaves. Pragmatic and instrumental, these representations were created from Whites' desires to oppress Black men and women, and some would say the remnants remain in more sophisticated ways.

I would contend that there are at least five depictions that have plagued the Black male image over the past 4 centuries and continue to shape the public perception, in subtle and not so subtle ways, of how Black males experience schools and the larger society today. These five depictions are (1) *the physical brute and anti-intellectual,* (2) *the shiftless and lazy Black male;* (3) *the hypersexual Black male;* (4) *the criminal-minded Black male; and* (5) *the slickster-pimp/gangster Black male.* In different ways, these depictions have contributed immeasurably to the physical, academic, psychological, emotional, cultural, and spiritual well-being of Black men and Black families. Not only have the breadth and depth of these images become so integral to the manner in which the wider society sees Black males, but the depths of the destruction run so deep that many Black people see Black males in a similar light. It is important to note that the depictions of Black males, much like racism, are tied to an ideology or a set of beliefs, and not limited to one particular racial or ethnic group harboring these beliefs (Solorzano, Allen, & Carroll, 2002). As a result, it is quite possible for people of color to internalize and act on these beliefs, just as Whites would. Therefore, the efforts to dismantle racism are tied to eradicating a system of beliefs, ideas, associations, and assumptions about individuals of a particular race. Each of these accounts is rooted in a legacy of slavery, racism, and racial stereotypes, and in many ways Black males have internalized the oppression. Moreover, they have engaged in behavior that frequently reinforces many of these characterizations, which has made the disruption of these depictions even more challenging.

The first depiction of Black males, the *physical brute and anti-intellectual,* is centered on the idea that Black males' greatest asset is their sheer physical strength, and the lack of strength when it comes to intellect. Hence, one of the most persistent acts that took place during slavery was to keep Black males tied to manual labor, which it was believed they were best suited to perform. This depiction is grounded in the idea that Black men, dating back to the inception of slavery in the colonies, were deemed necessary for their sheer physical and brute strength. The importing of millions of enslaved Africans, which served as an economic foundation for the emerging nation-state, has been noted in a number of works (Berlin, Favreau, & Miller, 1998; Morgan, 1998). Central to this reality, yet omitted from most accounts, is the notion that Black men (along with Black women) were primary pillars in the development and infrastructure of the nation and were the backbone of physical labor for sheer strength, heavy lifting, countless hours of moving, and engaging in back-breaking work (J. A. Anderson, 1988; J. H. Franklin, 1995; Shaler, 1884).

As much as the absolute physical strength of Black men was recognized, their intellectual capacity was seen as being child-like and far from the standard of their White peers. Moreover, the prevailing belief was that Black men were more muscular and had denser body mass than Whites, and as a result were innately less intelligent and could work longer, harder, and under more physically adverse conditions. A number of scholars have documented the manner in which "science" was done to prove the small brain and skull sizes of Blacks, which "proved" their intellectual inferiority and thus affirmed beliefs that Blacks should be relegated to menial, low-level types of labor (Butchart, 2010; Gould, 1981; Horsman, 1981; Selden, 1999). Elkins (1968) describes slave masters as having total control over Black males and removing all their human and legal rights because they were deemed mentally unable to make sense of understanding these rights. Patterson (1967) supports the account offered by Elkins, describing the type of psychological humiliation Black males encountered through seasoning, and the manner in which many believed that they lacked the "innate ability" of White men. Phillips (1918), considered one of the foremost historians on slavery, also writes about how the goal was to have Black men embrace values of White men; yet, as Black males fell short of this image, they were deemed as lacking the intellect, guidance, and resourcefulness to be self-sufficient in any way. So, from the outset, the clear narrative that exists about Black males is their innate inferiority, the lack of intellectual acumen, the inability to be a provider and emotional support for family, and the limited ability to make any type of meaningful contribution to the family or society writ large.

Popular culture and thinking of the time played a role in reinforcing the message of Black male inferiority. Perhaps no piece of cinema had as great an influence on the wider society's view of Black men as D. W. Griffith's *Birth of a Nation.* Situated in the early 1900s, *Birth* depicted Black males as unable to verbally express themselves, deeply unintelligent, and violent individuals with sexual frustrations, who were to be feared and loathed by Whites, who came to view the Ku Klux Klan as a heroic force to save the nation from this bestial deviant. The film became a nationwide success and is still considered one of the most influential pieces of cinematic work ever. *Huckleberry Finn*, considered one of the greatest novels of all time, also contributes to the notion of the Black male as anti-intellectual, with Huck's friend Jim, who is portrayed as docile, mindless, and in need of guidance. Many writers have criticized the work as being racist in nature and yet another example of a literary contribution to the image of Black males lacking in intelligence and mental fortitude.

The second historical image of Black men is that of the *shiftless and lazy Black male*. It is the image of the lazy slave, who did not want to work and required constant oversight and monitoring. This image is tied to an overseer who ensured that Black men would carry out the tasks that they were given. As previously stated, one of the dominant themes that developed about Black men was that they were savages who were subhuman and in need of control, structure, and order. This need for control, structure, order, and extreme discipline is a belief that many classroom teachers still have today when it comes to Black male students. Moreover, the belief historically was that Black men were averse to work and needed to be forced to engage in the intense labor for which they were suited. The irony in this depiction is compelling, given the inordinate amounts of physical labor that was required of Black men.

Popular radio and television shows help to develop this narrative further. *Amos and Andy*, a minstrel show that became wildly popular in the 1940s and 1950s played up the image of Black men as being lazy, dumb, inferior, and dishonest. The constant references to Blacks being "lazy" and "no good" became staples of the show, which was situated within a framework that showcased Black vernacular as being wholly incompetent, Black men being unable to figure out the most simple of tasks, and the promotion of individuals who were not fit to function in the larger society due to the lack of intellect and work ethic. Various terms were placed upon Black men, such as "nigger," "boy," and "coon," all of which became part of the American lexicon and reinforced this mantra of laziness. The term "coon" in particular was regularly applied to the blackface minstrels (who usually but not invariably were White men) of the mid- to late 19th century and was well established by the 1890s when the Black lyricist Ernest Hogan offered the song "All Coons Look Alike to Me" (a reference to Black men). He professed to be surprised by the hostility it aroused and claimed that as a Black man he could hardly be a racist. The word turned up again in such popular titles as *Every Race Has a Flag But the Coon* (1899), *Coon, Coon, Coon* (1900), and even *The Phrenologist Coon* (1901); all were written by Whites. Each of these labels often possessed implicit and explicit ways of framing Black men in a manner in which they were more concerned with levity and entertainment, and less concerned with or desirous of hard work. What is disturbing is the manner in which over the past decade there have been a series of accounts on college campuses where White students have mocked portrayals of Blacks with blackface depictions and stereotypical accounts as part of party celebrations.

A third account of Black males is that of the *hypersexual Black male*. The notion of the hypersexual male also has its roots within a 17th-century slavery context and connects Black males to stereotypical messages and images of deviant sexuality and unbridled sexual energies (Browser, 1994). The idea of Black male sexual superiority is also connected to the lack of intellect and rooted in the notion that Black men served on the plantation as the big "Buck" who was needed for procreation to bring additional human capital for the slave owner (Gutman, 1976). Related to the impression of the hypersexual Black male was that Black men were unable to control their sexual desires and were by nature rapists, and in particular had an uncontrollable and insatiable desire for White women (Jordan, 1968). This image of Black male sexuality was a constant fear in the eyes of many Whites, and one of the more persistent fears of White men was that of Black men pursuing sexual relationships with White women. This ultimately was a threat to Whites as a race because it would shatter the creed of the separation and purity of the races. Somehow lost in this fear of mixing the races is the reality that countless numbers of White male slave owners repeatedly raped Black women and frequently bore interracial children. Again, rooted in an ideology of fear, sexuality, and racism, it became apparent that for many Black men the mere accusation of looking at, discussing, or interacting with White women would be met with quick punishment of the harshest type. The brutal murder of Emmitt Till in 1955 for accusations of whistling at a White woman stoked many of these fears and reinforced the idea of Black masculinity being tied to hypersexuality and the inability to control one's sexual appetite. Moreover, the most common thread among the tens of thousands of Black men who were lynched during the 18th, 19th, and 20th centuries was the mere accusation that Black men had either raped, looked lustily at, or were interested in the sexual pursuit of White women, which explains the frequent practice of castration of Black men either before, during, or after their lynching (Allen, Lewis, Litwack, & Als, 2000).

Browser (1994) states that these observations of Black men were gross distortions and fueled what he refers to as the "myth of Black sexual superiority" (p. 143). Moreover, he raises the question of whether there is a relationship between the 19th-century racial beliefs about Black men's sexuality and contemporary social scientific studies that still describe Black males' sexuality in pathological terms (Fullilove, Fullilove, Haynes, & Gross, 1990). The more challenging issue is how Black men make meaning of deficit constructions of their sexuality. Staples (1978) discussed the dual dilemma of Black men, wherein they have to confront two different stereotypes when it comes to their sexuality: being viewed as hypersexual by the larger society in many circles, but also being viewed as victims of emasculation by domineering Black women in their own homes and communities. He also discussed how both messages contribute historically and contemporarily to destructive defense mechanisms to combat the stereotypes. One of the effects of this distorted notion of Black men has been the manner in which many Black men have tried to embrace or dismiss the hypersexual identity. Black male identity, to a large extent, stems from a distorted notion of masculinity, connected to the idea of being ultra-sexualized and being treated largely as one-dimensional and universal, and possessing a dearth of emotion and affective filters required for meaningful relationship (Majors & Billson, 1992).

A fourth depiction is the *criminal-minded Black male*. As stated earlier, the degradation of the Black male image has persisted over time, dating back to the 17th century. Russell-Brown (1998) discusses in her book the historical narrative that has rendered Black men as the "symbolic pillager of all that is good" (p. 84), and states that the construction of an image of Black men as criminals is more of a hoax than grounded in reality. She defines these hoaxes as "when someone fabricates a crime and blames it on another person because of his race or when an actual crime has been committed and the perpetrator falsely blames someone because of his race" (pp. 70–71). In addition to the idea or image of Black men as coons and jesters, the criminalization of Blackness and Black men in particular also emerged as a common theme.

Tucker (2007) argues that the representations of criminal Black men in popular culture help perpetuate the image of them as deviant, violent, and prone to crime. She writes that even throughout the 20th century, the portrayal of crime by conservative politicians during heated political campaigns was used as a metaphor for race and gender, with Black men being the primary culprits: Conservative politicians have often recast fears about race as fears about crime. She cites the Republican opponents of presidential hopeful Michael Dukakis, who used the case of Willie Horton to attack the Democrats' stand on law enforcement, suggesting that people would be safer if led by Republicans. She says that such politicians used Horton as a collective symbol of Black male criminality, deviance, and violence.

Muhammad (2010) writes about how the idea of Black criminality was vital to the making of modern America. His work chronicles how, when, and why contemporary notions of Black men emerged as their being exceptionally dangerous and prone to crime, and how the need for America to control, punish, and incarcerate Black men became a dominant narrative in many urban cities throughout the 19th and 20th centuries. Muhammad's work documents the manner in which social scientists developed a narrative that essentially would become part of the social fabric of U.S. Blacks in general, and Black men in particular. He cites Frederick L. Hoffman's seminal work, *Race Traits and Tendencies of the American Negro* (1896), and describes how it included Black crime statistics, and, tying issues of crime to morality and race, how it ultimately became one of the most influential works in the first half of the 20th century, and in many ways became the literary catalyst to the introduction of Jim Crow. Michelle Alexander (2010) documents the mass incarceration of Black men during the latter part of the 20th century as being focused explicitly on linking race and crime. Alexander documents how crime decreased in many urban communities in the late 1990s, while the incarceration of Black men reached unprecedented levels, yet again reinforcing the idea that Black men were to be viewed as more prone to crime, and that tougher laws were needed to crack down on widespread lawlessness perpetrated by them.

The fifth and final depiction that has emerged over the past half-century is the *slickster-pimp/gangster*. Given the reputation of Black men to be averse to hard work and lacking mental acuity, the slickster describes Black men that skirt the system, find ways around the law, and are devious, cunning, and skilled in illegal or criminal activity. These individuals avoid any and all circumstances that require hard work and commitment to accomplish goals. Thus, Black men at the turn of the 20th century frequently were seen as individuals who might lie, cheat, and steal to game the system designed by "the man." The hustler may have been a numbers runner, a gambler, a professional pickpocket, or an individual who spent countless hours at the speakeasy, at the bar, or on the corner looking for the quick dollar that would require little to no work, skill, or focus. The image of the Black man as a pimp became prominent during the 1960s with the advent of Blaxploitation films such as *The Mack, Cleopatra Jones, Superfly,* and *Sweetback's Baadasssss Song,* wherein the image of Black men and women was significantly damaged. Black men were fast-talking, quick-thinking, smooth manipulators who were able to convince Black women, who were portrayed as feeble, weak minded, and in need of male guidance, to sell their bodies to support their pimps financially. Needless to say, these constructions influenced an entire generation of individuals who believed that Black men were to be feared because they were out for a quick buck at someone else's expense and were quick to break the law to do so. The gangster image embedded Black masculinity in a way that was tied to violence, power, and money. Hence, the gangster was feared yet respected because of his ability to inflict physical harm upon individuals who invaded his turf for monetary gains or gang infiltration. The gangster image frequently included a particular bravado, often tied to a certain type of dress and lingo. Again, popular culture embraced this idea, and movies such as *Colors, Boyz N' the Hood,* and *A Menace II Society* reinforced it. Consistent with the movie portrayals were rap music accounts in which groups such as N.W.A, Above the Law, and Geto Boys assumed gangster images and produced lyrics frequently boasting of violence, lawlessness, misogyny, degradation of women, and an obsession with money. Here, Majors and Billson's (1992) theory of "cool pose" places Black males on a collision course with White social institutions. They posit "being male and black has meant being psychologically castrated—rendered impotent in the economic, political, and social arenas that whites have historically dominated" (p. 71). As a result of these depictions and the inability to assimilate or integrate into mainstream society, Black males create counterculture realities that enable them to gain economic power and control through underground markets centered on legal and illegal activities.

Each of these depictions has influenced Black men and the larger society in a multitude of ways. My contention is not that this is an exhaustive list of depictions. Needless to say, others exist. Black males also have been viewed as entertainers and athletes (as will be discussed in greater detail in Chapter 4) as well as lacking in emotion, callous, jokesters, absentee fathers, and a number of other less than flattering images. It goes without saying that as damaging as these portrayals have been, many of them have been embraced and glorified contemporarily by countless numbers of Black men. Hence the difficulty in shifting the paradigm. The challenge is how to move the thinking of the larger society of Black males, when many Black males continually reinforce these stereotypes.

BLACK MALES AND PUBLIC PERCEPTION

The characterizations of Black males undoubtedly influence the manner in which the larger society may frame its perception of the group. Most disturbingly, these same characterizations can be internalized by the group itself and subsequently have an impact on the manner in which they view themselves and become complicit in their own educational and social challenge. Without question, school personnel may operate on many of these beliefs about their Black male students, in some cases in extreme ways, and in others, subtly. But Du Bois's question, "How does it feel to be a problem?" is important to note for Black males here: What does it mean when you are viewed as a problem? And I pose several additional education-related questions: How does it affect one's behavior? How does one develop coping strategies? How does it influence teacher behavior? How does it affect placement for special and gifted education? And perhaps most important, how does it influence one's pursuit of academic success and social inclusion? It is also worthwhile to examine how the deficit-oriented construction of Black males presents major problems, and how even equity-minded researchers often may contribute to the manner in which Black males are viewed. Moreover, one can only begin to assess to what degree young Black males, after years of hearing these messages of what they cannot do and what they cannot be, internalize these ideas, resulting in a self-fulfilling prophecy that undermines any effort to improve their school outcomes.

Crucial to the paradigmatic shift is to understand the historical portrayal of Black men in the United States. Polite and Davis (1999) uncover the pathological manner in which Black males often have been described historically as brutes, criminals, entertainers, intellectually inferior, and physically superior.

The images of Black males, often characterized as docile and hypersexual, have been part of the DNA of the United States from the country's outset and have set much of the tone on race in the country for centuries (Gibbs, 1988). In one of the more illuminating works on Black males, and the narrative that has been woven over time, A. Brown (2011) offers an historical examination of the manner in which Black males have been portrayed in the social science literature. This examination raises important questions and concerns about how researchers have played a prominent role in the negative construction of Black males, even as they claim to disrupt some of the troubling accounts. Brown suggests that from the 1930s to the present, four recursive narratives about Black males have informed the general populace: (1) *absent and wandering,* (2) *castrated and emasculated,* (3) *soulful and adaptive,* and (4) *endangered and in crisis.* He identifies these four narratives as being staples in the normalized manner in which Black males are seen within popular media and describes the way in which much of social science research feeds into this characterization of Black males as being in need of intervention, lacking in emotional and social support, and in perpetual need of male mentorship and role modeling. Much of Brown's (2011) work is focused on how these narratives can be rewritten, reconceptualized in a manner that is asset-based, and show Black males from a position of possibility, and not one that continues to calcify them as directionless, hopeless, and deficient.

BLACK MALE INTERSECTIONALITY: REDEFINING AN IDENTITY

In 1989, Kimberléé Crenshaw introduced the concept of intersectionality in her work, *Demarginalizing the Intersection of Race and Sex: A Black Feminist Critique of Antidiscrimination Doctrine, Feminist Theory, and Antiracist Politics.* She describes the multidimensionality of Black women's experiences as being complicated based on their gender (patriarchal society), race (predominately White society), and poor (capitalistic society). Crenshaw's works spurred a plethora of works from dominated groups who argued that traditional approaches to examining equity and discrimination did not effectively capture the full spectrum of their experiences. Intersectionality conceptualized how oppressions are socially constructed and affect individuals differentially across multiple group categories. Crenshaw's explanation of intersectionality is central to understanding the complex and marginalized aspects of identity of which women in communities organizing for social change have long been aware.

Intersectionality, or interaction of multiple identities and varied experiences of exclusion and subordination, provides a suitable framework to examine the experiences of Black males because it not only centers race at the core of its analysis, but also recognizes and examines other forms of oppression and identity markers, namely, class and gender, which have important implications for Black males (Patterson, 1995). The concept of intersectionality is based on the idea that the typical conceptualizations of discrimination and oppression within society, such as racism, sexism, homophobia, and class-based discrimination, do not act independently of one another; instead, these forms of oppression interrelate, creating a system of oppression that reflects the "intersection" of multiple forms of exclusion, prejudice, and discrimination (McCall, 2005). The intersections of race, class, and gender have manifested themselves in a multitude of complex and harmful ways within the United States that have profoundly influenced the manner in which Black males experience schools (Polite & Davis, 1999). This intersectionality is rarely examined with men of color, and as a result opportunities to authentically capture the breadth and depth of Black males in this case are missed, and efforts to capture their stories and reform schools are misinformed and misguided.

Crenshaw (2009) contends in examining intersectionality and its influence on identity that "the problem with identity politics is not that it fails to transcend difference, as some critics charge, but rather the opposite—that it frequently conflates or ignores intragroup differences" (p. 213). Hence, one of the goals in disrupting age-old depictions of Black males is to shed light on the dynamic intragroup differences that exist among Black males and their respective identities.

The concept of *interlocking oppressions* (McCall, 2005) expands the idea of intersectionality, names the mechanisms of social construction more concretely, and explicitly allows for a deeper examination of intragroup differences among identities. The idea of interlocking oppressions considers how interactions between individuals and social factors shape individuals' subjectivities. Specifically, interlocking oppressions name how one person's sources of privilege or subordination can construct another's marginalized identity. In this way, the concept of interlocking oppressions explains how the oppressions associated with different socioeconomic locations are socially constructed and calls on individuals to take responsibility for their roles in the oppression of others. Examining the interlocking oppressions that Black males may be subject to, and explicating their experiences within those socially constructed locations of marginalizing subjugation, could prove fruitful in widening the discourse around Black male identity. Heterosexual Black men, for example, although oppressed in many forms for other identities, possess the privilege that heteronormativity brings (Yep, 2003) and may, consciously or subconsciously, participate in discriminatory or excluding practices toward homosexual men. This privilege, accounting for interlocking oppressions, can serve to marginalize homosexual Black men in unintended and largely unexamined ways (E. Brown, 2005; Collins, 2004; Hutchinson, 1999). Again, this intricate level of examination and discourse is necessary in order to better understand the complexity within the experiences of Black males.

Needless to say, the essentialization of any group presents a host of challenges. However, the failure to peel back the thick layers of oppression that afflict various groups ignores the complexity of identity in the 21st century. The failure to unpack the multiple layers of identity markers inadvertently leads researchers and practitioners to narrow and often misguided understandings of the lived experiences of certain groups—particularly those on the margins, in this case, Black males (McCready, 2004). As a result, inquiry, interventions, or means to disrupt their realities fall short because of the failure to see, describe, examine, and understand the rich differences that exist within groups.

Exploring the intersectionality of race, gender, and class in a more nuanced fashion for Black males is essential. In his book, *Thirteen Ways of Looking at a Black Man,* Gates (1997) unpacks the diversity and complexity of what it means to be Black and male in the United States. Gates's work is important because he attempts to capture through a narrative account the myriad variables that define the lives of Black men in the United States. He states:

> We agree that the notion of a unitary black man is as imaginary (and as real) as Wallace Stevens' blackbirds are; and yet to be a black man in the twentieth century is to be heir to a set of anxieties: beginning with what it means to be a black man. (p. xvii)

Gates speaks to the complexity of Black male identity, which is both located in a collective identity, yet influenced by individual experiences. The collective identity can produce a conundrum for researchers who seek to understand this group as a whole. A diversity of experiences influences the *individual* identity that Black males develop in the United States. Researchers would find that while obvious social identities such as race and gender are prominent, as provided in Gates's accounts, equally captivating are the ways that religion, social class, sexual orientation, political persuasion, ethnic origins, age, and geographical location also paint an intricate picture of how Black males define themselves and ultimately live their lives. Black males find themselves in perpetual negotiation as they seek to reconcile their own individual lived experiences with prescribed societal expectations and limitations. This negotiation can prove fatiguing and taxing mentally, physically, and emotionally for Black males (Smith, 2010; Smith, Allen, & Dantley, 2007) and may influence their social and academic outcomes in schools.

Disrupting deficit accounts of Black males and reconceptualizing diverse identities of Black males should include exploring what it is like to expand their *symbolic boundaries*. Researchers should engage in inquiry that encourages Black males to step outside of these restrictive constructions and instead create narratives from their standpoints, which can serve to disrupt the traditional narratives (Allen, 1996; Flennaugh, 2011). Researchers need to consider that efforts to disrupt Black male underperformance have fallen short in producing new knowledge and unique insights because the approaches taken historically have fallen short in incorporating, addressing, and examining the full scope, complexity, and diversity of Black male identity (Howard, Flennaugh, & Terry, 2011). Intersectionality has applicability in this discussion because it draws upon paradigms of multiple identities and calls for the exploration of these different perspectives to shift age-old paradigms. Delgado and Stefancic (2001) state:

> Perspectivalism, the insistence of examining how things look from the perspective of individual actors, helps us understand the predicament of intersectional individuals. It can enable us to frame agendas and strategies that will do justice to a broader range of people and avoid oversimplifying human experience. Another critical tool that has proven useful in this respect is the notion of multiple consciousness. (p. 55)

Recognizing that race and racism work with and through gender, ethnicity, class, sexuality, and nation as systems of power, contemporary critical race theory often relies upon investigations of these intersections (Collins, 2006; Solorzano & Delgado Bernal, 2001; Solorzano & Yosso, 2001).

Research on the experiences of Black males has to recognize the complexity that is Black male identity within the context of learning institutions and social spaces (Nasir, 2012). The intersectionality of race, class, and gender and other identity markers is fundamentally critical in research concerned with young Black males, as in the case of any other subgroup. Each marker in its own way profoundly influences identity construction, self-concept, interactions with the world, and meaning-making. Among the questions that need to be posed are: How do diverse notions of Black maleness play out in schools? What are the advantages and disadvantages of diverse masculinities in schools? Do school structures, policies, and practices suppress complex or strong racial and gender identities? I would argue that schools as social structures and institutions have their own culture, norms, and ideologies at work that affirm certain identities, yet silence and marginalize others. It is therefore crucial to investigate to what degree, if any, the wide range of cultural norms, ways of knowing, and personal/cultural knowledge that Black males bring to schools is at odds with the norms, values, and customs of the very structures designed to foster their development.

DOUBLE-CONSCIOUSNESS AND INTERSECTIONALITY

Du Bois (1903) paid particular attention to the internal conflict that Black people faced in the United States at the turn of the 20th century. His notion of double-consciousness recognized the psychological and sociohistorical realities of American oppression and sought to shed light on the complex ways in which Black people develop notions of self in a social, economic, and racial milieu that is hierarchical and exclusionary. Although Du Bois did not problematize

gender in his analysis of double-consciousness, his ability to raise the importance of multiple identities is salient in this context. More contemporary work
on Black males has encouraged educational researchers and identity theorists to
acknowledge the often complex ways masculinity, for example, plays out among
Black males in today's schools (Harper & Nichols, 2008). Harper and Harris
(2010) have suggested that there is a need to move "beyond singular notions of
gender" (p. 5), and state that this static understanding of what it means to be
Black and male excludes a large number of Black males who do not locate their
identities in such narrow characterizations. These works are important because
they operate from a framework in which Black males are not monolithic, but
walk in many spaces, have multiple identities, and negotiate identity with space
and place on a constant basis. Nasir, McLaughlin, and Jones (2009) note "the
need for a nuanced conception of . . . both the strength of the identity and the
local meaning of the identity" (p. 107). The local meaning of identity, therefore,
should consider space, place, age, race, ways of being, and ways of knowing,
among other factors. In their sociocultural and ecological theory analysis of
achievement, identity, and race for Black students, they discovered that African
American students endorsed a range of identity meanings and that these meanings varied according to the context in which they were shaped.

The exploration of intersectionality for Black males is complicated on several levels. Since they are racialized beings in a predominately White suprema-
cist society, issues tied to race and racism work to their detriment and bring a
multitude of challenges. It is important to identify the different ways that people
of color experience life in the United States (Solorzano & Yosso, 2001). In many
cases, Black people are more likely than other groups to be victimized targets
of racism, discrimination, and exclusion from mainstream opportunities. However, as gendered beings, Black males benefit from the privileges of living in a
patriarchal society, but because they are racial minorities, their male privileges
are not at parity with those of their White male peers socially, politically, and
economically (E. Anderson, 2008; Wilson, 2008). One of the challenges of these
complex intersections, in thinking about interlocking oppressions, is that Black
male privileges often lead to distorted notions of masculinity and can lead some
to overlook the manner in which sexism harms the life experiences of Black
men and women (hooks, 2004). Conversely, one has to wonder how some of
these forms of masculinity play out in classrooms. Given the feminization that
is present in many classrooms, some Black males may feel left out or pushed
out of schools if they are not able to negotiate their notions of masculinity in
feminized classroom spaces.

Black male identity to a large extent stems from a distorted notion of masculinity within the traditional context of many Black communities and has
been treated largely as one-dimensional and universal, meaning that men play
the role of primary provider, disciplinarian, and individuals with a dearth of

emotion and affective filters (Majors & Billson, 1992). Much of this construction is perpetuated within Black culture and life, and is a by-product of Eurocentric patriarchy, which has defined maleness in distinct and confining ways (hooks, 2004). Harper and Harris (2010) argue that definitions of masculinity contribute to the exclusion of Black males who do not fit the hyper-masculine construct.

McCready (2004) suggests that Black males experience troubling social conflicts that may affect their academic outcomes. He contends that researchers need to take into account multiple categories of difference and oppression in order to understand and suggest interventions for gay and non-gender-conforming Black male students in urban schools. Therefore, a more complete analysis of how Black males experience schools needs to engage a discourse about how masculinity often is defined narrowly within Black cultural contexts, thus making it difficult for many Black males to display alternative forms of masculinity. Furthermore, McCready (2010b) accesses Black feminist epistemology to apply intersectionality in documenting the experiences of Black males, while acknowledging the limitation of using a feminist framework to unpack the experiences of men. He states:

> The problem here is divorcing intersectionality from a distinctly feminist agenda and treating it instead as a normative enterprise. The persistence of uncritical, patriarchal, "additive," theoretical frameworks in urban education compels us to experiment and see what intersectionality, as a feminist framework, can bring in terms of developing a more socially just praxis for all stakeholders in urban schools. (pp. 14–15)

I employ intersectionality, despite its limitations, to further understand hypermasculine and heteronormative ideologies and practices that are pervasive in many Black communities and the larger society. These ideologies characterize what it means to be male and Black, in disturbing ways that are inconsistent with the manners in which countless numbers of Black males display their own racial and gender identities (Davis & Jordan, 1995).

Watts and Erevelles (2004) state that schools use oppressive ideologies associated with race, class, gender, and disability to justify the social construction of certain students as deviant or rule-breaking, thereby making it an individual rather than a social or systemic problem. Using an intersectionality analysis, Watts and Erevelles contend that material school conditions exist that compel students, especially African American and Hispanic students from low-income backgrounds, to feel vulnerable, angry, and viewed as resistant to normative expectations. Also incorporating aspects of critical race theory, Watts and Erevelles further assert that in U.S. public schools Whiteness continues to be constructed in such a way that material conditions produce and perpetuate difference to such a marked degree that both African American and Hispanic students, especially males, experience segregation and discrimination through schools' sorting practices and discipline.

Lacy (2008) argues that the intersectionality paradigm in most social science and legal research is limited because while it examines dual identities of subordinated groups (e.g., poor Black women), Black males usually are excluded from the paradigm even though they suffer the effects of racial and gender politics in a unique way. He contends that scholars have failed to take up the case of Black males in the intersectionality paradigm and he offers an "exponential framework" in response to this void. He contends that while Black men should enjoy the privileges that come with being male in a patriarchal society, the coupling of being male with *Blackness* creates a burden and undermines the privileges afforded to White men in the United States. He documents the disproportionality in educational outcomes, unemployment, and incarceration rates as indicators that even though this population is a dominant group (men), the intersectionality paradigm has utility in examining its suppression. Thus, he argues for an exponential framework, contending that as maleness and Blackness converge, evidence of prejudice and discrimination increases exponentially for this particular group in ways that it does not for others.

Purdie-Vaughns and Eibach (2008) contend that androcentric, ethnocentric, and heterocentric ideologies frequently cause people who have multiple subordinate-group identities to be defined as non-prototypical members of their respective identity groups. Their contention is that the debate about who suffers more, individuals from one subordinate group (e.g., Black males) or persons from multiple subordinate groups (e.g., Black women), is counterproductive; moreover, because of these multiple, subordinate, and frequently complex identities, people can suffer from *intersectional invisibility*. The prevalent and narrow ideologies will cause people who have narrow notions of identity, and engage in competition around degrees of oppression. Therefore, they suggest that the aim, then, is to engage in research on intersectionality that attempts to move beyond the question of "whose group is worse off to specify the distinctive forms of oppression experienced by those with intersecting subordinate identities" (p. 4). They contend that individuals who possess intersecting subordinate-group identities often are defined, described, and perceived as non-prototypical members of their constituent identity groups, thus rendering them invisible.

STRUCTURAL INTERSECTIONALITY

While competing forms of oppression can manifest themselves in problematic ways, another major layer of Black male identity is socioeconomic status. In a society where capital is germane to one's life opportunities and overall life quality, Black males find themselves at or near the bottom of most social and economic indices (E. Anderson, 2008). A thorough analysis of Black males' experiences in the United States needs to recognize interlocking forms of oppression that have had a profound influence on the ability of this population to become self-actualized. Perhaps no other system of oppression has had more of an adverse impact on Black males than capitalism and its most adverse manifestation—poverty. Different structures, systems, laws, and policies have combined to have a nefarious effect on how individuals participate in the nation-state (Massey & Denton, 1993). In a society that stresses the value of meritocracy, fairness, and egalitarian efforts, Black men have been one of the subgroups consistently on the outside, looking into the structures that contribute to economic and social mobility.

Structural intersectionality refers to the creation, operation, maintenance, and synthesis of various systems and structures in society that maintain privilege for some groups or individuals, while restricting or denying the rights and privileges of others (Swanson, Cunningham, & Spencer, 2003). Structural intersectionality also encompasses the political, economic, representational, and institutional forms of discrimination, oppression, exploitation, and domination; highlights the connectedness of systems and structures in society; and helps us understand how each system affects or impacts others (Wilson, 2008). To contextualize how structural intersectionality affects Black males in a capitalistic society, one need not look further than today's burgeoning prison industrial complex. Alexander (2010) unpacks how mass incarceration over the past 3 decades has disproportionately affected Black males more than any other group. Alexander also uncovers the varied obstacles that most Black males face as they attempt to re-enter society post incarceration. The prolonged stigma that comes with incarceration has a direct effect on the ability to access public housing, public assistance, political participation, and, most important, employment. Each of these systems has a devastating effect on Black men, their families, and their communities, and results in their frequently being denied options and opportunities for participation in mainstream society. Upon encountering repeated obstacles, many Black males, in a quest for survival, return to the same criminal behavior that led to their incarceration, thus explaining the 80% recidivism rate among Black men in cities across the country.

An additional reason to examine Black males within a more intersected context centers on the fact that much of the work on Black males has classified them as poor and residing in inner cities. Unquestionably, a large number of Black males are growing up in the midst of economic challenges that are part of urban and rural America. Absent from this discourse are explanations of upward mobility and how it has shaped the manner in which Black males experience schools and society. B. Gordon (2012) raises important questions that seek to understand the experiences of middle- and upper-class Black students in general, and Black males in particular, that have facilitated conditions under which they are woefully overlooked, ignored, and understudied in educational research. Her research reveals that even the promises of social and economic mobility do not seem to thwart the presence of race and racism when it comes to their schooling experiences. Gordon (2012) notes that "by living, growing up in, and attending schools in suburban communities, these students cannot help but absorb the culture of the schools and society of which they are a part, yet in which they remain the 'other'" (p. 10). Ogbu (2003) raises similar concerns in his analysis of the middle-class community of Shaker Heights, where he poses thought-provoking questions about how upward mobility influences the manner in which African American students view high achievement. Hence, just as race matters, so does social class. What is unique about these experiences is the need for Black males to negotiate the majority and minority cultures. The challenge for researchers, then, is not only to examine the lived experiences and school outcomes in overcrowded, low-performing schools, but also to document how Black males in high-performing schools, from middle-class to affluent neighborhoods, make meaning of these experiences.

Reynolds's (2010) work, for example, looked at the challenges that middle-class Black parents encountered when they sought to advocate on behalf of their children and discovered that the most notable obstacle was the issues that their sons faced from peers, teachers, and administrators. Parents in her study consistently noted the low expectations educators held for their Black sons. These parents distinguished between the treatment their Black daughters received compared with the experiences both they and their sons had working with educators who were primarily from the dominant group. In this study, class proved less a mediating factor in the disparate treatment Black boys received in predominately White middle-class schools. In this case, race and gender seemed to overshadow capital as an explanative factor in understanding discrimination that Black males face.

The intersection of race along with other identity markers raises important insights into how our questions, analysis, and understanding of Black males shift when social class shifts. Moreover, this analysis of class and race brings important considerations to bear, as research consistently reveals that Black and Brown students in middle-class and affluent schools find themselves at a distinct disadvantage compared with their White and Asian counterparts (Howard, 2010). Thus, inherent in the analysis is that while the dominant community has its fears and concerns about poor Black males, there is a degree of comfort in seeing them as restricted within a poverty context. However, when Black males are not located exclusively within a poverty context, the response to race and class can have deleterious effects for them. Thus, we find that complexifying race and class in educational theory and practice contributes to a unique analysis and a richer, more comprehensive examination of the challenges Black males encounter in schools. This type of examination is imperative if we wish to engage in the authentic democratic tradition upon which the educational system was founded initially.

CHAPTER 3

Who Really Cares?

The Disenfranchisement of African American Males in Pre-K–12 Schools: A Critical Race Theory Perspective

In his noted 1992 work, *Faces at the Bottom of the Well*, legal scholar Derek Bell tells a fictitious story about a group of "Space Traders" who have arrived in the United States. In this most intriguing account of extraterrestrial invaders landing on the Earth's shores, Bell describes a scenario in which this group of Space Traders have come equipped with natural resources, special environmental cleaning chemicals, money, gold, and other commodities that are desperately needed for a financially and natural resource–strapped United States. The traders are willing to provide these items to the U.S. government in exchange for all of its African American citizens, who would be taken to an unknown location. Bell's Space Traders story is fascinating because he walks readers through a 2-week travail of the agonizing debate in which governmental leaders and the American public engage around a central question: What is the worth of African Americans in the United States? Bell's work is mentioned here because over 2 decades after his story of the Space Traders, the question may very well loom for educational practitioners, researchers, and scholars around a group of students whose value and worth seem to be called into question every day in schools across the United States, and who are the focus of this work—African American males.

One of the subtexts to Bell's story about the Space Traders is, Who would really care if African Americans no longer existed in this country? Would there be an uproar and mass protest about their removal? Or would there be silence and indifference from many citizens that would send a strong message of complicity and agreement with the decision? Again, Bell's work is mentioned here as a backdrop for delving into a hypothetical, yet seemingly real, conundrum facing the field of educational research: How would educational researchers and scholars react if a particular group of students no longer existed? What if there were a group of students whose educational prospects and life chances seemed

47

in such dire straits that their viability as a group was in serious question? How would the educational research community react? Would there be a strong call for funding and research to probe potential interventions and solutions to stem the tide of hopelessness for this group? Would we seek new paradigms that might provide the needed insight into helping improve the schooling experiences and ultimately the quality of life of this group? Or would the disenfranchisement of this group be greeted with a loud silence that would seem to convey a general lack of concern about their education and life prospects? These questions are raised because a close examination of the current state of education for African American males in pre-K–12 schools reveals that these students' underachievement and disenfranchisement in schools and society seem to be reaching pandemic and life-threatening proportions.

One of the disturbing realities about the plight of African American males in pre-K–12 schools has been the relative silence from the educational community at large, and the educational research community in particular. While an increasing number of African American scholars have addressed this issue (Brown & Davis, 2000; Fashola, 2003; Foster & Peele, 1999; Garibaldi, 1992; Hopkins, 1997; Noguera, 2001; Polite, 1993b; Polite & Davis, 1999), it would appear as though others have accepted this widespread failure as business as usual, thus echoing an old phrase from Marvin Gaye's famed song, "Save the Children," in which he asks the poignant question about the fate of our children: "Who really cares?"

This chapter examines the underachievement and disenfranchisement of African American males in pre-K–12 schools, using critical race theory (CRT) as a conceptual framework. CRT is a lens that enables a discourse about race, class, and gender to be the centerpiece for an analysis of African American male underachievement. This particular analytic lens acknowledges the presence and perniciousness of racism, discrimination, and hegemony, and enables various cultural and racial frames of reference to guide research questions, influence the methods of collecting and analyzing data, and inform how findings can be interpreted. A number of scholars have argued about the value of race-based epistemologies and methodological approaches for educational research (Delgado, 1999; Delgado & Stefancic, 2001; Parker & Lynn, 2002; Solorzano & Yosso, 2002). Race-based epistemological approaches are important analytic lenses, particularly within qualitative research, because they offer the opportunity to challenge dominant ideology, provide transdisciplinary modes of inquiry, and suggest a space for insiders' accounts of their experiences (Solorzano & Yosso, 2002). Equally important is that theoretical approaches such as CRT seek to illuminate the voices of individuals that historically have been silenced in educational research, thus providing a counterscript to mainstream accounts of their realities (Tillman, 2002).

THE STATE OF AFRICAN AMERICAN MALES IN PRE-K–12 SCHOOLS

The academic achievement of African American males in pre-K–12 schools has been the subject of a growing number of scholarly works over the past 2 and a half decades (Brown & Davis, 2000; J. E. Davis, 2003; C. W. Franklin, 1991; Gibbs, 1988; Hopkins, 1997; Madhubuti, 1990; Noguera, 1996; Polite, 1994; Polite & Davis, 1999; Price, 2000). Much of this work has been concerned with the identification of informative research, effective strategies, and critical concepts that seek to address two concerns: (1) explanations for the persistent underachievement of African American males in U.S. schools and society, and (2) potential interventions that can help improve the educational aspirations and life chances of African American males. This research has been much needed given the troublesome state of many African American males in pre-K–12 schools. A multitude of statistics underscores the severity and persistence of the academic underachievement of many African American males. Consider the National Center for Education Statistics data over the past decade, which reveal that a majority of African American males in the 4th, 8th, and 12th grades did not reach grade-level proficiency in key subject areas such as reading, mathematics, history, and science. In addition, less than one-quarter of African American males were at or above grade level in these same subject matter areas. Furthermore, fewer than 3% of African American males performed at advanced levels in these areas. Advanced-level performance would make them eligible for gifted and talented or advanced placement courses, which are important gatekeepers for postsecondary education (U.S. Department of Education, NCES, 2012).

In 2006, the Schott Foundation for Public Education revealed startling statistics in a national report card titled, "Public Education and Black Male Students." According to the report, during the 2003–2004 school year, 55% of African American males did not receive diplomas with their classmates 4 years after beginning high school. A number of states scored worse than the national average. For example, Florida and Nevada failed to graduate a third of their Black male students. Seven states (Delaware, Georgia, Illinois, Michigan, New York, South Carolina, and Wisconsin) failed to graduate more than the national average for Black males. Furthermore, the study found that Black males who dropped out of school were heavily concentrated in those cities, such as New York, Detroit, and Chicago, that failed to graduate between two-thirds and three-quarters of their African American males. The report's authors stated that they studied African American males because "as a group, the cumulative consequences of school failure are most severe for this group of students . . . and to understand that this enormity of school failure has created a rip tide of negative results for Black male students and society as a whole" (p. 2).

A preponderance of evidence shows that academic underachievement exists for many African American males in pre-K–12 schools; however, social and emotional challenges face them as well. Consider the fact that African American males currently make up approximately 7% of the nation's pre-K–12 student population, yet they constitute a disproportionate percentage of students who are in special education, alternative schools, and remedial classrooms (Office for Civil Rights, 2000). This overrepresentation is most prevalent in the classification of students with high-incidence disabilities; namely, mental retardation, learning disabilities, and serious emotional disturbances (Yates, 1998). These categories require a high degree of professional judgment for consensus, however, and in many ways could be interpreted subjectively, with different outcomes depending on the cultural competence of the assessor.

Not only do the school failures of African American males have implications for them in pre-K–12 schools and higher education, but, more disturbing, the widespread failure has a direct correlation with the quality of life they face after an unsuccessful school experience. There is an increasing correlation between African American males who perform poorly in school, many of whom ultimately drop out, and their subsequent involvement in the penal system. According to the 2005 Bureau of Justice statistics, African American males outnumber all other ethnic groups of the prison population and have a rate of incarceration that is five times higher than the rate of White males. Moreover, one in every eight African American men in their 20s and 30s was behind bars in 2003 (Elsner, 2004). Department of Justice statisticians project that based on current demographics, one in every three African American men can expect to spend time either incarcerated, on probation, or under some type of jurisdiction of the penal system during his lifetime.

Longitudinal research done by the U.S. Bureau of Justice and the Justice Policy Institute revealed that in 1980, 463,700 African American men were enrolled in higher education compared with 143,000 who were incarcerated. By 2004, the study found that 758,400 African American men were enrolled in colleges across the United States compared with approximately 924,000 who were in the nation's jails and prisons. The Justice Policy Institute estimates that over this 24-year period, for every one African American male who entered a college or university, three entered jail or prison. In California, African American males are five times more likely to go to prison than enter one of the colleges in the state's university system (Conover, 2000), and in Illinois there were 10,000 more African American men in prison than in college. Even today, such staggering numbers paint a sobering reality that suggests that a young African American male who started kindergarten in the fall of 2013 had a better chance 12 years later of finding himself under the supervision of the penal system or being incarcerated than enrolling in a college or university. To quote Alan Elsner (2004), who has done extensive work examining the crisis in the U.S. prison system, "For many young black men, prison is their college" (p. 13).

THE NEED IN RESEARCH FOR NEW PARADIGMS FOR
AFRICAN AMERICAN MALES

Much of the recent research that has been concerned with African American males has sought to counter the stereotype of their being inherently undereducated, underemployed, criminal-minded, oversexed, and pathological in nature (J. E. Davis, 1994; E. W. Gordon, 1996, 1997; Noguera, 1996; Price, 2000). These works have provided alternative portrayals of African American males that disrupt the hegemonic notion that they are socially and academically deviant. Furthermore, these works have sought to identify frameworks that will allow more African American males to reach their full potential. I share similar concerns of previous scholars in identifying important variables of the problems facing African Americans in general, but more important, I am concerned with identifying meaningful interventions and useful research paradigms that offer ways to improve the educational experience for African American males.

As a researcher, I am interested in more probing and critical theoretical frameworks that will invite a more penetrating analysis of the dismal state of affairs for many African American males in pre-K–12 schools. As an African American male scholar who has endured the challenges that scores of young Black men face from preschool through postsecondary education and beyond, I am seeking to identify a theoretical framework that will enable researchers to ask, "How do race and racism influence the current state of affairs for young Black men in pre-K–12 schools?" I am in search of a theoretical framework that does not have to "make the case" or "explain beyond a reasonable doubt" how and why race matters in the schooling experiences of African American males, but that accepts race and racism as integral parts of life in the United States. Equally important, as a father of three young Black males, this troubling state of affairs not only has professional interest for me, but sets forth real, personal, and tangible issues that I, and scores of other parents of young African American males, face on a daily basis as we seek to identify and implement protective and nurturing strategies to enable our sons to experience school and society in a manner similar to that of their non-Black peers.

DOES RACE STILL MATTER?

Some may ask, "How do we know that race plays a factor in examining the disenfranchisement of African American males?" It goes without stating that important issues such as class, gender, home and community environments, parental education and involvement, disabilities, language, ethnicity, and culture all play important roles in access to education in this country. However, race still remains one of the least understood, yet most provocative and divisive, elements of our society. Cornel West (2004) reminds us that race still matters and is "America's most explosive issue and most difficult dilemma" (p. 1). In many ways, our failure to honestly and critically examine race and all of its manifestations has led only to further tension, discrimination, and hostility along racial lines. James Baldwin often referred to the "rage of the disesteemed" that would occur if the United States did not acknowledge the destructive roles that race and racism played in this country. According to Balfour (2001), Baldwin argued that the United States is guilty of

> a willful ignorance, a resistance to facing the horrors of the American past and present and their implications for the future. This unwillingness to confront these horrors accounts for the resistance of racial injustices to remedy by formal, legal measures. For innocence sustains a mind-set that can accommodate both an earnest commitment to the principles of equal rights and freedom regardless of race and a tacit acceptance of racial division and inequality as normal. (p. 27)

This is one reason why race still matters and must be a central aspect of any discussion that is concerned with racial inequities, because as a country, and as a community of researchers, we have yet to engage one another in an authentic, honest, and sustained dialogue about race and racism. Our failure to engage in this most important dialogue about race, racism, power, and all of their manifestations, significantly limits the manner in which various individuals can talk about their experiences in the United States. This failure also prevents us from hearing and empathizing with the pain, frustration, and deep-seated anger that resides in the hearts and minds of many U.S. citizens, particularly our young people, because they have been told that race is unimportant. Yet, in so many ways they find their experiences and opportunities being shaped largely by issues of race. Our failure to engage in a conversation about race and to suggest that we now reside in a color-blind society is problematic and potentially destructive (Bonilla-Silva, 2003; Tatum, 1997). Such shortcomings only further silence the voices of those on the margins who continually seek inclusion in schools and society. Thus, a theoretical framework centered squarely on the salience of race, racism, and power, and the education of racially diverse students in this country, would allow us to have a conversation that is desperately needed, most certain to be uncomfortable, and long overdue.

Why such a critical focus on African American males? Beyond the wide range of statistics that reveals their social, educational, political, and economic disenfranchisement in this country, there are democratic reasons why this examination is necessary. If the United States is to hold true to its democratic creed of life, liberty, and the pursuit of happiness, do we as social scientists have the privilege of sitting idly while a large group of our citizenry continues to be excluded from these core aspects of society? As educational researchers whose goals and aims are, as David Larabee (2003) states, to "make sense of the socially complex, variable rich, and context-specific character of education" (p. 14), how can we not engage in meaningful dialogues and critical inquiry about severely disenfranchised groups? Gary Orfield (2004) posits, "When we see a problem as a serious threat, we don't wait until we have scientific proof about the solutions. We start experiments and try to figure out what works and how to refine our efforts" (p. 9).

If one of our tasks as scientific researchers is to improve education through scholarly inquiry for the public good, it is essential that our work deal with those populations who have not benefited from the good that the public has to offer. While the focus of this work is on African American males, equal concern should be given to a plethora of other ethnic groups who continue to under-achieve in U.S. schools. Latino students, the nation's largest non-White group, in particular underachieve at a level comparable to many African American students. These startling figures are most prevalent with Mexican American students in the western and southwestern United States and Puerto Rican students in the northeast, the majority of whom are below grade-level proficiency in reading, math, and science (National Center for Education Statistics, 2009). Despite the prevailing construction about Asian Americans being high achievers, a close examination of the achievement of Hmong students in the Midwest, as well as other Southeast Asian students, namely, Vietnamese, Laotian, Cambodian, and Taiwanese students in pockets of the west coast and the Midwest, reveals that their school performance is far from acceptable, and deplorable in many circumstances (Allen & Nee, 2003). These disturbing educational trends affecting large numbers of students of color require researchers to probe into the salience of race as a factor in school achievement.

I propose using CRT as a theoretical framework for examining the educational experiences of African American males because race has been, and remains, by and large undertheorized in education (Ladson-Billings & Tate, 1995). Race is also a topic that individuals frequently avoid when discussing the experience of life in the United States. Cornel West (2004) states, "To confront the role of race and empire is to grapple with what we would like to avoid, but we avoid that confrontation at the risk of our democratic maturation" (p. 41). The failure on the part of researchers to critically examine the role that race plays in the pursuit of an equitable education may reveal insights into why previous measures have had limited effectiveness for marginalized student populations.

An explicit acknowledgment of race and racism in educational theory and practice may contribute to a unique analysis and a richer, more comprehensive explanation of the educational challenges facing African American males, who, perhaps more than any other student population in the United States, may be most negatively affected by distorted constructions of race and gender. As a result, these students are the victims of detrimental racial politics that play out in many U.S. schools. It is also necessary to recognize that race and racism have been and remain central cultural and structural forms of oppression that permeate every social, economic, and political institution in the United States. Thus, unpacking their historical legacy and their contemporary remnants for all citizens is critical. This unpacking has obvious implications for the victims of racial oppression and inequity because many of them have experienced schooling in a manner that has had negative consequences for them, and educational researchers can play an important role in examining these circumstances in order to improve their educational and life chances. Equally important, however, is for this examination to inform those who have been beneficiaries of racial privilege to recognize their connivance in a social order that has produced institutional structures and ideological paradigms that have directly and indirectly contributed to the disenfranchisement of various groups in this country.

CRITICAL RACE THEORY

Initially developed primarily by scholars of color who were concerned with challenging racial orthodoxy in the legal arena, critical race theory emerged from the field of critical legal studies (Delgado, 1995; Matsuda, Lawrence, Delgado, & Crenshaw, 1993). CRT was a response to the slow pace of racial reform in the United States in the post–civil rights movement era, and the emergence of neo-conservative policies of the 1980s (Bell, 1992, 1995; Crenshaw et al., 1995; Delgado & Stefancic, 2000). According to Delgado and Stefancic (2000), the CRT movement is a "collection of activists and scholars interested in studying and transforming the relationship among race, racism, and power" (p. 2). Critical legal studies also criticized mainstream legal ideology for its portrayal of American society as a fair and just meritocracy that seeks to legitimate and maintain existing institutional arrangements (Crenshaw et al., 1995).

One of the basic tenets of CRT is the normalcy and permanence of racism (Bell, 1992). Critical race theorists assert that racism is and has been an integral feature of American life, law, and culture, and any attempt to eradicate racial inequities has to be centered on the sociohistorical legacy of racism (Delgado & Stefancic, 2000). It is through this lens of race and all of its manifestations that CRT is able to pose this challenge to racial oppression and subjugation in legal, institutional, and educational domains. A central part of this analysis is the notion of Whiteness as property, wherein historically the law has been used as the primary vehicle to protect the interests and rights of Whites over the rights of persons of color. Thus, CRT interrogates the positionality and privilege of being White in the United States, and seeks to challenge ideas such as meritocracy, fairness, and objectivity in a society that has a legacy of racial discrimination and exclusion.

CRT within education is an evolving methodological, conceptual, and theoretical construct that attempts to disrupt race and racism in education

(Ladson-Billings, 1998; Solorzano, 1998). It enables scholars to ask in unique ways the important question of what racism has to do with inequities in education. CRT examines racial inequities in educational achievement in a more probing manner than do multicultural education, critical theory, or achievement gap theorists, by centering the discussion of inequality within the context of racism (Sleeter & Delgado Bernal, 2004). CRT within education also serves as a framework to challenge and dismantle prevailing notions of fairness, meritocracy, color-blindness, and neutrality in the education of racial minorities (Parker, Deyhle, & Villenas, 1999).

Critical race theorists in education anchor their interrogation of racism in four primary ways:

1. By theorizing about race along with other forms of subordination and the intersectionality of racism, classism, sexism, and other forms of oppression in school curriculum.
2. By challenging dominant ideologies that call for objectivity and neutrality in educational research. CRT posits that notions of neutrality typically serve to camouflage the interests and ideology of dominant groups in the United States, and that they should be challenged and dismantled. Ladson-Billings (2000) argues that "there are well-developed systems of knowledge, or epistemologies, that stand in contrast to the dominant Euro-American epistemology" (p. 258).
3. By offering counterstorytelling as a liberatory and credible methodological tool in examining racial oppression. Counterstorytelling has a long and rich history in communities of color, which have utilized oral means of conveying stories and struggles that often are overlooked by those in positions of power, and it draws explicitly on experiential knowledge.
4. By incorporating transdisciplinary knowledge from women's studies and ethnic studies to better understand various manifestations of discrimination (Smith-Maddox & Solorzano, 2002; Solorzano & Yosso, 2001).

CRT has the potential to enable a discourse to take place in the educational research community that has occurred in Black homes, neighborhoods, churches, barber shops, and communal gatherings for years. Among scores of Black men, this dialogue, or the counterstory, has occurred within school locker rooms, on street corners, and in basketball gyms. It is a conversation that this research community should hear as we continue to seek interventions for complex problems in educational research, theory, and practice. The inclusion of a CRT framework is warranted in education when one considers the perennial underachievement of African American males in U.S. schools (U.S. Department of

Education, NCES, 1998, 2000). The severity and persistence of underachievement for African American males and other non-White students in U.S. schools lead critical race theorists to ask the question, "What's race got to do with it?" (Parker & Lynn, 2002). This is a question that we as an educational research community have failed to engage on a large scale, but when we listen to certain voices on the margins, they would suggest that "race has a lot to do with it." It is this viewpoint that we must allow to be a part of our data sources, methodologies, and analyses; CRT can be a useful lens to better understand these omitted voices and viewpoints.

CRT provides a suitable framework because it not only centers race at the core of its analysis, but also recognizes other forms of oppression, namely, class and gender, which have important implications for African American males as well. Parker (1998) argues that:

> The critical centering of race (together with social class, gender, sexual orientation, and other areas of difference) at the locations where the research is conducted and discussions are held can serve as a major link between fully understanding the historical vestiges of discrimination and the present-day racial manifestations of that discrimination. (p. 46)

The intersections of race and gender have manifested themselves in a multitude of complex and harmful ways within U.S. society. Grant and Sleeter (1986) argue that there needs to be further analysis of the intersection of race, class, and gender in student academic achievement and social adjustment. Moreover, they argue that the failure to examine the complexity of race, class, and gender intersections may lead to oversimplification of theory and the perpetuation of bias about groups based on single areas of identity. The intersectionality of race, class, and gender for African Americans is necessary in the analysis of what Collins (2004) refers to as Black sexual politics. She defines Black sexual politics as a theoretical framework that views race, class, gender, sexuality, ethnicity, and age as mutually constructing systems of power. Furthermore, she maintains that this intersectionality permeates all social relations in society and has particular ramifications for African Americans. Collins maintains that "developing an intersectional analysis of Black sexual politics has tangible political ramifications for anti-racist scholarship and activism" (p. 11). She also suggests that this contemporary and complex mix of race, gender, and class must be mindful of the "new racism" apparent in the United States. She asserts that globalization, transnationalism, hegemonic ideology, and mass media have created an environment where "Black youth are at risk, and, in many places, they have become identified as problems to their nation, to their local environments, to Black communities, and to themselves" (p. 54). Therefore, it is important to identify specific locations, practices, and paradigms where this "new racism" manifests itself.

It is important to delve into the constructs of race and gender for African American males for several reasons. First, the exclusive use of race in the analysis of African American males does not set their realities apart from the experiences of African American females and of other racial minorities. Although there has been research that has chronicled the experiences of African American females (Paul, 2003) and other racially diverse students (S. Lee, 1996; Moll, 1996; Pang & Cheng, 1998; Valenzuela, 1999), one could argue that these groups do not seem to have the same degree of exclusion and disenfranchisement from schools as do African American males. An analysis of African American males strictly through a gendered lens does not allow race to be examined. While there is extensive research that examines the social, emotional, and educational challenges that males of all ethnic groups face in schools, there is a clear racial hierarchy among those groups that requires examination. The race and gender nexus is important because individuals wear multiple identities that typically are shaped by both race and gender in all of their manifestations. More important, the social construction of these identities plays out in unique ways that have critical implications for racial and gender minorities, in particular African American males. Anne Ferguson (2003) writes:

> Sex is a powerful marker of difference as well as race. While the concept of intersecting social categories is a useful analytical device for formulating this convergence, in reality we presume to know each other instantly in a coherent, apparently seamless way. We do not experience individuals as bearers of separate identities as gendered and then raced or vice versa, but both at once. The two are inextricably intertwined and circulate together in the representation of subjects and the experience of subjectivity. (pp. 22–23)

A conceptual framework with an explicit examination of the ways that race and racism manifest themselves, and their juxtaposition with gender, in education may offer new analysis into the underachievement of African American males and provide new insight and direction for reversing their school underachievement. Moreover, an investigation of what it means to be Black and male in the pursuit of education in the United States is critical given many of the distorted racial and gender norms that frequently offer narrow constructions of each group (Davis, 2003). All too often African American males have been caught in a web of stereotyped notions of race and gender that place them at considerable disadvantage in schools and ultimately in society. The mere exploration of the social construction of the Black male image in the United States over the past 4 centuries reveals a highly problematic depiction ranging from the docile or the bewildered slave, to the hypersexed brute, to the gregarious Sambo, to the exploitative pimp or slickster, to the super athlete and entertainer. The social and political ramifications of each of these images still influence the perceptions of scores of young Black men today, including through their own perpetuation of these images. These characteristics all contribute to what Hutchinson (1994) has referred to as the "assassination of the Black male image" and undoubtedly play a role in the racial and gender politics that play out in schools across the country.

COUNTERSTORYTELLING AS A METHODOLOGICAL TOOL TO RECONCEPTUALIZE RESEARCH WITH AFRICAN AMERICAN MALES

One of the central tenets of CRT that can have important implications for educational research concerning African American males and other marginalized populations is the importance of counterstorytelling and narrative theory as a methodological tool (Clandinin & Connelly, 2000; Delgado & Stefancic, 2001). The idea of counterstorytelling and the inclusion of narratives as a mode of inquiry offer a methodology grounded in the particulars of the social realities and lived experiences of racialized victims (Matsuda, 1993). Delgado (1999) refers to counterstorytelling as a method of telling stories of individuals whose experiences have not been told, and a tool for analyzing and challenging the stories of those in power whose story is a natural part of the dominant discourse. Given the troubling state of affairs experienced by an increasing number of African American males in pre-K–12 schools, paradigms must be created that will allow their voices to shed light on the day-to-day realities in schools and challenge mainstream accounts of their experiences.

One of the glaring absences of much of the research associated with African American males is that it has not included firsthand, detailed accounts from African American males about the roles that they believe power, race, and racism play in their educational experiences. It is the value of experiential knowledge that may offer important opportunities for new research paradigms, particularly those centered on the manifestations of race and racism. The use of narrative and storytelling offers what Tillman (2002) refers to as "culturally sensitive research approaches" for African American students. Tillman describes these approaches as "interpretive paradigms that offer greater possibilities for the use of alternative frameworks, co-constructions of multiple realities and experiences, and knowledge that can lead to improved educational opportunities for African Americans" (p. 5). According to Sleeter and Delgado Bernal (2004), CRT "view[s] experiential knowledge as a strength, they draw explicitly on the lived experiences of people of color by including such methods as storytelling, family history, biographies, [and] parables" (p. 22).

A small number of works have documented African American students' perspectives of their learning environments (Howard, 2001; P. W. Lee, 1999; Noguera, 2003; Price, 2000; Waxman & Huang, 1997), but even fewer have used CRT or comparable theoretical frameworks to examine how African American males interpret their schooling experiences. To highlight examples of how such work is critical and informative, consider the work of Duncan and Jackson (2004), which used a post-critical approach to examine the schooling inequities of African American males at a Midwest high school. Informed by a theoretical framework that was mindful of various ethical and moral considerations in the schooling of Black males, their post-critical approach sought to "privilege the voice of those who bear the brunt of inequalities in schools and grant them an opportunity to inform the analytic and conceptual categories we bring to our research" (p. 3). Furthermore, Duncan and Jackson state that they used an approach that went beyond traditional critical analyses and that "privileges the subjective ontological categories that inhere the language of the students" (p. 3). Thus, by centering the voices of young Black males and their accounts of schooling, this study highlighted the political nature of language in schools, and how African American males made sense of schooling in an environment that many of them felt was inherently unjust. This work offers useful ways to practitioners and researchers who seek to understand choices that many Black males make in their schooling process.

In another example of scholars using a CRT lens to critique the schooling experiences of African American males in U.S. schools, Watts and Erevelles (2004) used internal colony theory to expand the scope of CRT's critique of racism. Watts and Erevelles maintain that internal colony theory as a theoretical framework offers a different insight into the existing literature on African American and Latino males that blames them for violence in U.S. schools and labels them as "natural born killers" (p. 284). Moreover, they assert that internal colonization explains how "colonizing education is both violent and oppressive because of its psychological impact on the colonized, who have had to struggle against the illusion that everyone is operating under a fair but competitive market" (p. 284). Borrowing from the works of Paulo Freire and Frantz Fanon, Watts and Erevelles suggest that African American males, as a racially oppressed population in schools, begin to "imitate the behaviors and attitudes of their oppressors" (p. 287), and that their outward expressions of violence and resistance in schools are not the real problem. Rather, they believe that if authentic possibilities for troubled groups are to be identified, the racist practices and ideologies that are institutionalized and normalized within schools, but that "are not recognized as violent or dangerous because they are so normalized," need to be examined (p. 287).

Another example of the use of CRT as a methodological tool to shed light on the experience of African American students is highlighted in DeCuir and Dixson's (2004) examination of the racial climate at Wells Academy, a private school located in a predominately White, affluent southeastern city. Undertaking a CRT analysis of African American students' experience at the elite school, DeCuir and Dixson use a counterstorytelling approach to uncover the persistent and subtle acts of racism that students experience at the school with regularity. Moreover, the analysis of this work is instrumental in documenting the normalcy in which racism occurs. The African American students at Wells elaborate on the tacit and explicit acceptance of racism by school teachers and administrators, stating that school staff "aren't that surprised that it is there" (p. 26). This work is critical in highlighting the pervasiveness and normalcy of racism, in addition to the Whiteness as property principle, which among other things sanctions the exclusion of perspectives and ideologies that are not consistent with a Whiteness paradigm.

COUNTERSTORYTELLING FROM AFRICAN AMERICAN MALES

To provide an additional account of counterstorytelling, I spent the past year documenting the experiences of African American males in an attempt to allow them to shed light on their experiences in schools. As part of an ongoing study, 200 African American middle and high school males were surveyed about their schooling experiences and the potential roles that race may play in them. A subsample of this larger group was interviewed to gain a more in-depth analysis of their perceptions of and experiences in schools. Ten African American males who were part of this smaller sample, and who were middle or high school students during the 2005–2006 academic year, serve as the participants for this work. The young men whose counterstories are offered here represented five different schools in a large metropolitan area on the west coast of the United States. Part of this study was to investigate the young men's experiences within different social class school settings. Therefore, five of the young men attended schools in urban, primarily low-income areas that were made up largely of African American and Latino students. The other five participants attended more racially mixed schools located in suburban communities, which were predominately White and middle class.

One of the central themes to emerge across each of the stories offered by the young men was their keen awareness of negative racial stereotypes about African American men. Critical to each of these young men were explicit attempts not to reinforce widely held beliefs and stereotypes about African American males. Most of the young men in this study attributed much of their academic success to their desire to challenge negative stereotypes about young Black males. Many of the young men discussed peers they knew who were incarcerated at some point, made bad choices, or had dropped out of school; these students had a strong desire not to follow a similar path. I probed their thoughts about the choices many young Black males make, and why they felt it was critical not to reinforce these stereotypes about Black males. Jawan, one of the respondents, offered this commentary:

I always have to think, "What are they thinking about me?" If they think I am going to gang bang, rap, and act stupid, then I just work on doing the opposite. So when they see me on the honor roll, they seemed surprised, and I just trip off that.

Several of the young men talked about the perception that is held about young Black males in schools, and how they try to disrupt these beliefs. Jelani commented:

I play football, so you know they expect you to be good in sports. But when you are on the ASB [Associated Student Body] council, like I am, and being a school leader, have good grades, and talking about going to college on an academic scholarship, then they look at you like, Whoa!! I didn't think that they [Black males] were into those kind of things. One teacher even told me once, "You're not like the rest of them." I didn't ask her what that meant, but believe me, I knew what that meant.

The types of accounts provided by the young Black men from this work are rarely shared in the educational discourse. DeCuir and Dixon (2004) assert, "The use of counterstories allows for the challenging of privileged discourses . . . serving as a means for giving voices to marginalized groups" (p. 27). While several of the young men who attended predominately White schools discussed the manner in which they felt they were viewed by White peers and teachers, several of the respondents at the predominately African American schools also discussed the importance of shattering stereotypes. As Christopher stated:

It's hard, because so many of us [Black males] are messing up at this school, and I know the teachers look at us like, "Why should we care, when they don't?" And I work hard to let them know that not all of us are messing up. A lot of us are doing homework every day, studying, working hard, so that we can improve ourselves.

Most of the young men stated that they believed that race was frequently a factor in how they were dealt with by their teachers and school administrators. Rodney stated that "teachers never let you forget that you are Black." Akbar, a middle school student, maintained that being Black at his predominately White school was difficult because "the minute something goes wrong at the school, the first people that get looked at are all the Black boys, and it ain't even that many of us around here. You just get tired of that." A similar sentiment was provided by Richard, who was a high school senior during the year of the study, when he stated:

I watch it all the time. One of us (Black males) do something, and we get suspended or expelled. A White kid does the exact same thing, and he gets a warning, or an after-school referral. Sometimes it's so obvious that they treat us different than them.

Essential to the power of counterstorytelling are the insidious accounts of discrimination or racism that many of the respondents stated occur at their schools with regularity. Vann discussed an example that occurs in his racially mixed school, commenting:

Mr. Paulsen [an English teacher] will have White or Asian kids who talk in class by challenging stuff in the book, or disagreeing with some of the readings, and he says that they are being "critical thinkers" and he praises them for that, but each time I say something that I disagree or don't like something we've read, he says I am being disrespectful, or I don't understand the text. Why are they critical thinkers, but I am disrespectful?

In examining each of the works mentioned, it is imperative to recognize that African American males discussed and defined their own realities on their terms. The young men were the center of these analyses based on their own interpretations of their experiences and were offered frameworks that allowed them to critique schools as institutions and the people within them. Moreover, each of these works did not solicit or invite its participants to provide "safe" or politically correct responses. To underscore the salience of using CRT as a methodological tool to glean insights from African American males about their learning environments, future research must give credence to the power and insight that comes from their naming, describing, and analyzing their own realities. New paradigms also must be cognizant of how insider or cultural knowledge, which is an essential part of qualitative research, can be revealed through first-person accounts of reality. Moreover, appropriate theoretical frameworks are necessary for race-specific research because they are critical in identifying relevant concepts and constructs to guide the research. They also offer specific questions to be queried, methods of analysis, and means of interpreting the findings (Merriam, 1998).

At least two of the young men challenged the way in which students were assessed, and how access to a quality education, along with race, may be a factor in that process. Kenji stated:

I mean, think about it. We have this exit exam now, and a lot of kids are not passing it. I passed it after the third time I took it. But when I first took [it] I was like, "none of this stuff, we never were taught," so how can you test us on it now? The only way I passed was that my dad got me a tutor. But what about the kids who can't afford a tutor? They are not gon' pass, and it's not because they are dumb, it's because they haven't been taught that stuff at this school.

Greg, another high school student, was more explicit about the racial disadvantages and stated:

I mean, . . . look at this school. You have to go through metal detectors just to get in. Half the teachers don't care. Just walk in their classes and you can tell. In my geometry class, we had subs the whole year. How can you have a school, and you don't even have teachers to teach the kids? I mean, come on now. I think that we are Black and poor have a lot to do with it. Show me where they have a school with White kids that have it like we have it. You can't prove that it's racism, but how can it be anything else?

Consequently, as researchers seek to identify useful interventions for improving the educational opportunities for African American males, they must be mindful that insider perspectives may provide different and often more condemning accounts about the schooling process than mainstream versions.

To highlight other examples of research concerned with African American males' perceptions of their schooling environments, Noguera's (2003) research found that African American males had vastly different experiences in schools from their White counterparts. He discovered that the overwhelming majority of African American males believed that education was important and had strong desires to attend college; however, they were the group least likely to believe that teachers cared about them and their learning. Noguera posits that the hostile and nonsupportive feelings that African American males experience in schools merit an examination into structural and cultural explanations of how identity is constructed within racial and gender terms for this population. Needless to say, in light of the various portrayals of African American males through mainstream media, researchers could be informed by the myriad factors that African American males employ in constructing their identities and could inquire whether these factors could be manipulated in order to create more positive and self-sustaining identities.

IDENTIFYING RACIAL MICRO-AGGRESSIONS THROUGH COUNTERSTORYTELLING

What must be clear as researchers examine the role that race and racism play in the educational experiences of many African American males is that the manifestations of individual and institutional racism are not always blatant, overt, and easy to observe. Frequently, acts of racism in schools are innocent, subtle, and transparent, but harmful nonetheless. Solorzano (1998) has discussed using CRT as a theoretical framework to uncover racial micro-aggressions that frequently affect students of color. Solorzano cites Chester Pierce's (1974) work on racial micro-aggressions wherein he describes them as "the chief vehicle for proracist behavior. . . . These are subtle, stunning, often automatic, and non-verbal exchanges that are put-downs of blacks by offenders" (p. 526). Other scholars have written about the insidious nature of racial micro-aggressions and a pressing need to uncover them. P. Davis (1989) defines micro-aggressions as "stunning acts of disregard that stem from unconscious attitudes of white superiority and constitute a verification of black inferiority" (p. 1576). For African American males, racial micro-aggressions from classroom teachers can manifest themselves in numerous ways.

Justin, a high school senior, provided an account of these subtle, yet harmful, put-downs that students may feel:

> We had an assembly at school for all the seniors who were going to college. They had the students come up on stage and said what college they were going to. For whatever reason, they forgot to call me up during the assembly, so I asked Mr. Matthews [the assistant principal] after the assembly why I didn't get called up, and he said that they were only calling up the kids who were going to "good colleges," and they didn't think that Morehouse was a really good college. That was like a slap in the face to me. Morehouse is a good college. I'm one of the first kids to go to college in my family, and he says that it is not a good school. How does that make me feel?

Future research centered in a CRT framework involving African American males could question whether and how racial micro-aggressions are present in low teacher expectations for African American males, suspicion or surprise about their academic success, common acceptance of their underachievement, lack of positive reinforcement for their accomplishments, differential forms of punishment, demeaning comments, failure to place them in leadership positions, and reluctance to refer them for advanced classes. In short, racial micro-aggressions are tantamount to what Joyce King (1991) refers to as dysconscious racism: "an uncritical habit of mind that justifies inequity and exploitation by accepting existing order of things as given" (p. 135). To reinforce this point, Richard offered his experience with taking an AP class on the first day at his new school:

> On the first day in class, I showed up a little late to this AP chemistry class. The teacher said, "You must be in the wrong class, this is AP chemistry." I said, "No, I am in the right class," and showed her my schedule. She looked

at it, and said, "This must be wrong, you cannot be in here." She didn't even know me, but she assumed that I didn't belong in her class. She called down to the office, and took about 15 minutes calling down to the placement center, talking to counselors and everything, and when it was all over, I was in the right class. Am saying, if I was Asian, would she have gone through all of that?

As many African American males attempt to come to grips with racial micro-aggressions that may be present in school policies, curricular programs, and teacher practices, researchers can play a vital role by providing nonthreatening platforms that allow them to offer uninhibited descriptions of these instances, which vary from the dominant script about them, their performance, and their potential. Delgado and Stefancic (2001) state that the concept of the differend is much needed in critical research. They state that the differend occurs when the pursuit of justice is complicated by two competing explanations from various positions. The differend helps explain the value of narratives from marginalized persons and allows them to tell their stories and offer a counterscript to the dominant paradigm. In her work *Yearning*, bell hooks (1990) talks critically about the dangers of White interpretations of the Black experience, and the mainstream's suspicion of the Black experience as told by Black people. Kristopher, a middle school student, stated that he had to attend a different school because of a fight he had with a White peer:

We got into this fight. I said he started it, he said I started it, but the principal believed him. I had never been in trouble at school before, and this kid got in trouble a lot. But I am the one who got kicked out, and he stayed at the school. They said that I was "too hostile and aggressive," and I never caused trouble, but it was like they didn't want to hear nothing me and my mother had to say.

Counterstorytelling, or the differend, gives agency to African American males to offer narratives that can counter many of the rhetorical accounts of their identities that frequently describe them as culturally and socially deficient, uneducated, unmotivated, prone to violence, and anti-intellectual. According to Delgado and Stefancic (2001), counterstorytelling can serve as a cure for silencing those who have been the targets of racial discrimination. They state:

Many victims of racial discrimination suffer in silence, or blame themselves for their predicament. Stories can give them voice and reveal that others have similar experiences. Stories can name a type of discrimination; once named, it can be combated. If race is not real or objective, but constructed, racism and prejudice should be capable of deconstruction. (p. 43)

If race and racism are social constructs that can be deconstructed, particularly within the context of education, educators must be informed by reliable research that documents where, how, and why race-related problems persist in schools. Researchers should be careful not to either underestimate the ability of African American males, or any other group of students, to name their experiences; or question the veracity of students' accounts; or dismiss students' notions of how their schooling experiences can be improved. One of the enamoring aspects of this work has been the young men's surprise about someone wanting to hear about their experiences. This was best summed up by one of the high school participants:

> I'm kinda shocked that you are asking us about this kinda stuff, because we never get asked about racism and stuff. Because you just assume that nobody's gonna believe you when you tell them about it. But this stuff is real. I was tellin' one of my friends about the stuff we were talking about, and they were like, "Where is he [the interviewer]? Can we talk to him too? Cause we got some stuff to tell him too." It's like a lot of dudes got a lot of stuff they want to get off their chest. You know it's like being in the desert and everybody's thirsty, and you bring a big thing of cold water, everybody runs to get some. You being here, just asking about this stuff, makes a lot of dudes want to talk to you about what they go through. The way we get talked to, the way teachers treat you, the stuff they want you to learn, I mean I could go on and on.

A deconstruction of race and racism has to take into account new realities, different voices, and the uncovering of silenced viewpoints. One of the criticisms made of CRT, and the idea of counterstorytelling and narrative theory as a methodological tool, is its perceived lack of analytical rigor and objectivity, and the inability to verify or confirm the accuracy of the accounts offered by the victims (Farber & Sherry, 1997; Posner, 1997). Some scholars believe that the stories may be intentionally atypical in order to garner greater attention and sympathy for the victims. At least one account from a middle school participant seemed to offer a retort to this claim:

> I talk to my cousin who goes to Countrywood [another suburban middle school], and he tells me the same kinda stuff that happens to us [Black males] there. First to get blamed, surprised when you do good in school, expect that you are good in sports. It's like different school, same stuff. It seems like we get it no matter where we are.

To combat this criticism of atypical stories, one must acknowledge the permanence of storytelling from the dominant paradigm when it comes to ideas such as meritocracy, democracy, and equality: ideas and concepts that many citizens in this country believe are just that—ideas and concepts, not realized ways of life. Thus, from a CRT perspective, the notion of storytelling comes down to Sleeter and Delgado Bernal's (2004) comment, "At issue is the question of what counts as truth and who gets to decide" (p. 249). The critics also contest how representative these accounts are of all members of the group, or what Rosen (1996) refers to as "vulgar racial essentialism." Although CRT situates race at the center of its analysis, it recognizes the fluidity and multifaceted nature of identity for all individuals, and does not attempt to create monolithic constructions or experiences of any group. All theoretical frameworks have their share of strengths and weaknesses, and CRT theorists recognize that the framework is not a panacea for all that ails children of color in U.S. schools and that it will be subject to various critiques. However, these critiques should not prevent a much-needed examination of race and racism in education from occurring. More important, future research concerned with CRT can directly address these critiques conceptually and empirically, which will only strengthen the paradigm as it continues to emerge in educational research.

CRITICAL RACE THEORY AND ITS CHALLENGE FOR AFRICAN AMERICAN MALES

This chapter began with Derek Bell's parable of the Space Traders who essentially challenged the United States to contemplate the value of African Americans. In many ways, the plight of African American males in pre-K through postsecondary education may ask educational scholars how much we value young Black males in this society; if they are valued, how can so many of them encounter such unsettling experiences in schools? How can their pleas for help go seemingly unheard? Where is the plethora of research and funding opportunities to identify meaningful interventions for this group?

The CRT challenge in education should be centered on several fronts that may provide interventions for the state of affairs of African American males. CRT has played an important role in legal decisions. Crenshaw et al. (1995) contend that one of the common interests of critical race theory in the legal arena is not to "merely understand the vexed bond between law and racial power but to change it" (pp. xiii). Critical race theorists in education must be willing to adopt a similar stance: a stance that is centered not only on ideology, but on reliable research, useful strategies, and effective interventions that will improve the day-to-day realities, educational prospects, and life chances of African American males and other disenfranchised student groups.

As previously mentioned, CRT can be applied in key aspects of the schooling experience of African American males in tangible ways. Ladson-Billings

(2004) argues that there are several areas of education that are amenable to a CRT analysis, namely, curriculum, instruction, and assessment. She contends that a close examination of each of these areas suggests that students from racially diverse backgrounds experience significantly different accounts of what is taught, how it is taught, and the ways schools evaluate what students know. Traditional curriculum that does not reflect the experiences, histories, and issues that are germane to African American males, could be re-evaluated for its relevance to various student populations. A multitude of scholars have made the call for curriculum revisions that are multicultural (Banks, 1997; Gay, 1994), critical multicultural (McLaren, 1994), and anti-racist (Brandt, 1986). Similar claims can be made for revising instructional approaches. The intricacies of human variation as manifested by culture tell us that students vary widely in their modes of communication, cognitive development, modes of expression, motivation, and world views, each of which influences learning (Rogoff, 1990). As a result, teacher pedagogy should be reflexive and culturally responsive to these differences.

So where else can CRT position itself in the field of education? How does it challenge the status quo regarding racial justice in ways similar to the legal field? Where are the racial tensions in education that allow CRT to be utilized? Two areas that would be ideal for a critical race examination of African American males would be standardized testing and school discipline. In the most recent era of educational accountability where No Child Left Behind has become the law of the land, the implementation of standards-based learning and high-stakes testing has become the vehicle used to sort and stratify students in the name of school reform. Ladson-Billings (2004) states that "from a CRT perspective, current assessment schemes continue to instantiate inequity and validate the privilege of those who have access to cultural capital" (p. 60).

A perusal of the national data shows that an increasing number of states have adopted high-stakes testing for their students, with a growing number of them using these tests to determine important decisions such as grade promotion, retention, and graduation. Conversely, recent research has found that reliance solely on high-stakes testing as a graduation or promotion requirement may increase inequities and dropout rates among students by both race and gender, with African American males the student group most likely to drop out because of high school exit exams (Dee & Jacob, 2006). Some accounts assert that tests by themselves do not improve student achievement (Brennan, Kim, Wenz-Gross, & Siperstein, 2001). Thus, an area of increasing concern is that there seems to be a high correlation among test performance, socioeconomic background, and the race of students. It is no accident that student performance on high-stakes tests frequently is tied to students' socioeconomic background and the level of teachers' experience and overall school quality. Given the fact that students of color and from low-income backgrounds are more likely to come from poorly funded schools, and have underqualified and inexperienced teachers, one can only question the wisdom of evaluating those students on similar measure as students who come from schools with greater resources and more qualified teachers. Consequently, the more poorly students perform on standardized tests that serve as gatekeepers to grade promotion and retention, the more likely they are to drop out—a reality that increasingly has affected African American males. More troubling is the reinforcement of racist and classist normative beliefs that students who perform poorly on such tests are therefore less capable, less intelligent, and inherently less prepared to do well in school and society. The test scores are viewed as reliable "evidence" to make such claims about particular populations. CRT must contribute to other works that help to uncover the ways that race, class, gender, and overall structural inequities play a significant role in student performance.

The second area where CRT may bring attention to issues affecting African American males is school discipline. The "zero-tolerance" policy that was designed in the mid- to late 1990s to curb school violence seems to have clear racial overtones in terms of who is most affected. According to the 2000 Department of Education's Office for Civil Rights (OCR) report, African American students are 2.6 times more likely than White students to be suspended from school. The OCR data also reveal that African American males are more likely than any other racial or ethnic group to be expelled from school. The U.S. Department of Education reported that in the year 2000, African American students accounted for 34% of all out-of-school suspensions and 30% of all expulsions, with the overwhelming majority of these students being male—a disproportionate percentage for a group who make up 7% of the total student population.

The growing rates of suspensions and expulsions in the name of zero-tolerance may make get-tough and no-nonsense policies appealing to administrators; however, the fallout seems to be that students' academic prospects suffer when they are suspended or expelled. Research shows that students who have been suspended or expelled are increasingly likely to drop out of school and subsequently more likely to become juvenile delinquents. Using data from 2000, Skiba and Noam (2001) looked at zero-tolerance in 37 states to assess its relationship to achievement, behavior, and youth incarceration. They found that schools with high out-of-school suspension rates had lower achievement in 8th-grade math, writing, and reading. Moreover, the data revealed that states with higher rates of school suspensions were more likely to have higher incarceration rates among their students. Most troubling was that Skiba and Noam (2001) found that in almost every state, African American males had higher suspension, expulsion, and incarceration rates than the general population by far.

The confluence of persistent low achievement and soaring suspension and expulsion rates of African American males may suggest an emerging "school-to-prison" pipeline that is becoming a mainstay in many schools across the country (Skiba et al., 2003). Critical race theorists can interrogate the criminalization of young Black males in schools today and ask, "How and why have zero-tolerance policies had a disproportionate and more punitive effect on young Black males than any other student group?" This is particularly disturbing when the zero-tolerance policy was largely in response to the spate of random school shootings that occurred in the mid- to late 1990s, none of which, coincidentally, were perpetrated by African American males. How can policies be evaluated to assess their fairness, and be reconstituted to ensure that particular groups are not disproportionately punished? Methodologically, CRT-based research not only can examine the racial disparities in testing and school discipline, but also can provide qualitative studies that allow students to talk about the ramifications that policies and practices have on their perceptions of school and about how they believe their lives are influenced by those policies and practices.

I began this chapter using Derek Bell's parable of the Space Traders and posed the question, What would happen if young Black males were no longer in existence—how would the educational research community react? Or perhaps the more poignant question that R&B legend Marvin Gaye poses, "Who really cares?" I maintain that the educational research community must engage in serious soul-searching about the work that we do and the utility that it possesses in the lives of everyday citizens. Not only must we ask what relevance our work has to the larger society, but another question we should ponder is, Does our work in any way contribute to the transformation of disenfranchised populations? Some would argue that it is not our purpose to save the world, but that it is our task to responsibly and reliably investigate various phenomena in education, identify meaningful interventions, and contribute to new knowledge about how education works. Nonetheless, I would maintain that we have an obligation to do more than merely talk about, or theorize, the real challenges that scores of young people courageously live through every day in our society. Our challenge must be to listen to the stories, experiences, challenges, setbacks, successes, and triumphs of those on the margins.

NOTE

This chapter originally appeared as an article in the *Teachers College Record, 110*(5), May 2008, pp. 954–985. Reprinted by permission.

CHAPTER 4

Black Males and Sports
Opportunity or Obstruction?

Haven't you ever wondered why the [W]hite man genuinely applauds a [B]lack man who achieves excellence with his body in the field of sports, while he hates to see a [B]lack man achieve excellence in his mind.

—Eldridge Cleaver, 1968, p. 151

Four years ago, my oldest son, who was an all-league, all-area football player in high school, was invited to participate in a Nike-sponsored combine. The purpose of the combine was to bring some of the top football talent together in southern California so that talent evaluators, college scouts, and assistant coaches could see them up close in person and assess their speed, strength, agility, and jumping ability, among other things. Being told that we had to report to the community college where the event was to take place at 7:30 A.M. was a bit of a surprise to me and also led me to believe that the event would not be well attended, given that 16- and 17-year-old young men were asked to wake up early on a Saturday morning. To my amazement, my son and I arrived at the combine where approximately 200–250 young men (90% of whom were Black) were aligned in an orderly and patient fashion, preparing to display their physical prowess for the ogling eyes of the mostly White male audience, complete with stop watches, tape measures, and the like. Over the course of 4 hours, Black male bodies were instructed, marveled at, prodded, analyzed, and sized up, in a fashion that was almost similar to what enslaved Africans encountered prior to being sold on auction blocks. This scene included a flood of parents, siblings, and other concerned family members who were hoping that their sons, brothers, and grandsons would catch the eye of a talent or college scout who might deem them worthy of a college scholarship. The scene was intriguing to me in many ways, because well-wishers cheered when their sons did well, groveled when they did not, and held lots of conversations about their loved ones' football abilities in a beaming and prideful manner.

My immediate thought upon observing this scene was how and why Black parents, family members, and caregivers seemingly make such extraordinary efforts (especially on a weekend) to attend, support, celebrate, and encourage young Black boys' participation in football, basketball, track and field, and other athletic endeavors, yet seemingly do not exert the same level of commitment and effort to support these young men academically. I say this because I reflect on my days as a classroom teacher in Compton, California, and the countless back-to-school nights and open houses that were poorly attended, which frequently left me confused as to why more parents were not in attendance. My aim here is not to indict parents, because I believe the overwhelming majority of parents care deeply about their children's academic well-being. I also understand the reasons why many parents may find it challenging to attend school-based events. Nonetheless, I wondered why so few come to schools, yet so many attend athletic events.

A visit to a little league football field on a Saturday morning or afternoon during football season, or a trip to the local gymnasium during basketball season, would provide a glimpse into the phenomenon that I maintain is doing persistent harm to countless numbers of Black males in the United States. I refer to this phenomenon as the *athlete seasoning complex* (ASC), which affects a growing number of Black males, particularly those growing up in urban and low-income communities. I define the athlete seasoning complex as a process in which youth are provided early, intensive, and persistent access to sports, and thus expected to participate and excel at high levels. The process, which usually is introduced explicitly and implicitly by parents or caregivers, can envelop young boys, especially, in a culture of sports and athletics that can blind them to other areas of development such as academics or the arts. The process also may entail an expectation that immersion and excelling in sports may result in college scholarship opportunities, or perhaps even professional stardom. I will elaborate more on the ASC later in this chapter, but before I do, I will provide a backdrop of the nexus that is race and sports in the United States, and then discuss some of the more pressing issues in today's context and what they mean for Black males.

RACE AND SPORTS: A COMPLEX RELATIONSHIP

Dating back for 2 centuries, there has been a unique nexus between race and sports in the United States (Donnor, 2005; Edwards, 1983, 1998; Entine, 2000; Harrison & Lawrence, 2004; Hoberman, 1997, 2000). The ability of individuals to use sports as a platform for athletic excellence, competition, racial pride, and greater social equity has been essential to American life and culture. African Americans in particular have a long, arduous, yet glorious history within the field of sports. The triumphs of sports icons and American heroes such as Jack Johnson, Joe Louis, Wilma Rudolph, Arthur Ashe, Jesse Owens, Althea Gibson, Jackie Robinson, and Muhammad Ali all have served as symbols of Black pride, excellence, and resilience in the face of sordid racial ideologies, racism, and outright discrimination (Rhoden, 2006). Their triumphs have carried accomplishments that often seem to go beyond the playing field to convey a larger message to the wider society about Black promise and potential in the elusive quest for racial equality. William Rhoden (2006) states that "Black athletes have symbolically carried the weight of a race's eternal burden of proof" (p. 3).

Given the salience that sports have played in the African American cultural tradition, it would seem illogical to consider sports to be a harmful or detrimental element to the Black experience. Yet a growing body of evidence would suggest that it may be. Some have ridiculed sports for centuries as a form of exploitive racism used to showcase Black bodies for the purpose of the entertainment and enjoyment of White spectators. Dating back to the 18th century, some Black leaders have questioned the value of sports and their social ramifications. Frederick Douglass stated that "boxing and wrestling, drinking and other merriments during holiday periods were the most effective means slaveholders had for keeping down insurrection" (quoted in Sammons, 1988, pp. 31–32). Booker T. Washington raised further questions about the utility of sports, stating that "all men should be educated along mental and spiritual lines in connection with their physical education. A man with muscle minus brains is a useless creature" (quoted in Gilmore, 1973, p. 25). Raising the question about the utility of sports is not new, and given contemporary circumstances, there is a strong case to be made about how sports may be doing irreparable harm to young Black males today (Beamon & Bell, 2006). Undoubtedly there is a complex relationship between young Black males and sports. Moreover, I ponder whether the lure and pursuit of sports today is doing unequivocal damage to Black males academically in a manner that no other subgroup experiences.

Sports have served as an excellent venue for Black males to learn invaluable lessons about teamwork, competition, sacrifice, discipline, and dedication. Needless to say, all of these characteristics go beyond the field of competition and can provide life lessons that are essential for being productive and contributing members to society. In the spirit of full disclosure, I acknowledge my positionality as someone who participated in high school and Division I athletics. Sports helped me to learn the value of dedication, commitment, and hard work. I am forever indebted for the experiences I had through my participation in sports. Understanding the importance of teamwork, self-sacrifice, and time management also have served me well. Furthermore, having three sons who also have participated in sports (one currently at a Division I level), I understand the paradox of being critical of an entity that my sons and I have benefitted from. However, a closer look at the current sports industrial complex reveals unprecedented troubling, harmful, and outright immoral practices that are undermining the future of young Black boys. My goal is to put forth theoretical and practical cautions about the detrimental role that sports, and the pursuit of stardom through sports, plays on young Black males and subsequently their families and communities. Although this stand may be challenged in many circles, without a doubt sports have a complex and troubling influence on the societal landscape in countless ways—and at the center of this phenomenon are young Black males.

What is needed are further examinations into the lure of sports for Black males, the commodification that occurs for many, and how this pursuit of athletic stardom frequently comes at the expense of their academic development and educational attainment. The burgeoning sports industrial complex that sells the idea of fame and fortune, which is a billion-dollar industry, has Black males at its very core. Patricia Hill Collins (2006) contends that "athletes and criminals alike are profitable, not for the vast majority of African American men, but for people who own the teams, control the media, provide food, clothing and telephone services, and who consume seemingly endless images of pimps, hustlers, rapists, and felons" (p. 311). There are a number of intersecting economic, political, educational, and social imperatives that are driving the expansion of the sports industrial complex on the very backs of Black bodies at the turn of the 21st century, much as slavery did at the turn of the 18th century. Not only are public and private entities profiting immensely from the mass movement of Black talent through the system, but Leonard and King (2011) maintain that the commodification of Black athletes "also functions as an ideological and discursive commodity used to sell the American Dream and colorblindness in post-civil rights America" (p. 9).

SPORTS: WHY THE QUEST?

Much of the appeal of athletics for young Black males is obvious. In a society that largely portrays Black males as problematic, inept, and lacking intellectually (despite having a Black male as president), the athletic domain is one of the few settings in the United States where Black males see their excellence acknowledged, their creativity cheered, their bravado and masculinity replicated on a major stage and promoted globally. In many cases they are outright revered as folk heroes, and the appeal of million-dollar contracts remains a large carrot as well. Moreover, the manner in which athletic prowess is embraced in a cross-racial and cultural context is intriguing; it is one of the few spaces where much (but not all) of the racial baggage that plagues Black males seems to be ignored, dismissed, or overlooked. Some of the most recognizable individuals in the world are Black male athletes, such as Kobe Bryant, LeBron James, Michael Jordan, and Usain Bolt, all of whom have become global icons. Seemingly, they not only have transcended race, but have shattered the deficit notions that define many Black males as angry, threatening, and unintelligent. As a result, the goal for many young men is to become the next superstar basketball or football player. Hence, from the time many young Black boys are toddlers, any semblance of speed, agility, or athleticism leads to discussions about the potential that may lie right beneath the surface. Can he be the next Michael Jordan? Is he the next Robert Griffin III? These thoughts are often in the forefront of doting parents' minds as they witness the physical development of their sons.

While I raise questions here about the academic–athletic balance, I recognize that Black males are not monolithic, and I am aware of the large numbers of young Black males who do excel academically and athletically. Without question there are many young Black males who have been able to identify that precious balance of time commitment to academics and sports in a manner that has allowed them to excel at both. L. Harrison (2001) has documented these realities in a number of works and spoken to the manner in which many Black males embody the true element of what it means to be student-athletes, or what he refers to as "scholar-ballers" (individuals who excel in the classroom and on the playing field). Many young men are to be commended for demonstrating a unique ability to master two difficult terrains—regardless of grade level. They are not the unit of analysis for this discussion. The focus of this chapter is on young Black males who have been either unwilling or unable to devote precious time to their academic *and* athletic development. This inability or unwillingness to commit time, focus, and attention to both of these endeavors has resulted in an alarming number of young Black males choosing one at the expense of the other (Hodge, Burden, Robinson, & Bennett, 2008; Harrison & Lawrence, 2003; Hartmann, 2000). This is particularly problematic given the inordinate amount of time that is required for participating in high school athletics, and how many young males see it as worth their while to put the lion's share of their time investment into athletics and a paltry investment into their academic development (Benson, 2000). The tragic reality is that often this decision is supported or even encouraged by adults, whether parents, family members, or teachers and coaches who explicitly and implicitly convey a message that prioritizes athletics over academics.

To further expound on the challenges between sports and race, Edwards (2000) states that Black males are victims of a triple tragedy that functions in many Black communities: (1) youth's obsessive pursuit of sports, (2) personal and cultural immaturity of many sport aspirants, and (3) cultural and institutional underachievement of their communities. He asserts that these factors are cyclical, intense, and persistent, and often drive Black youth toward a narrow-minded focus on selected sports (e.g., basketball and football) and away from other occupational and educational pursuits (Edwards, 2000; Taylor, 1999). Some scholars assert that Black males are simply products of a socialization process that deliberately guides them toward athletics. Beamon (2009) suggests that social imitation theory affects Black males in the creation of a strong athletic identity. Her assertion is that many Black males learn the values, beliefs, and norms of socializing agents, such as parents, extended family members, siblings, peers, and coaches, who convey to Black males that they are best suited for athletics. Winbush (1987) claims that Black males, more than any other group, are intentionally geared toward athletics. Taylor (1999) talks about the effect that imagery has on Black males when it comes to athletics and states that "although fewer than 2,000 African Americans are in the NBA and more than 30,000 African Americans are physicians, we would never know it from the images that surround our children" (p. 75). It has been suggested that the reason many Black males overidentify with sports is that they are intentionally and intensively geared to sports more than any other group (Beamon, 2009; Beamon & Bell, 2006). A number of scholars have argued that Black males place an inordinate amount of time, effort, and emphasis on sports pursuits, with less attention given to academics (Benson, 2000). The growing body of research that suggests that Black males' participation in sports often results in the underdevelopment of nonathletic skills raises important questions about the saliency of sports in 2014. Although this is a difficult topic to probe, it is necessary to do so, given current trends and realities that I attempt to lay out in this chapter.

BLACK MALES AND SPORTS: PAST AND PRESENT

Dating back to the 19th century, lingering stereotypical beliefs about Black males usually—and disturbingly—have depicted them as athletically superior while intellectually inferior to Whites (Harrison & Lawrence, 2004; L. Harrison, 2001; Hodge et al., 2008; Kane, 1971; Miller, 1998; Sailes, 1991, 1993; Wiggins, 1989). The notion of Black male athletic superiority has been written about in a number of different outlets. The premise has been simple: Black males, due to genetic dispositions and larger muscular structures, have body types that make them run faster, jump higher, and exhibit greater agility (Hoberman, 1997). Coupled with the idea of Black physical superiority is intellectual inferiority. Dating back to the 18th century, ideas about the smaller brain size of Blacks were rampant in professional literature (Horsman, 1981; Selden, 1999). Therefore, while sports seemingly provided an outlet for Blacks in general and Black males in particular, the image became complex and troublesome in ways that continue to have lingering effects.

Within a contemporary context, some scholars assert that young Black males are still haunted by the social constructions of Black male stereotypes. Taylor (1999) maintains that schools are "saturated with images of Black athlete stereotypes. . . . Not only does the reinforcement of physical ability over intellectual capability diminish the potential of young Black men, but it also perpetuates the myth that the road to success is paved with sports contracts, not diplomas" (p. 75). Hence, there is a need to disrupt the notion that Black males are suited only for the athletic domain, but this task has been complicated by sociocultural factors that continue to place a large emphasis on sports in many Black homes and communities.

High school sports participation remains as high as ever, with many purported benefits. According to the Child Trends DataBank, which tracks data on school participation in athletics, there are social, emotional, and academic benefits to high school sports participation. Their data show that high school students who participate in sports have healthier eating habits, better cardiovascular fitness, and higher levels of parental participation, and are less likely to use tobacco, drugs, and alcohol. From an academic standpoint, sports participants have higher GPAs than their non-sports-participant peers, have lower dropout rates, fewer disciplinary referrals, and higher graduation rates (Action for Healthy Kids, 2004; Beets & Pitetti, 2005). Lastly, the data show that sports participants have higher self-esteem, motivation, and overall psychological well-being. However, a closer analysis of these data reveals that gender and race matter when it comes to high school sports participation and academic outcomes. In short, frequently Black males do not receive many of the benefits, in particular in the academic domain, that their peers do when it comes to sports participation. Black male student-athletes are the only group to have lower GPAs and academic outcomes than their Black male peers who are non-athletes. Zeiser (2011) recently examined the influence of sports participation in high school across race and gender and found that for Black males, participation in basketball and football resulted in lower grade point averages and test scores compared with their White peers in the same sports. Other studies have found similar results (Eitle & Eitle, 2002; Melnick, Sabo, & Vanfossen, 1992), which points to disturbing questions about why Black males are not receiving the benefits that their peers from other racial and ethnic groups receive from sports participation.

ATHLETE SEASONING COMPLEX: DETRIMENT TO ACADEMIC DEVELOPMENT?

One of the most damaging aspects of Black male development is the powerful and persistent role that sports have on them and their families. I refer to this process as the athlete seasoning complex (ASC), whereby young Black boys as early as 4–5 years old are encouraged to play basketball, football, or baseball; follow the sport in an intense and persistent manner; compete at all costs; and practice to achieve perfection or a high degree of proficiency—often at the expense of their academic development. The ASC is built on four key components that put these young boys and men on a pathway that has become increasingly commonplace in Black communities, hinders academic development, and has long-lasting ramifications for Black males: (1) early and persistent exposure to sports, (2) inordinate time commitment to developing high-level competency in sports, (3) the holdback phenomenon, and (4) the save the family syndrome. It is my contention that while sports play an instrumental role in developing lifelong skills for many participants, the ASC plays a major role in the arrested development of Black males academically and socially.

Early and persistent exposure to sports. This concept is tied to the idea of exposing young boys to the allure and attraction of sports at an early age. While many children, especially boys, across all racial groups often are exposed to sports at an early age (5–7 years of age), there is evidence that this exposure is more intense and more persistent for Black boys than it is for other subgroups (Edwards, 2000; Eitle & Eitle, 2002; P. C. Harris, 2012). Black males are reported to be engaged in sports-related activities and to feel pressured to compete in them at levels that are not seen in other groups (Beamon & Bell, 2006; Benson, 2000). Conversely, research informs us that Black boys are often lacking in other areas, namely, the academic arena. For example, while Black children at young ages are engaging in sports, and are aware of the teams, names, and uniform numbers of professional football's and basketball's biggest stars, disturbingly they do not show similar command in rudimentary academic areas. Black children have less exposure to literacy instruction and environments compared with their peers from other backgrounds. Research shows that at 4 years old, Black males score significantly behind White children in their proficiency in letter, number, and shape recognition (U.S. Department of Education, NCES, 2010). On average, Black children arrive at kindergarten and 1st grade with lower levels of school readiness than White children (Flores, Tomany-Korman, & Olson, 2005). They have fewer books in their homes, know fewer words, and are less likely to be read to by their parents (Duursma, Pan, & Raikes, 2008; West, Denton, & Germino Hausken, 2000; West, Denton, & Reaney, 2001). These types of early academic disparities are rarely recovered, and for Black males, data show how the gap grows increasingly worse over time, one of the fundamental reasons why the dropout rate for Black males is over 50% nationally (Schott Foundation for Public Education, 2010).

One can question why such early exposure, concentration, and participation in sports appear to be commonplace for many young Black males. The reasons are frequently part of the cultural framework that exists in many homes and communities, where not only is participation in sports expected, but excelling in them often is demanded. I would pose that similar approaches be used in the academic domain at an early age. The attraction to sports is obvious for Black males. It is one of the few areas where young Black males receive affirmation and praise, and are not met with the types of exclusion and angst that they encounter in classrooms. In many ways, there is a seasoning process that occurs for young Black males, wherein they are led to believe that their strengths lie in athletics, and not academics. The realities on this matter are the following: African American males are grossly overrepresented in the sports world (Beamon & Bell, 2006; Spigner, 1993). Some scholars posit that Black males "don't treat academics with the same intensity as they do basketball or football" (Powell, 2008, p. 73). C. K. Harrison (2000) noted that "the struggle for equality by African-Americans is often hidden through the spoils of race, sports, and professionalism" (p. 37). Edwards (2000) argued that African American families often encourage males to pursue a sports career at the expense of education. The research has been consistent that sports play a dominant role in the lives of many young Black males. It is critical to note that for many young men, sports serve as a vehicle to keep them out of trouble and away from other social challenges, but the larger picture must be analyzed in a way that interrogates early socialization of Black males around sports and schooling.

Inordinate time commitment to developing high-level competency in sports. One of the most concerning aspects of the ASC is the sheer amount of time that many Black males invest in sports. Given the increasing demands now placed on little league teams from grade school all the way through high school, and college, the time factor may be most debilitating for young Black males and is a cause for deep concern. O. Harris (1994) reported that many African American males believe that doors to success in non-sports-related occupations such as business, science, and politics are only slightly ajar in comparison to those opportunities in professional sports, and that the time investment has greater odds for paying off. This could be supported by the fact that less than 2% of doctors, architects, attorneys, and business professionals are Black (Spence, 2000). One of the problems is that many African American male athletes invest a great deal of time and energy in their sport and have very little time to spend on "preparation for non-sport careers" (Harris, 1994, p. 49), which perpetuates the underemphasis on achievement in the non-sports careers. Eitle and Eitle (2002) contend that disadvantaged African American youth, who have limited educational resources, are more likely to perceive sports as the primary vehicle for social mobility, therefore placing more emphasis and time on sports and less emphasis on academics.

An analysis of young Black males' interest in sports reveals many layers and high levels of complexity surrounding how sports influence them. In a recent study that my graduate students and I conducted on high school–age Black males, we questioned 38 participants about their career aspirations, and 70% of the respondents stated that they were interested in pursuing athletic careers or careers in the music industry. In another study, this one involving young Black males who excelled in basketball and football, approximately 80% of the 120 8th-graders we sampled contended that they were good or excellent because they put in excessive hours to excel. One young man stated, "I work at least 2–3 hours every day on my game"; or another stated, "My uncle says that I need to practice at least 5–6 hours a day." Many of these responses would appear to reflect a deep and sincere commitment to athletic excellence. And one can only applaud the type of discipline, diligence, and focus that many of the young men in our study discussed. But what is troubling is the manner in which these young men stated that they devoted smaller amounts of time to their academic pursuits. While there were young men who stated that they were committed to academic and athletic excellence, a concept that has been documented in other works (Comeaux, & Harrison, 2011; L. Harrison, 2001; Harrison et al., 2002), these responses were in the minority.

Overwhelmingly, the young men conveyed a message that their athletic excellence was directly correlated to their investment of time into crafting their ability to run, jump, shoot a basketball, or throw a football. One young man made reference to Malcolm Gladwell's (2008) 10,000-hour principle, contending that for him the surest way to athletic dominance was to "put in more time than my opponents." Gladwell mentions the 10,000-hour rule in his book *Outliers*, claiming that the key to success or world-class status in any field is, to a large extent, a matter of practicing a specific task for a total close to 10,000 hours. This inordinate amount of time reveals a high degree of intellect and insight on the part of the young men who mentioned this commitment. Recognition that their talents and skills can be honed through persistent practice and disciplined repetition is commendable. It also disrupts the notion that Black males are lazy, unfocused, and not committed to improvement. Yet while this increasing amount of time is devoted to athletic excellence, one has to question how a similar amount of time can be invested in the academic domain.

It is important for educators to recognize the level of focus and intensity which young men display when they are focused on what they believe to be an attainable goal. When we asked these same young men how much time they devoted to studies, the responses revealed a stark discrepancy, one wherein they discussed time as a factor that limited their ability to commit to academics. The responses included the following: "Don't have as much time as I should for the books," "I usually give it [studying] about an hour or so," "I do all my homework during 6th period, before I go to practice," and, the quote that may have been most telling, "Sometimes I am so tired after practice, I want to study, but I just don't have the energy to do much of it." All of these reactions seem to create a narrative that conveys an uneven distribution of time committed to sports over academics. The question is where and how does this process start. There seem to be both implicit and explicit messages that tell many young Black males that this uneven time distribution is acceptable, with little conversation about the long-term ramifications of not investing increased time in the academic domain.

Holdback phenomenon. One of the more disturbing occurrences with Black males in the education domain has been the increasing numbers of them who are retained a grade or more for what appear to be sports purposes. Researchers have reported few beneficial effects of retention on achievement (e.g., Arthur, 1936; Hong & Yu, 2007; Jimerson, 2001; Jimerson & Ferguson, 2007; Silberglitt, Appleton, Burns, & Jimerson, 2006), and negative effects on high school completion (Alexander, Entwisle, Dauber, & Kabbani, 2004; Eide & Showalter, 2001; Jimerson, Anderson, & Whipple, 2002; Rumberger & Larson, 1998), social adjustment (e.g., Jimerson & Ferguson, 2007; Nagin, Pagani, Tremblay, & Vitaro, 2003), college attendance (e.g., Fine & Davis, 2003; Ou & Reynolds, 2010, 2013), and wages (e.g., Eide & Showalter, 2001). It is disturbing that many parents are choosing to hold back Black males, who academically are able to matriculate, to repeat a grade for increased strength, growth, and talent on the playing field. The data have been clear that grade retention as currently constructed has far more drawbacks than benefits. Yet, the process of retaining young Black men not for academic, social, or emotional reasons, but for athletic advantages, has become increasingly commonplace in many sports (particularly basketball and football). The thinking is that one may increase a young man's prospect for athletic stardom if he has the ability to compete against younger, smaller, and less developed competitors.

The hope for many families is that this athletic advantage will translate into athletic scholarship opportunities. The holdback phenomenon has resulted in countless numbers of Black males not only being retained for athletic reasons, but often finding themselves attending multiple high schools in an effort to find the school that will provide the best athletic opportunity. Therefore, it is not uncommon to find young men who have attended three or four different high schools; this mobility is tied not to family mobility, but often to promises made by athletic coaches about the types of training, opportunity, and exposure students will receive at different high schools. Unfortunately, most of this movement and upheaval does not guarantee or result in the majority of these young men earning athletic scholarships or having a solid academic footing. The pursuit of sports for this group often results in their having no college degree or work experience to lead to upward mobility. In some cases, these movements across schools can be across counties, and even from one state to another.

Some contend that the pursuit of sports, while seemingly beneficial on the surface to young men, has ties to racism and exploitation. Hoberman (1997) wrote that athleticism contributes to overt racism and unconscious assaults on Black males from Whites and the larger society. Moreover, Hoberman (2000) contends that the dream of many African American males to achieve stardom through sports leads to many of them rejecting, ignoring, or outright dismissing educational opportunities, and that many adults play proactive roles in the process. In short, honest conversations are long overdue about the potential damage grade retention is doing to the academic, social, and long-term economic development of young men.

Save the family syndrome. A large challenge that must be confronted with Black males and sports is the manner in which the larger society continually has socialized them into thinking that the only or primary way to professional and economic success is through sports and entertainment. Not only do many Black males subscribe to the idea that they must master sports, but many of them who grow up in economically challenged neighborhoods believe that sports is the most feasible vehicle for upward economic mobility, and hence saving the family. It must be recognized that there are startling data that support the notion of sports as a way for many young Black males to escape poverty.

Sailes (1998) stated that sports participation is an integral part of African American male socialization. For many Black males, athletic participation has been considered a means to social mobility for disadvantaged youth (Miller, 1998; Riess, 1980; Sabo, Melnick, & Vanfossen, 1993). The Center for the Study of Sport and Society at Northeastern University reported that African American families are seven times more likely than White families to encourage males to participate seriously in a sport (Spence, 2000).

To help provide a larger context tying Black males to poverty and the quest for upward mobility, consider that nationally during 2010, 52% of African American youth under the age of 18 were living in a single-parent household compared with 26% of White youth who lived in a single-parent household (Pew Research Center's Internet & American Life Project, 2012). Madyun and Lee (2010) argue that African American males who live in single-female-headed households tend to live in chronic poverty, attend low-performing schools, and do not fare well academically when compared with those living in two-parent households. The types of family and internal pressures bestowed on young men can become intense, persistent, and outright destructive, when the subtle and not-so-subtle charge is to save the family. The save the family syndrome is centered on a set of beliefs that contends that young Black males will excel in athletics, earn a full athletic scholarship, and then parlay that opportunity into a multimillion-dollar contract that will help to alleviate all the family's financial woes. Images of young Black men at NBA and NFL drafts are frequently etched in the minds of countless numbers of young men. As these newly minted millionaires hug overjoyed family members, friends, and significant others, one of the more common statements made is, "I plan to buy my mom a big house," or "move her out of the hood." So the narrative that is communicated to young men, especially those growing up in poverty, is that if you work incredibly hard at sports and excel in them, you too will attain the riches that are at the end of the road, which will help quell the ills of generational poverty, hopelessness, and despair that often afflict many Black neighborhoods. The narrative becomes ingrained in the minds of family members, who encourage, support, and often demand efforts in pursuing athletic excellence at the expense of academic excellence. Eitle and Eitle (2002) found that economic variables were strong predictors of participation patterns of Black and White youth. They reported that Black high school students were 1.6 times more likely than their White peers to participate in football and 2.5 times more likely to play basketball. When other factors are controlled for, Black males are actually 2.5 times more likely than White males to play football and 5.7 times more likely to play basketball. Their research discovered that one of the primary motivators for pursuing sports was the potential for upward mobility.

DO HIGH SCHOOL SPORTS BENEFIT ALL?

African American males sometimes are viewed as both victims of and participants in their own educational demise (J. E. Davis, 2003). One example of this is when sports participation is given greater credence than academic pursuits. What is vexing about the ASC phenomenon is that there is overwhelming evidence showing that high school students who participate in athletics have higher academic achievement, have better educational attainment, are more likely to attend college, show higher levels of civic engagement, and have greater success in the labor market, compared with their peers who do not participate in sports (Barron, Ewing, & Waddell, 2000; Eccles, Barber, Stone, & Hunt, 2003). What seems to be clear from the literature, though, is that African American males tend to focus less on intellectual pursuits in favor of devoting more time to a sport (Spence, 2000). Disproportionate to White athletes, more African American males aspire to professional careers in basketball and football as a means to economic and social mobility (Burden, Hodge, & Harrison, 2004; Butler, 2007; Sailes, 1996; Weatherspoon, 2007). At the professional level, basketball and football have the greatest percentages of African American players. Hartmann (2008) suggested that African American youth—especially boys—are not only more likely to play football and basketball but also to be negatively impacted by their participation in these activities. They contend that "rather than sports serving simply as a drain on energies that could be spent maximizing academic achievement, [Black] males may end up pursuing some sports because they lack the resources to perform well academically, which only serves to disadvantage them further in achieving academic excellence" (p. 142). While I would object to the idea of Black males "lack[ing] the resources," what seems to be abundantly clear is that for many Black males, participation in sports does not coincide with academic participation, and in many cases happens in lieu of academic participation.

In addition to the manner in which many Black males seem to place sports ahead of academics, perhaps the tawdriest aspect of the current phenomenon of Black males and sports is evident in the current Amateur Athletic Union (AAU) High School Basketball arrangements that have become prevalent in almost every major U.S. city. For years, high school basketball has been the sport of choice for tens of thousands of Black males; however, the dynamics of college recruitment have changed in a manner that has made many young Black males the object of affection of countless high school and college coaches. In *Play Their Hearts Out*, George Dohrmann (2010) chronicles an 8-year journey in the cutthroat, and often immoral, world that is AAU basketball. He documents the manner in which aspiring AAU coaches seek to find the "next LeBron James" in inner-city neighborhoods. Dohrmann unpacks how, when promising young talent has been located, boys (mostly Black) as young as 9–10 years old become the subject of bidding wars by shoe companies, AAU travel teams, and rival coaches, all in an effort to land the next superstar. Dohrmann's work is compelling because he documents the persistent exploitation of young Black males at an early age, with promises of stardom and riches, only to see so many of them fall incredibly short of unrealistic expectations. What is evident in Dohrmann's work is that Black males with exceptional athletic talent quickly can become objectified in a manner that is wholly unacceptable, particularly when many, if not most, of these young men will not make the professional ranks, let alone earn an athletic scholarship. Dohrmann also examines how academics are a non-entity for the adults who coddle these young men and only reinforce the idea that sports are the way out for talented high schoolers. What has intensified these efforts even more is the increasingly common practice of many colleges and universities offering exceptional student-athletes college scholarships before they enter high school. Several high-profile universities have offered football scholarships to students as young as 12 and 13 years old, thus creating an intense level of commodification of increasingly young males.

Other scholars have raised concerns around the issue of Black males and sports. Donnor (2005) uses a critical race theory analysis and contends that Black males are deliberately exploited for their athletic talents, and that universities do not concern themselves with the academic mission that they are charged with for these students but rather see the financial windfall that Black males bring with their athletic talents. Harper's (2012) research has revealed gross inequities when it comes to educational outcomes, namely, graduation rates for Black male student-athletes at predominately White institutions (PWIs). This pipeline of exploitation and academic shortchanging of young men seems to be growing larger by the day and pulling in countless students in the process.

IMPLICATIONS

There are some sobering realities that must be addressed when discussing the prospects of Black males playing at the professional level, or, for that matter, even earning a Division I athletic scholarship. With a narrow focus on "making it" through sports, studies show that this is unlikely to occur. In the 2008 National Collegiate Athletic Association President's Report, Myles Brand reported that "1% of all high school [basketball] players ever realize an opportunity to play in Division I. Thus, the likelihood of being drafted by the NBA is about 1% of 1% for high school players" (p. 1). On the other hand, during the 2008–2009 season, 82% of players in the NBA were African American (Gonzalez, 2009). This is where the conflicting messages come into play. Many young men see overwhelming numbers of Black males participating at the professional levels of the NFL and NBA, but seemingly do not see the overwhelming odds facing their getting to those same levels. According to the High School Athletic Association, only .09% of high school seniors playing football—less than 1 in 1,000—end up in the professional ranks. Among basketball players in high school, it's only 1 in 3,400. Among all college athletes, 1% go on to play at the professional level. These numbers suggest that it is critical that parents, teachers, coaches, and other concerned adults have a sobering dialogue with young men about the almost insurmountable odds they face in the pursuit of athletic professionalism.

As stated earlier, the explanations for Black males being connected to and involved in sports are understandable, yet they are complex and numerous. Some suggest that the exploitation of young Black males must be called into question, as they play roles that provide so few of them with real opportunities for upward mobility, while aiding in the creation and expansion of multimillion-dollar corporations. Economist Boyce Watkins (2013), who writes on the intersection of race, sports, and economics, contends:

> In order for African American males and black athletes to understand this system, they must be educated about it. The culture that grabs our boys at an early age is one that is based on profuse amounts of mis-information, peer pressure, tradition and self-destruction. A man can be an athlete and still be an intelligent, productive and capable member of the community in which he lives. In fact, there is quite a bit of room for black male athletes to become part of our nation's black leadership. (p. 1)

It is important that parents, teachers, coaches, academic advisors, and Black males themselves understand how race–sports stereotypes can influence the aspirations of youth toward or away from various athletic pursuits at the expense of their academic success (Harrison, Azzarito, & Burden, 2004; Harrison & Belcher, 2006).

There are a number of areas that should be considered and explored further, if serious attention is to be given to the academic prospects of young Black males. I would offer the following as a starting point:

- Parents and teachers must develop a culture of celebrating academic achievement and success, much in the way that athletic success is revered. The idea of cheering athletic accomplishment, yet overlooking, ignoring, or being complicit in academic mediocrity or underperformance, has to change. Pep rallies are held before football and basketball games to encourage performance of student-athletes, yet we seemingly take academic excellence for granted. A similar commitment to and display of excitement about high academic achievement need to be part of the educational fabric of schools.

- The construction of Black male images must go beyond sports. While there are many admirable professional Black male role models, they become the only representation of Black male success. There must be a concerted effort to highlight Black male excellence in non-sports domains. Many schools have career days and encourage Black male participation. But there needs to be a more explicit effort to put Black male adults in viable non-sports careers in frequent contact with and presence of young Black males.

- Additional research is needed to examine school experiences and outcomes for Black males who are student-athletes at the high school level, and those who are not. While the topic has been studied, there is more to be understood that unpacks this phenomenon. How and why are parents making decisions about grade retention? What messages do Black males contend they receive from family about the pursuit of sports?

- Another contention that must be considered is an increase of the minimum grade point average that is required for participation in sports at the high school level. In many districts and states across the country, students need to earn and maintain only a 2.0 GPA for participation. I would contend that this sets a standard for academic mediocrity. I would recommend that students have to have a 2.75 or 3.0 GPA to participate in sports. In this way, the message would be loud and clear that high levels of academic performance are expected before they can participate in sports. I believe that most young men are capable of rising to this challenge.

- A concerted belief that student-athletes can perform at a high level is needed. Teachers, coaches, and parents must demand the same level of commitment, discipline, and focus from young men in the classroom that is expected on the playing field. Many parents pay for athletic training, special camps, and one-on-one supports to increase athletic prowess; the same efforts must be made for academic performance, if the message is to be conveyed that Black males are capable learners.

Sports will continue to play a notable role in U.S. life. It also would seem as though sports will continue to play an instrumental role in the lives of countless numbers of young Black males. My purpose here is not to discredit the value of sports, but to challenge all stakeholders in the development of young Black males to give careful thought and consideration to the increasingly prominent role that sports play in the lives of young Black men. While sports help to build confidence, hope, and opportunity for many young men, we also must help them realize that there is a long and rich history in which education has done the same for millions of African Americans over the past 3 centuries, and that legacy must not be ignored or forgotten.

CHAPTER 5

Black Male Perspectives

One of the goals of this work has been to center the perspectives, opinions, and insights of Black males as part of the school reform discourse. This intentional step is taken because a multitude of voices have been part of the narrative on how to transform schooling experiences for Black males. Scholars, practitioners, parents, policymakers, legislators, and community-based advocates have all offered recommendations, best practices, special initiatives, and policies on how to disrupt the chronic exclusion and underperformance of Black males in U.S. schools (Noguera, 2008; Polite & Davis, 1999). Glaringly absent from this discourse have been the voices of Black males themselves. In this chapter, I seek to insert their voices, their standpoints, their sentiments, and their own unique thoughts about schools, teachers, learning, and the perceptions that they believe are held about them by school personnel and the wider society. Most critical to this chapter is having Black males offer their recommendations on how schools can be improved. The voices captured in this chapter were generated through a series of interviews and focus groups over the past 3 years tied to several different projects in which I have been involved. Each of these projects focused on Black male achievement in some capacity. In total, approximately 119 young males were interviewed from grades 6–12 over the 3 years. The goal was to identify young Black males who come from a multitude of different backgrounds and lived experiences. While all of these young men are from the west coast, it should be noted that approximately one-third of them live in what could be considered middle-class or upper-middle-class, predominately White or Asian communities, and attend schools in suburban areas. This was done deliberately because the typical characterization of Black students has them attending urban, low-income schools. Some scholars have reminded us that approximately one-third of Black families live in what could be considered middle-class, suburban neighborhoods, yet these students are seldom part of the discussion on Black students (B. Gordon, 2012; Reynolds, 2010). This work seeks to expand the notion of who Black males are and what they see in schools where they are the minority.

Some of these interviews were conducted in one-on-one settings. Most were done in focus-group settings, while some of the students responded in writing to a four-question prompt that was provided to them (shown below). A number were informal conversations that were follow-up discussions, as some of the young men wanted to provide additional clarity to the responses given in previous settings. Approximately 50 of the interviews were conducted as part of a summer outreach program that I am involved in at UCLA. This program identifies students from urban communities in Los Angeles county schools who show high academic promise and provides them with an intensive summer enrichment experience. This group of young men I classify as high academic performers (HAPs), meaning that they had grade point averages that were 3.0 and higher. This sample of participants was instrumental because I wanted to be deliberate in capturing the perspectives of Black males who defied the notion of academic underperformance being normative for them. If the narrative currently constructed around Black males is to be more holistic and inclusive, it is essential that the full spectrum of Black male performance be captured. There are a disproportionate number of Black males who are not performing to the levels of their peers, yet the discourse should highlight and hear from those who are thriving, who are outperforming their White and Asian peers, and who are successfully navigating the rigorous terrain of schools, in spite of the challenges that many Black males encounter in schools. Their voices are crucial to this work and should be an integral part of the discourse.

A second group that was intentionally selected for this work were (approximately 36) students that I identify as middle of the road (MOTR) performers. These are young men who had grade point averages between 2.0 and 3.0. The overwhelming majority of these students were not on college-prep tracks; most had never been in trouble at their schools and seemed to be doing just fine academically. This group included students from both urban and suburban schools. One of the problems in studying any group of students, but in particular Black males, is that there is a tendency by researchers and practitioners to pay particular attention to those who are at the bottom end of the academic continuum. While it is important to identify useful interventions for those students who are struggling academically, the tendency is to overgeneralize for some groups in a manner that suggests that the entire group is performing below a particular standard. Conversely, a growing body of research has been concerned with students who are identified as gifted and talented. A small number of researchers have studied gifted or high-performing Black students, and Black males in particular (Ford, 2011). Thus, a polemic construction of achievement is becoming prevalent in educational research, especially around students of color. The middle group of students, much like many other students from other backgrounds, are not high performers, but not low performers either, and often are either overlooked, ignored, or understudied. It was vital to capture their perspectives on school and schooling.

Finally, approximately 33 of the young men who participated in our interviews had GPAs that were below 2.0. This group was included for academic balance in our sample and also because this is the group that often seems to be most targeted, studied, and analyzed. It should be noted that when the focus groups took place, the students were not grouped by GPA. The groups were diversified to create a more open and conversational tone. The students were not asked directly about their GPAs in the interviews or the focus groups. However, if they mentioned their academic performance, they were probed further about the academic outcomes.

The participants included in this chapter come from a total of four middle schools and seven high schools. The Academic Performance Index for these schools ranges from 530 to 920. The responses from these young men are laid out here based on the following four research questions that guided these conversations:

1. How do you describe how you are doing academically?
2. What can schools do to improve academic outcomes for Black male students?
3. What can Black males do to improve their academic achievement?
4. What do you think school personnel and society most misunderstand about Black males?

The responses provided here were centered on these four key questions that each of the participants was asked. The first question was focused on having the students provide an account of how they were doing academically, and to delve into why they were where they were academically. The purpose was also to gain a sense of what attributes they gave to their current state of affairs academically. We received a wide range of responses on this particular question, which generated a number of intriguing conversations. By and large, most of the respondents explained their current academic status in a straightforward fashion, without offering explanations to give further depth or breadth. One of the most thoughtful responses was from Jonathan, a MOTR, 10th-grade student in a suburban high school. He offered the following response to the question:

> I would say that I am pretty much an average student. I take school seriously, but I don't believe in taking all these hard classes, and being a nerd. But I also don't blow it off either, you know what I mean? If I wanted to be a straight A student I probably could. But for me, I want to enjoy my life and not make school my whole life.

This type of sentiment also was expressed by Ray, a high performer at a suburban high school. He commented:

I mean I have a 3.5 GPA, and I am cool with that. I am a good student, but I look at some of the kids in my school, and they stress out over grades, and trying to get a 5.0, and I am like, ain't no way I would be like that. So I'm cool with being a good student. I know I will get into college somewhere, but it don't have to be like Harvard or something like that. I enjoy having a life.

The notion of "having a life" was a sentiment that was mentioned throughout our interviews. A number of the young men stated that having the opportunity to be social and have friends was just as important to them as being high-achieving students. Jason, a high-performing, 9th-grade student who attended a school where most of the students were White and Asian, contended:

I look at them Asians and they seem like they don't have any fun . . . it's just school, school, school . . . that ain't good. They have no social life. I was talking to this one kid and he was like, "My parents put a lot of pressure on us." It's like, man, these kids are gonna just flip out one day, because they have no outlet. I would never get like that.

What is important to note is that some of the students who were not high performers offered keen insight into why they were not. Astin, an 11th-grader and low performer at an inner-city high school, stated, "I don't really trip off my grades, because I have life issues to deal with." The sentiment of life and family challenges was quite prevalent in the interviews with students who attended schools in low-income communities. One of the major take-aways from these responses is that the social context of education, or non-school matters, plays an important role for many young men. Furthermore, a number of the young men expressed a desire for more educators to understand why they arrive at school late, why homework is incomplete, or why they often appear to be disengaged in school when there other issues that occupy their minds. Daveon, a 10th-grade MOTR, provided an insightful commentary when he offered the following:

I'm okay, you know. I get mostly Cs and few Bs, but life is hard. My mom is going through so much with her health, so I gotta do a lot with my brothers and sister, like help them get fed and all that. . . . So I don't always do my homework . . . I'm not making excuses or anything, but life is stressful. I think about my mom a lot. Like if something happens to her, where are we going? Don't want to go through that whole foster care system thing. So I'm like, school just ain't a big priority right now, and I'm cool with that. Life is a priority.

Brandyn, a 7th-grader and a high performer at an inner-city school, offered a similar assessment. He stated:

My grades could be a lot better, but I have just not been focused since my dad went to jail and all that. I kinda miss him, and now my mom has a new boyfriend, and he kicked my big brother out the house . . . [so] I really don't like him, and he moved in with us, so I can't focus of my grades. I know I should, but I just wish some things were different.

Throughout our interviews, a number of the young men spoke about home issues, family challenges, peer pressures, health concerns, and financial considerations that explained why they were not as strong academically as they would like to be. A number of the young men who were high achievers indicated that their family members were vital to their academic success. For example:

I am a pretty good student. I would say that I am because my mom stays on me about my grades. She is like, "How'd you do on that test today?" or, "Are you studying your notes?" So I do better than a lot of my friends, just because my mom stays on me.

Andre, a 8th-grade, high performer at an inner-city school, reinforced this idea.

My parents said that they will not accept anything less than a B on my report card. So I have been like a straight A student most of my life. I know school is important, and my grades are important so I just make sure that I stay on top of them.

WHAT CAN SCHOOLS DO TO IMPROVE ACADEMIC OUTCOMES FOR BLACK MALE STUDENTS?

Identifying ways to improve schools is not a new. More recently, student voices have been introduced into the conversation to provide a fresh, yet overlooked, perspective into this critical dialogue (Hill, 2009; Howard, 2001; P. W. Lee, 1999; Noguera, 2008). The voices of Black males have been less prevalent in the student discourse, and one of the aims of this work has been to augment those perspectives. When we probed Black males to offer ways that schools could improve their outcomes, the majority of the responses fell into three categories: (1) teachers, (2) curriculum, and (3) personal ownership. I will highlight some of the data from each of these perspectives.

Teachers

The single most repeated comment about ways to change schools that could offer improved outcomes for Black males was the need for better teachers.

Almost half of the participants made some reference to the ways that teachers could make schools more inviting, or less inviting, places to be as learners. In addition, participants made references to the type of attitudes, direct and indirect comments, as well as overall inability of teachers to make learning an interesting endeavor. Many of these young men believed that improved teaching and teachers could be an important factor in engaging them in the process. Alex offered his assessment:

> Man, I will tell you right now, if you got better teachers it would help us out a lot. I mean most of them are boring, don't care about teaching us, and just act like they don't want to be there, so okay, you don't wanna be here? Neither do I.

There seemed to be a general theme around teacher apathy that was repeated throughout these responses. Jordan, a middle of the road achiever from an urban high school stated:

> They [teachers] just act like they don't wanna be there. So if you got new young teachers who are excited, maybe you could get better test scores and stuff.

Ayende, a high achiever from a suburban high school, said:

> The number one thing you could do to improve schools is get rid of like 90% of the teachers. Bottom line, they are horrible. . . . They don't know us, don't care about us, and don't try to help us out. I do well in school because my parents get me tutors and I study hard, but our teachers [pause] . . . just bad.

Benjamin commented about how the good teachers get stretched because so many of their peers are not up to par.

> I would make more teachers like Ms. Riad, my English teacher. You go to her class before school, during lunch, and after school, and there's a bunch of students in her room. Why? Because she is helping kids in all different subjects. If more teachers did what she does, like encourage you, help you, teach you, and show you, it would help a lot of people. . . . Why is she helping us with algebra problems? Because the algebra teachers don't want to help you. But I know she gets tired because she does so much for a lot of students.

Throughout the series of interviews and focus groups, the students continued to offer their sentiments that schools could benefit from an influx of caring teachers. Some of the participants even mentioned that they frequently had teachers who "did not know how to teach," or recommended that schools would improve if they "get better subs [substitute teachers] because we have them all the time."

Samuel, a lower performer from an urban middle school, stated the following:

> If you wanted to help Black boys, all you have to do is make the principals come in our classes all day. I swear, when the principals come in our room, the teachers act all nice, and explain stuff real clear, and act like they care. But when the principals ain't in there, it's just the opposite. It's the teachers that make things bad for us.

It is essential to note that there was a cross-section of participants who saw teachers as the primary individuals in turning schools around. From low performers to high performers, students saw teachers as vital parts of what worked, and what did not work, in schools. Much has been written about how teachers are the most critical influences on students' performance in schools (Darling-Hammond, 2010; Rist, 1970; Rong, 1996). Most of the high performers talked about learning in spite of teachers, and not because of them. Researchers consistently have shown how teacher turnover harms student achievement, and that the most detrimental effect of teacher turnover and ineffectiveness occurs in schools where Black students are most prevalent (Ronfeldt, Loeb, & Wyckoff, 2013). What is important to note were the occasions when the young men talked about teachers who really made a difference in their lives. One of those statements was offered by Jackson, a high performer from an urban school.

> If you want to make schools better, just take Mr. Harvey and clone him for every school. Every school and student would do better. You just want to learn in his class . . . he explains why biology is important. He is funny, we do lots of projects, he treats us like we are adults and not little kids or something with all these rules. He knows if you are having a bad day to give you some space. He talks to us a lot after school. He really makes me wanna do better.

One of the intriguing parts of listening to Black males in the course of this work, was that while many of them dismissed teachers as being non-factors, or contributing to their lack of interest in schools, many of the participants also suggested that if teachers would hear them out, it would make them better teachers. Markus, an 8th-grader, commented that:

> Sometimes these teachers should just listen to their students. . . . I mean if we are saying that we don't understand something, don't say, "you need to pay more attention"; reteach it. That kinda stuff just makes you not wanna learn.

Isaac, a 6th-grader who is a lower performer at a suburban middle school, maintained that his teacher, Mrs. Waxman, "has it in" for a lot of the Black students in her class. He explained:

> I was talking to my friend asking him a question about the assignment, and she pulled my card sayin' I was being disruptive. I tried to explain what I was doing, and she was like, "I don't wanna hear it, I don't wanna hear it." I'm like, "will you just listen to me and let me tell you what happened." She is like that with all the Black students; that's why we don't like her.

Curriculum

Aside from teacher apathy and expectations was the sentiment that much of what is taught in school is not interesting, is irrelevant, is not connected to social realities, and seems to be intensely centered on testing. A number of scholars have discussed the manner in which school curriculum often is disconnected from students' day-to-day realities and should be more centered on topics, issues, and themes that students are interested in (Camangian, 2010; Duncan-Andrade & Morrell, 2008; Milner, 2010). The call for a more relevant curriculum has been made by other scholars who have asserted that cultural attributes should be incorporated into classroom curriculum (Banks, 1992, 1993; Gay, 1994, 2010; Hill, 2009; Ladson-Billings, 1994). As participants responded to the question of how schools could be improved, Joey, a middle of the road student from a suburban high school, recommended the following:

> You come to the after-school program and they teach us stuff like computer graphics, and gaming . . . things that we are interested in. You never have anybody messing up there, because everything we learn is interesting and fun.

A consistent sentiment around curriculum was boredom. More interesting or stimulating content was suggested by at least 25 of the young men whom we queried about what schools could do to improve academic outcomes for Black males. Benjamin stated that sometimes he is "so bored in class it's hard to stay awake." Tariq, a high school sophomore, stated that the main thing that could be done would be to "make us want to come to school, with things that are interesting to learn." Some students raised questions about literature ("Why do we always read about White people?"), while others questioned the portrayal of Blacks in their U.S. history classes. Travis stated:

> If you changed what we learned in class that would help a lot of us, so at least it would be interesting. We always talk about slavery and the Civil

Rights Movement, but what about Obama, how about the Black Panthers, why can't we talk about that? If we did, I bet dudes would be a lot more into it.

Excessive testing was mentioned throughout the conversations with the young men. A number of participants stressed that many of their teachers "teach to the test" and "talk about testing" quite often. Elton noted, "I like how things are better after testing, because then we get to real interesting topics in English." Brandyn stressed how schools could "make things a lot better if we just stopped testing all the time . . . it's this assessment, this benchmark, the CST test, always another test." Thus, reducing the prevalence of testing was repeatedly suggested as a way to remedy schools.

Ownership

The third category that was most referenced by the young men in our work was that schools by and large do not control their efforts and outcomes. A number of participants stated that their outcomes could be improved if they increased their effort, focus, or discipline. Taking personal ownership of their educational outcomes seemed to be a way these young men could not allow their fate to be determined solely by schools and school personnel. In many ways, these young men accepted the fact that their schools were subpar, that teachers were noncaring, that curriculum was nonresponsive to them and their realities, and that resources were limited. Yet, they believed that in light of the various challenges that they faced, they, and they alone, were most essential to their academic prospects. Malcolm offered the following reply on what schools could do to improve school outcomes:

Really nothing . . . it's all on me. I mean, I know what I have to do, it's just a matter of me doing it, you know? Studying, managing my time . . . schools are gon' be what they are . . . but that won't stop me, it's just grinding every day.

The sentiment of self-effort also was offered by Ryan, a high-performing senior at an urban high school.

Look, you know that some teachers are bad, and you know some students are bad, so what are you going to do about it? Complain and cry? Or just handle your business? My schooling is all on me, and nobody else. Is my school perfect? No, but at the end of the day, it ain't changing, so I have to get mines. I have to study, go to the Internet, do my homework, take care of my college apps, all without the school, and that is what I did. I tell my friends that all the time. Don't complain about them [school officials], just handle your business.

These types of responses offer a stark contrast to the notion of victimization that some scholars have suggested is prominent for Black youth (McWhorter, 2000) and suggest more agency-driven responses that squarely place students— and in this case, Black male students—in full control of their educational destinies. When many of the young men were probed, they seemed to offer a sentiment that suggested that they succeeded in spite of schools and not because of them, which speaks to the level of resilience that many of them displayed. DeMont, a senior from an urban high school and a high performer, contended that he sought resources outside of his school.

> I got a lot of my help for college from the VIPS program [a college-prep program at a local university]. They helped me with classes to take, SAT prep, taking classes at community colleges, and overall counseling. My school doesn't have any of that stuff and I knew that so I had to take responsibility and find out where I could help myself, because Woodworth [his high school] sho ain't gon' do it.

DeMont's response builds on Yosso's (2005) notion of community cultural wealth. She suggests that many students of color possess the types of capital that allow them to navigate trying circumstances. Her contention is that the counternarrative to the Eurocentric frame of reference about what types of capital matter most needs to be rethought, and informed by the cultural capital of diverse groups. The six types of capital that she offers in response to the dominant paradigm (aspirational, linguistic, familial, resistant, social, navigational) all seem to be evident, in different ways, in the young men that we interviewed. As it relates to gaining access to college, several of the young men seem to exhibit the type of navigational capital that Yosso (2005) asserts is common for many people of color, and youth of color in particular. Throughout many of our focus groups, a number of the young men stated that "somebody told me to . . . ," or, "I found out from . . . ," or, "my dad knows someone who . . ." These references to friends and family who knew about opportunities to help with academic pursuit were common.

Equally intriguing were the relatively large numbers of low-performing students who offered responses to the self-effort and ownership notion. The attitude that many of the students seemed to possess was centered on their recognition of the importance and value of education, yet they struggled for a variety of reasons and were either unable or unwilling to apply the maximum effort for school success. This was much like the attitude–achievement paradox that Mickelson (1990) discusses, in which Black adolescents understand the importance of education, yet often do not put forth effort due to their beliefs that opportunity structures for them can be limited. Alex, for example, stated the following:

> Yeah, I know I could do better in school, but for what? I see dudes on my block, and they went to school and got good grades, you know what I'm sayin', and they not doing any better than I'm doing, so does school really pay off?

Several other young men, when probed about what schools could do to better engage young Black males, questioned the value of school. Many of them had the foresight, and a well-crafted response, to contend that they "just put up with school" or that "it's a place to hang out," and that they put forth the effort they do because their parents or caregivers urge them to, but they have little confidence in the payoff that education promotes. But more than offering a critique of schools, several of the young men had critiques of the larger society that creates conditions that turns them off of schools. The clarity with which some of these young men articulated their assessments was insightful, analytic, and poignant. Malcolm, a middle of the road student at an urban high school, commented:

> You look at the dropouts from poor schools, nobody cares about that, because they have a school-to-prison pipeline, just lock us up, and blame us for it. Nobody says anything about crime and violence in the hood, or no jobs for people, or no services to help people who need it, so, yeah, I mean schools are messed up, and that's because the neighborhoods they are in are messed up, and it makes you wonder if it's done on purpose.

The complexity and diversity of Black male thought on what schools can do to enhance their outcomes is evident. While many of the young men had sharp critiques of schools, namely, teachers and outdated and irrelevant curriculum, others were more introspective and saw themselves as being complicit in their own underperformance. Attempts to disrupt the underperformance of Black males must be cognizant of all of these perspectives. Simplistic overtures that are based on victim blaming (Ryan, 1976) will fall short, for obvious reasons. Our data suggest that many of these young men deal with complex life realities and still put forth effort to be the best they can be. Others believe that schools remove creativity and deep levels of analysis, and stifle innovation. Yet despite these circumstances, these young men have firm opinions, insightful ideas, and well-thought-out responses to what ails their schooling experiences. These voices merit further analysis, these approaches need further replication, and these ideas merit full consideration.

One of the key take-aways from our conversations with the youth was that while they had various criticisms about schools, they also recognized their complicit roles in their underperformance. The students were not persistently critical of schools, but were willing to hold themselves accountable. As students spoke about "needing to try harder," "working more," and "not messing up in class," it became apparent that many of them seemed frustrated about their lack of core requisite skills to be academically successful. Tevin, a 9th-grader at an urban school, offered the following:

> I need to try harder. My algebra class is hard, some of it I just don't get, and I try hard. . . . I try to do my homework, ask questions in class and everything, but I still get Cs and Ds on my tests. I think it's because I didn't get all the stuff in pre-algebra, but I guess I gotta just keep trying.

Andre commented:

> My parents gave me everything I need to be successful in school . . . so it is up to me. But it would help sometimes if our teachers taught some of this stuff better. . . . I'm not blaming them, saying it's all their fault . . . because it's up to me, but when some teachers can't teach, and can't control the class, it's hard to learn.

Tevin's and Andre's frustration seems to reflect a reality that is often understated, but seems to be a prevalent part of the achievement discourse. While each of these young men appeared to accept complete responsibility for his learning, they all spoke to various challenges they encounter academically. For Tevin, it almost seemed to be an issue of lacking core academic competencies, while for Andre it seemed to be a teacher effectiveness issue. A number of the participants from urban schools seemed to articulate similar themes along these lines (e.g., "I try hard, but just can't understand," "I try my best, but some of these things I was never taught"). These types of responses highlight students taking accountability for their learning; however, they also lead one to question how sufficient their teachers are in preparing them. In short, there could very well be significant disparities in the extent to which certain students have learned or been appropriately taught, at an earlier age, the rudimentary concepts and key academic skills that are critical to future academic success. This point becomes even more salient when many students have teachers who often are not equipped to adequately teach them. Scholars have documented the degree to which many low-income schools have teachers who are frequently underprepared, and often unqualified, to teach, particularly in high-needs schools (Darling-Hammond, 2010). Thus, while it is refreshing and encouraging to hear many of the young men take ownership of their learning, it is essential that this personal responsibility be coupled with institutional accountability as well. It becomes paramount that as educators encourage students to work hard, focus, be disciplined, and be resilient in pursuit of academic success, we also hold states, districts, and schools accountable for ensuring that students have safe and orderly schools to enter, qualified and competent teachers, committed school leaders, and adequate learning materials. In summary, individual responsibility *and* institutional accountability would appear to be important foundations to ensure academic success.

BLACK MALES BEING MISUNDERSTOOD

One of the questions that we posed to the young men was centered on perceptions that they believe the wider society has toward them. We were interested in this because of the manner in which many young Black males are viewed through media and how these images shape the discourse about them. Moreover, some have discussed the negative consequences of social imagery and how Black males are harmed by these constructions more than any other population (Reynolds, 2010). Furthermore, we wanted to hear the young men speak about their own interpretations of how they are viewed by the wider society, and we wanted them to be able to offer their own narratives about how they would like to be viewed. The responses ran the gamut, from some young men who stated that they really did not care about how they were misunderstood, to one young man saying that he would like to write a manifesto titled "Black Boy Blues" to provide insight into the multitude of ways that schools and society misunderstood them.

The general sentiment that came across from most of the young men was the manner in which they seemingly were dehumanized or viewed as being less than others because of their consumption of popular culture. Dante, a high achiever from a suburban high school, contended that "people think because we listen to rap music or whatever that we still don't have feelings and don't want to be treated like regular people, and we do." Astin offered a similar assessment but thought that fear was also a motivating factor in the misunderstanding.

> One thing that people don't get is that we don't want to rob you, steal your purse, or beat you up. Yeah, we might listen to violent lyrics, but we know how to make the difference. So the main thing is "don't be scared of us." Just leave us alone and we will leave you alone.

David, a middle of the road senior, stated that he believes his size plays a role in how his teachers and others see him.

So I'm a big dude (6 ft. 2 in., 280 lbs.) so people automatically think I play football, which I do, but they I think that I'm like this big dumb jock you know . . . so then when I can have a conversation with them about my interest in learning about investments or stocks, they are like shocked . . . like "you know how to think? You have ideas?" So don't judge a book by the cover.

Throughout the series of conversations with the young men, phrases that consistently came up were "treat us like others" or "just be fair" or "we're not all athletes." It became apparent that many of these young men believe that there is a dual system of justice, one where they often are held to a different standard than many of their non-Black peers. Several of the young men expressed frustration at constantly seeing young Black males being disciplined or reprimanded for infractions that they knew other students were guilty of committing. Justyn, who attends a suburban high school, provided his experience.

I go to the dean's office and all you see is Black and Mexican dudes in there . . . it's like, are we the only ones that get in trouble? I don't think so, these White boys act like fools all the time, but why don't they go the dean's office? So my thing would be just treat us all the same.

The notion of fairness and equal treatment was a common theme. When pressed as to why they believed school officials or others held them to such a different standard, young men generally responded that they believe that media-generated images of Black men permeate the minds of many individuals and that makes it hard for Black male students to get a fair shake in many instances. Miles, a high school junior, said:

What I would tell people is to stop watching *Cops* and *America's Most Wanted*, where every criminal is a Black man, then they come here [to the school], and think we are the same way. . . . I hate that. We see White people do bad stuff, but we don't think that they would do that.

Kevin, a high school junior, who by his own admission has been a "f--k up in school," added a layer of complexity to the conversation around perceptions of Black males when he asserted that many teachers of color are equally culpable in their negative depiction of Black males. He offered an emotional and astute critique that seemed to be saturated with a need to be understood, cared for, and humanized.

I expect White people to be scared of us, but it's when the Black and other people of color don't treat us right. Mr. Smith [who is Black] treats us like s--t . . . he don't try to help you, encourage you, none of that . . . he just is full of self-hate or something . . . always talking down to the Black kids, sayin' stuff like "y'all goin' straight to prison" or "I got mine, y'all ain't gonna get yours." Who says that to other Black kids? He is a straight racist. So I would say to him, "look in the mirror." I know it had to be hard for him growing up, so help us out, don't put us down. We have feelings like anyone else. That's why I never went to his class.

As the young men continued to offer opinions about how they believed that they were misunderstood, issues of race and all of their complexities became ever present. Justyn talked about a biology teacher suggesting that there was no such thing as race and that he saw all of his students the same, with which Justyn disagreed, saying, "He knows he sees African Americans in here . . . just 'cuz biology says something different, don't act like we ain't Black." The color-blind notion was mentioned frequently by the young men who attended pre-dominately White and Asian schools; they stated that teachers often told them things such as, "I don't see color," or "You're not Black to me, you're a person just like me." These color-blind approaches seemed to bother most of the young men, which theorists have argued has a number of problematic implications. Guinier and Torres (2003) explain:

> In response to those who take a colorblind approach, we argue, as a practical matter, that it is impossible to be colorblind in a world as color-conscious as ours. Moreover, efforts to be colorblind are undesirable because they inhibit racialized minorities from struggling against their marginalized status. The rule of colorblindness disguises (sometimes deliberately) or normalizes (sometimes unwittingly) relationships of privilege and subordination. (p. 42)

As color-blind issues arose, students in middle-class, predominately White schools spoke to the manner in which they became spokespersons on the Black experience. Todd provided a sentiment that at least a half-dozen of the young men spoke to.

> What teachers misunderstand is that when we talk about slavery or the civil rights movement, don't always look at me, or ask me questions . . . if I want to say something about it, I will, but when you're the only Black person in the class, don't put me on the spot and expect me to say something. I hate that.

The idea of essentializing the Black male experience has been discussed previously in this text, and the young men who attended more racially integrated schools attempted to convey how important it was to not be the "Black person, who knows everything about Black things and Black people." The notion of individualizing experiences was important to the young men whom we spoke to in focus groups. Key to the idea of misunderstanding, we also discovered that the young men wanted to ensure that school personnel, if they were uncertain or unsure about who these young men were, and what motivated them, would merely engage the young men about various issues as opposed to assuming, inferring, or generalizing. Kenyon spoke to this point.

> I would say, just don't judge us, talk to us, we laugh, we cry, we hurt like anybody else, you know what I'm saying? Don't assume. Talk to us, like you would talk to anyone else. I mean . . . we don't bite.

A cry for being humanized is the way that I would characterize what many of the young men were saying in response to this question. A number of scholars have documented how Black males often are analyzed, scrutinized, and dissected, and in the process not seen in a more humane context as in need of encouragement, support, and mentorship (Duncan, 2002; Hopkins, 1997; Noguera, 2001). Young men throughout our conversations commented about the importance of certain mentors in their lives, whether fathers, mothers, siblings, uncles, cousins, or school personnel who spent time with them, talked to them, and helped them with life challenges. Over the course of the conversations, when young men discussed individuals who were helpful to them, they were probed to say more about the roles that these individuals played. Overwhelmingly, these individuals seemed to be what Kleinfeld (1975) labeled as "warm demanders." Kleinfeld coined this phrase to describe the type of teachers who were effective at teaching Athabaskan Indian and Eskimo 9th-graders in Alaskan schools. These teachers, who insisted that students perform to a high level, communicated personal warmth and used an instructional style Kleinfeld called "active demandingness." The individuals who were helpful to the young men in our study were explicit in their expectations, expected much from them, held them accountable, were swift with constructive criticism, but also were willing to provide nurturance and support when needed. A number of the young men said that the individuals who were most salient in their success academically and personally often gave them "tough love" or made them "responsible." It should be stated that some of the young men commented that a different approach worked best for them. Jason commented, "Don't keep telling me I messed up. I know it. I feel bad about it, so don't keep saying it. I will fix it."

THE COMPLEXITY OF BLACK MALENESS

The voices of the young men were rich, complex, diverse, at times encouraging, and at other times concerning. While Black males are often complicit in their marginalization, they also are victims at the same time. Thus, Black males undoubtedly can play a role in helping to reverse underperformance in schools and ostracization in society writ large. Much like their counterparts from different ethnic, racial, and gendered backgrounds, they often question the relevance of schools and wonder whether the payoff is what often is promised. These young men have hopes and aspirations, have had successes and setbacks, and continue to persevere to become self-actualized. Moreover, the young men we spoke with made continual pleas for caring educators, greater relevance in their school curriculum, and more explicit connections between course content and their interaction with social media, popular culture, and current issues and challenges. In many ways, for scholars and practitioners to get a much more insightful and authentic account of Black males' realities requires less theorizing and more day-to-day engagement with these young men in their worlds. Critical race theory scholar David Stovall (2013) builds from work in critical legal studies by incorporating tenets of action and engagement into education work. What he offers is the type of framework that can be more useful to understanding the complexity and diversity of Black male identity. He states that there is a need for more

> commitment to on-the-ground work. Our theorizing should deal less with abstract concepts and should be rooted in a tangible commitment to the physical/material, social, and intellectual support of communities that are experiencing educational injustice. (p. 294)

This commitment to "on-the-ground work" that Stovall speaks about is what seems to build trust, display care, and demonstrate a level of commitment to understanding challenges that youth face. Several of the young men mentioned how pleased they were that we took the time to talk with them about their education, engage them in conversations, and spend time with them at their schools or after-school programs. In many ways, these small efforts send a key message—caring—and can go a long way in creating the types of relationships that are essential to youth success. Gladwell (2000) states that "it is not the heroic actions of tackling complex societal problems that count; instead, the power of context says that what really matters is the little things" (p. 150). Much of what these young men spoke about was adults understanding their contexts and being mindful of the challenges they face on a regular basis in and out of schools. Delpit and Dowdy (2002) speak of the importance of listening to youth before we respond to what we think ails them.

> Listening . . . requires not only open eyes and ears, but open hearts and minds. We do not really see through our eyes or hear through our ears, but through our beliefs. . . . It is not easy, but it is the only way to learn what it might feel like to be someone else and the only way to start the dialogue. (p. 139)

Milner (2007a) builds on Delpit's point when he says that teachers play a critical role in helping Black males to reach their full academic potential. He says effective teachers of Black males

> value Black male students' perspectives and provide them space to have voice in the classroom. They empower the students to speak about what could be in their lives, and the teachers themselves speak about future opportunities and possibilities for their lives. (p. 243)

Education professor Marc LaMont Hill (2009) talks about the need to listen to urban youth because listening can help healing to evolve. He contends that healing can lead to the "therapeutic dimensions of personal and collective story-telling . . . that exposes and produces new possibilities" (p. 65). Much of the work covered in this chapter was directed at hearing the voices of Black males, giving them a space to discuss how they saw themselves in schools, and perhaps most important, helping them think about what could be, or imagining themselves in schools in a different and perhaps transformative light. Louis, an 8th-grade, middle of the road student, stated that "it would be cool if when we came to school we could learn about stuff we want to learn about." The manner in which Louis's eyes lit up as he talked about this educational utopia was intriguing, because he talked about it in a manner that seemed so elusive, yet would be gratifying if it to came to fruition. A growing number of scholars have begun to engage in the power and potential of the arts, for example, to engage urban youth, and in particular Black males, in schools. Childs-Davis (2013) discovered in her work that the use of arts in an urban high school was the biggest lure, next to athletics, for many Black males to even attend school on a consistent basis. She discovered that many of the young men that she studied and worked with saw the arts (namely, music and drawing) as forms of therapy and an outlet for them to express their pain, misery, suffering, and overall frustration with growing up in a community that was plagued by crime and violence. Her contention was that so much can be learned about how young Black males feel about their realities by studying their artistic expressions. In particular she cited the prominence of rap music as a medium that should be analyzed for developing a sense of how many Black male youth think, feel, and see the world. Over the past 2 decades, a growing number of scholars have examined the role that rap music and hip-hop culture can play in engaging urban youth, and Black males in particular, in the learning process (Alim, 2006; Camangian, 2010; Dimitriadis, 2001; Duncan-Andrade & Morrell, 2008; Hill, 2009). There is an appeal to these forms of expression that seems to resonate with many young Black males that should be understood and incorporated into how we teach and talk with them.

I would contend that it is important for schools to find spaces for all students, but in particular it is important for those who find themselves on the margins to have spaces where they can discuss out-of-school issues, which undoubtedly influence their performance and disposition in school. I would offer the following recommendations to better engage Black male youth:

Recommendation #1—Create spaces for dialogue. Based on the conversations we had with students, there is a clear need for them to talk, emote, and share some of the daily challenges they confront. Ideally, these spaces would be facilitated by school personnel who are able to listen to, engage with, and offer meaningful support to these young men in a nonjudgmental way. Issues around trust and expressing emotions can be a challenge for any student, but tend to be more difficult for males of color (Conchas & Vigil, 2012). Therefore, breaking the mode of silence with young men can be challenging at times, and may be met with silence or resistance, but ultimately it can be therapeutic and instructive, and can lead to improved relationships with school personnel and potentially better academic performance. In a previous study we conducted on single-sex learning spaces for Black males, we discovered that the most significant outcomes of single-gendered classes were the *counterspaces* that were created that allowed for more thoughtful and insightful dialogue about the young men's day-to-day challenges and realities (Terry, Flennaugh, Blackmon, & Howard, in press). These spaces can be before- or after-school programs, lunch settings, Saturday academies, or bimonthly special meetings, but their impact has the potential to be invaluable.

Recommendation #2—Reduce the stigma of remediation. Many of the lower performers that we spoke with expressed the sentiment that they believe they were placed in classes that were extremely low-level, nonstimulating, and highly tracked. At least a handful of the lower performers that we spoke to talked about being "in the dumb class" when they were younger. While it is important to help all students obtain the skills that they need, many students clearly recognized that they were not expected to be in more challenging classes, and in many ways seemed to internalize the low expectations school personnel had for them. As Roland, a 9th-grader, told us, "You think I'm a f--k up, then I will act like a f--k up!" School personnel must evaluate school data and take a close look at the gender and racial breakdown of students' academic placement. Students will not engage if they believe school personnel do not believe in them. Dance (2008) talks about the "weighty bag of stigmatization" often faced by Black male youth, wherein teachers "do not go beyond the official curricula to teach more complex content, and treat . . . [a student] like a troublemaker when he requests a more advanced, culturally relevant curriculum" (p. 142). The answer here is not an easy one, but requires a complex analysis of early intervention when students are young so that less remediation is necessary in middle and high school. While it is clear that a disproportionately high number of Black males have shown lack of proficiency in core academic areas, an emphasis on rote memorization and one-dimensional instructional practices that are often unengaging, uninspiring, and reductive is a surefire way to turn students off from learning in particular and schools in general.

Recommendation #3—Rethink and revise discipline policies. One of our most pressing concerns in our conversations with young Black males was that they seemed to have a keen sense that school discipline was often excessive, disproportionate, and meted out for minor infractions. Many of the young men seemed to express anger, frustration, or resentment toward school officials who adhered to these policies in a harsh and inflexible manner. Thus, one way to re-engage young Black males in schools is to give careful consideration to the manner in which zero-tolerance and other discipline policies are implemented, and to take a close look at data on school suspension, expulsion, and referral along racial and gender lines. The research on Black males and discipline has shown disturbing disparities consistently for the past 3 decades (Artiles et al., 2004; Harry & Klingner, 2006). This must change if young Black males are ever to authentically re-engage in schools. As I have discussed in previous works (Howard, 2010), many young Black males believe that they are often guilty until proven innocent when it comes to their behavior, and that school personnel are looking for them to be disruptive or waiting for an opportunity to send them to the office. Communicating with young people in an attempt to engage them in schools must be centered on a framework that sees their assets, recognizes their possibilities, and attempts to identify their academic, social, or cultural strengths in an effort to connect them to learning.

Recommendation #4—Learn from athletic coaches. What became apparent for many of the students that we spoke with, was the salience of sports. While there are a number of cautions that come with sports, as outlined in Chapter 4, there are models that offer insight into what is required for connecting with and re-engaging Black male youth. Athletic coaches were referenced by many of the students as key individuals at the school who seemed to care about them, understood them, pushed them to be their best, and did not view them in such a negative light. Previous work has looked at the important role that many athletic coaches play for males of color, urban youth, and Black males in particular (Duncan-Andrade, 2010). This is one of the few areas on the school campus where young Black males are likely to interact with individuals who look like them, may have been reared in situations similar to theirs, and thus have a level of cultural synchronization that is uncommon in most classrooms that they enter. The roles that coaches can play are multiple, even for those young men who do not participate in sports. Coaches often can serve as intermediaries between students and teachers, their relationships with students may be strong enough to encourage students to put forth their best effort in classrooms, and in some cases they may be one of the primary male role models in young men's lives. At least several of the young men that we spoke to discussed their basketball or football coaches as being like father or big brother figures to them. The nature, arrangement, and intricacies of these relationships between coaches and young Black males should be looked at and analyzed by school personnel who are seeking to engage with this student population. Among the questions that should be pondered are: What do coaches do? How do they do it? How do they deal with resistance? And perhaps most important, What, if anything, can I learn from these interactions in an attempt to connect with the Black males in my classrooms?

Recommendation #5—Incorporate the role of social media and popular culture. For the past 5 to 6 decades, youth culture has been shaped and influenced by various inventions and occurrences of the day. Arguably the biggest influences have been television, radio, music, and technology. Today's youth are no different. In an information age driven by advancing technology, young people are more media and technologically savvy than any generation of young people this country has ever seen. Kellner and Share (2009) state that there is a need for a more complex and refined notion of understanding and engaging youth in media literacy and popular culture, and that this can have unlimited benefits. They state:

> Critical media literacy is an educational response that expands the notion of literacy to include different forms of mass communication, popular culture, and new technologies. It also deepens the potential of literacy education to critically analyze relationships between media and audiences, information, and power. (p. 282)

In short, they make a call that can serve as an ideal way to connect with Black male youth. Some researchers have shown the manner in which urban youth are prominent daily users of social media and social network sites, and see them as a communal space to learn, commune, socialize, and engage around current topics. In short, much can be learned about young people in these spaces. Therefore, it is vital for educators to learn, think about, and possibly incorporate into their course content information tied to platforms such as Facebook, Twitter, and Instagram, which Black youth are shown to engage in at levels higher than their White, Asian, and Latino peers (Pew Research Center, 2013). Becoming informed about the mechanisms and platforms where millions of youth are connected is a no-brainer for educators looking to better understand youth. Moreover, a cursory level of knowledge on contemporary music and movies also becomes a platform for engagement. While there is definitely a generational gap between most educators and students when it comes to these platforms, students are often more than willing to inform, invite, and engage interested parties. Thus, it requires practitioners asking, learning, and suspending judgment about these formats, which hold high importance in the lives of many young people.

The power of voice, the power of listening, and the power of learning from youth cannot be overstated. Our current reality is that young people have unique knowledge, insights, opinions, and perspectives that need to be heard. Frequently we tend to dismiss or ignore youth perspectives for the underlying reason that their youth, immaturity, and lack of lived experiences do not give them much credibility. I would hope that this small sample of voices from Black male youth would cause adults to think differently about them. Many of our young people have lived much more complicated and complex lives than many adults could ever imagine. They have experiences from 15 years of living that adults two and three times their age have; thus, they are wise, skeptical, thoughtful, and equipped to see the world in a very different manner than most adults did at their age. Much of what ails our attempts to connect with and engage young people in learning rests in their hearts and minds. The challenge is whether we are willing to listen. Moreover, if we are willing to listen, we must be prepared for the honest and often harsh assessment that young people may have to offer adults about how we often dismiss and marginalize them, sometimes consciously, much of the time unconsciously. I frequently am reminded of a statement from a former 4th-grade teacher of mine, who frequently stressed the importance of listening. She often would tell us that "there is a reason why God gave you two ears and one mouth, so that you can listen twice as much as you speak." The call is before us now, when it comes to young Black males, to listen to them a lot more than we speak.

CHAPTER 6

Black Male Success

Throughout this book, I have chronicled, documented, and analyzed much of what ails countless numbers of young Black males in schools and society, and attempted to offer some insights and recommendations as to what can improve their educational prospects. There have been seemingly endless data on how and where Black males trail their counterparts from different ethnic and racial backgrounds. I will not belabor those data in this chapter, as they have been discussed in earlier chapters. The focus of this chapter is to build on the idea of the paradigm shift that I discussed in Chapter 2. The need for a paradigm shift is critical in an attempt to alter, or radically change, the discourse on Black males in U.S. schools. I raise this point because if the narrative on Black males remains the same, the general sentiment that emerges and becomes reified locally, nationally, and globally is that "Black males are a problem." Furthermore, if Black males are continuously seen in problematic terms, any efforts to disrupt their educational challenges will be anchored in problem-based and deficit terms (Valencia, 1997), and be largely unsuccessful. Such approaches often are tied to "fixing," "disciplining," or "changing" Black males, without any interrogation into the historical, institutional, economic, or social structures that shape their realities. A number of works have documented the types of resistance, or refusal to learn, that students are inclined to demonstrate when they believe their intelligence, dignity, identity, or integrity is compromised by a teacher, an institution, or a deficit-driven mindset (Kohl, 1994; Kushman, 2003; Solorzano & Delgado Bernal, 2001). A deficit-driven approach can be seen in schools all across the country, wherein approaches to "fix" or "deal with" Black males are often dealt with by placement in opportunity rooms, discipline rooms, detention centers, or other spaces designed to punish students until they change their ways, without any attempt to authentically understand their behavior and engage them in a meaningful way.

In fairness to Black males, and to provide an honest assessment of the larger landscape of students, there are strong arguments to be made that students from all ethnic, racial, and gender backgrounds struggle academically, socially, and emotionally. Yet, it seems that Black males often are treated more harshly, for similar shortcomings, than their peers from other racial and gender backgrounds (Noguera, 2008). In short, academic and social challenges are not unique to the Black male experience. Practitioners and researchers must be explicit that there are Black males who are doing well on multiple fronts and disrupting the idea that they are all struggling to find their way in schools. I make a call for a more asset-based examination of Black males. An asset-based approach operates from the standpoint of identifying strengths, seeing their potential and promise, and designing interventions around their academic and social potential and possibilities. This chapter on Black male success will address individual and programmatic accounts of success that operate from an asset-based approach. As in Chapter 5 where I documented Black male voices, here I will highlight more student accounts to build the narrative from the individual level, but I also will identify school and community-based programs that are helping to create or sustain Black male success. These cases will be laid out in an attempt to inform the larger discourse on what is happening at the individual (micro) level as well as the institutional (macro) level where Black male assets are seen as a conduit to academic success and not viewed as a threat.

BLACK MALE SUCCESS: WHY IT MATTERS

One of the reasons that Black male success will be discussed further in this chapter is to transform the narrative in framing how Black males are viewed. It is also critical for Black males to know what is possible and what is required for success, and to affirm those who are doing well. One of the issues that emerged in my interviews with the high-achieving Black males was what could be considered an attempt to conceal or apologize for academic exceptionalism. Several of the young men talked about their stellar academic records almost in dismissive or embarrassing terms. Two young men, when talking about their GPAs that were over 3.5, labeled their high performance as "not a big deal." Another young man talked about how he was "made fun of" when he was in elementary school because he did well academically, while two other participants said they did not like to talk about their high grades around their peers because they would become the subject of peers' scorn and ridicule. Thus, it is essential for practitioners, researchers, and policymakers to know that there are a number of critical ingredients that contribute to Black male success and to understand these ingredients—and there is no better source from whom to hear about them than Black males.

The following are excerpts from interviews with Black male high school students who were participants in an academic enrichment program. These young men, who were rising high school seniors and juniors, provided insights into the ingredients that explain their academic success. By no means are these accounts meant to be generalizable to all Black males, but they do provide a glimpse into a paradigm that is not heard enough. In short, these young men were asked to respond to one question: To what, or whom, do you attribute your academic success? This question was posed to evaluate how students themselves gave attributions to their academic successes. Much has been written in the psychological literature about attribution theory (Gordon & Graham, 2006). The concept of attribution is tied to the notion that people frequently seek ways to explain various types of behavior. Moreover, people make explanatory attributions to understand the world around them and to seek reasons for a particular event. Some researchers on the topic have made the argument that one of the fundamental errors typically made when it comes to attribution is that people tend to overestimate the power of the person and underestimate the power of the situation (Malle, 2004; Weiner, 1992). In short, when young people tend to fall short of stated goals or objectives, there is a tendency to point the finger at or blame the individual for lack of effort, persistence, or intellect (Ryan, 1976). I do not dismiss the importance of individual attributes to academic success, but I raise a question about the importance of context to learning and performance. In our exchanges with high-achieving Black males, there seemed to be three key responses given concerning their high achievement: *resilience, high expectations others had for them,* and *upward mobility potential.* Each of these concepts was stated repeatedly by these young men. In speaking about issues tied to resilience, Aaron commented:

> I am successful because my priorities are in order . . . education comes before anything else. School is my first priority. I don't involve myself in drama. I am not discouraged to ask questions or get extra help if I need it. I know what is best for me and I take all the right steps to get where I need to be. I may not do well on a test, but then I know I need to study harder to do better on the next one.

The idea of prioritizing education, asserting oneself, and responding to setbacks was a common theme and is tied to this idea of resilience and achievement outcomes. D. J. stated:

> I am successful because we have this saying in football: "hard work pays off." So I use that in school too. I work hard on my studies, and I think the grades show that. So for me, it's just working hard, not getting distracted, not making excuses, and not messing up my future . . . some things may not go well, but how do you bounce back? How do you respond?

The notion of resilience has been mentioned as vital to success in any endeavor, but is more prevalent in education. Education scholar Mike Rose (2012) states that "people who do succeed . . . often tell stories of success mixed with setbacks, of two steps forward and one back. Such stories reveal anger and nagging worry or compromise and ambivalence or a bruising confrontation with one's real or imagined inadequacies" (p. 25).

High expectations that others had for them was also cited as a reason for academic excellence and school success. A number of these young men talked about the types of environments in their homes where there were explicit expectations about their school performance. Mark commented:

> I am successful in school because I have a mother who pushes me to do better. When I settle, she doesn't. She has taught me to be hungry for As . . . given me motivation to push harder. She knows how hard it is for Black males to succeed in the world; she wants me to show the community how a Black man can succeed in life.

The role of expectations cannot be overstated. As highlighted in the previous chapter, many of the young men talked about apathetic teachers with low expectations of them, who did not challenge them or hold them to high academic standards. So what seems to be a key ingredient to these young men's superior performance was a belief that adults expected them to do well—not only said it, but coupled those words with persistent actions. Cedric, a rising high school junior, stated the following:

> My household is responsible for a lot of my success. Everybody has contributed in some way. From my dad's pestering me to do more than required, my brother and sister being role models, and everybody just expecting me to do well.

Winston built on this sentiment when he commented:

> My friends, family, and everybody plays a role and tells me to persevere and get my education. From elementary school I was expected to get good grades and go to college. So that has been my support group, friends and family. When everybody around you expects you to go to college, that's what you do.

The idea of Black males growing up in dysfunctional and unsupportive families has been chronicled in a number of works (E. Anderson, 2008). These accounts have been persistent and paint a picture that suggests that most Black males grow up in turmoil, in dysfunctional homes and communities, and thus lack the skills and the supportive environment needed for academic success. However, absent from the portrayal are family members, even in trying circumstances, who still put forth immeasurable time and effort into ensuring these young men's success. Although many of the circumstances were far from ideal, young Black males still find an ethos of care, love, expectations, and support in their homes. It is these types of assets that many Black males possess that cannot be overlooked, dismissed, or ignored. They are present, and it is vital for education practitioners to identify them and build on them. It seems that for many students adversity can serve as a source of motivation that can lead to better outcomes. DeMont contended:

> The fear of failure encourages me to work hard, that's why [I am successful]. My older siblings stay on me and expect me to try harder, and never give up, so I don't and it makes a difference.

Another sentiment that several of the young men mentioned was their desire to move their families out of trying circumstances, and dispute the notion that Black males see sports as their only way to upward mobility. Thus, education was seen as a vehicle that could create access to better life opportunities. Lorenzo, an 11th-grader, said:

> I am successful because I want to get me and my grandmother out of poverty, and I know education is the way to do that. My grandmother has done so much for me that I owe this to her, so I will not let anything stop me, or get in my way. I have to study hard, manage my time, and hang around the right people who also have goals . . . so it's just never giving up.

Another student, Antonio, spoke about the upward mobility potential that education offered.

> We have a lot of things that are not good with my family . . . dad locked up, mom has problems, my sister messing up . . . so somebody has to do well to change that. Getting my education will do that for us. So I am successful in school because I need to help my family and I cannot do that without an education.

Antonio's response offers an account of how the challenging circumstances at home were used as motivation to do better academically. The key is to seek a better understanding of how and why difficult circumstances motivate some young men to do better, but derail others. In short, this speaks to the importance of demonstrating resilience, or developing coping mechanisms in pursuing goals while navigating difficult terrain. Educators at all levels need to identify approaches that can help students develop an inner sense of determination to respond to obstacles and adversity. What many of these young men offered were additional data to support the notion that not only is Black male success possible, but that it is occurring with frequency in a number of unexpected places.

It is important to take note of these messages, support young men in these circumstances, and create environments in homes, communities, and schools that expect academic success of Black males and seek to remove any obstacle that hinders that possibility.

RACE, GENDER IDENTITY, AND ACADEMIC SUCCESS

An interesting discovery that emerged in some of the conversations with the young men centered on complex notions of identity tied to academic success. Previous researchers have spoken to the idea that academic success for many Black students seemed to be a sign of racial or cultural abandonment, and the concept of "acting White" (Fordham & Ogbu, 1986). Several of the young men we talked to seemed to suggest that racial abandonment was not an issue for them as much as issues of masculinity and gender identity were. At least a half-dozen of the young men we spoke with, who were high achievers, contended that one of the charges that they encountered from their peers (especially Black and Latino male peers) was that they were gay, "acted gay," or seemed to display behavior that was not viewed as masculine. These students made mention of how, for them, doing well in school often was coupled with questions about their masculinity. Anthony elaborated:

> Yeah, some of the guys say that I act a certain way, or talk a certain way that they don't like . . . I guess . . . and I'm like, "I'm just being me, and I'm not gonna change that for nobody. Just because I don't push up on girls, and I handle my business in class, that makes me gay?"

A growing body of research has examined the complexity of masculinity (McCready, 2009, 2010a, 2010b; Skelton, 2001; Weaver-Hightower, 2003). What has been most prevalent in this work is the problem of narrowly defined notions of masculinity that many Black males operate on. While several of these young men were asked to elaborate further, none identified as being gay, bisexual, or transgender, but what they seemed to reject was any attempt to have their academic success minimized because of socially defined rules of male behavior. Anthony elaborated further on this point.

> So, some of these guys try to say that I only get good grades because I am a suck up to my teachers, or I go their classrooms at lunch, and I'm in there with all these girls and that real dudes don't act that way, but you know what? That's where I get extra help, that's where I find out what's coming up on the test, and that's where we study together. . . . So instead of hating

on me, and calling me a suck up, they need to be in here getting theirs, like I am getting mine.

A more complex analysis interrogating academic performance and social identities tied to masculinity is desperately needed. One has to wonder whether masculinity or one's gender identity has now replaced race as the identity marker that is essential to academic success for males of color. While a body of work has unpacked much of the hostility that non-gender-conforming individuals encounter, there remains a need to understand this better and see how it plays out for Black males in classrooms. But also, a statement from at least one student we spoke to raised questions about how, for many male students, classrooms have become feminized spaces that penalize certain young men and the ways in which they manifest their masculinity. The student, Frank, a low-performing 10th-grader at an urban school, commented that "if you come in here and act all passive, soft-spoken, and quiet, teachers love you, but if you come in class like a real man, they don't like that . . . they are scared of you then . . . and you get treated differently, that's what I don't like." When I pressed Frank to say more about what acting like a "real man" was, he seemed to be at a loss for a clear definition, stating, "You know what I'm talking about . . . a real man don't hang out with girls all the time, join the dance team, and all that kinda stuff . . . like act nerdy and dress a certain way . . . like feminine like." This statement was loaded on multiple levels that require further analysis. What seems to be evident is that the young men who embody Frank's ideas of a "real man" represent certain ideals and beliefs that are problematic due to the way that they marginalize certain ways that students behave. Conversely, he also raises an important point about how certain behaviors by young men are viewed in problematic terms. There is a need to inspect both of these approaches because they reveal deep-seated concerns about the way in which many young men may be experiencing schools. Moreover, it is crucial to disrupt the beliefs of some high-achieving males that they are type-cast in a certain box due to their academic performance that calls into question their masculinity and gender identity. More research is needed to hear these voices, but there also is a need for practitioners to provide safe spaces for young men who find themselves in the cross hairs of limited and harmful notions of masculinity, learning, and identity.

PROGRAMS SERVICING YOUNG BLACK MALES

I have been fortunate to work with school personnel all across the country, in addition to parent groups, social service agencies, and community-based organizations. Much of this work has been tied to school reform, improving teacher efficacy, understanding culture and learning, community enhancement, and parental empowerment, among other topics. One of the questions I am asked most frequently when working with educators and parents in urban communities is, "What programs are out there for Black boys?" In many ways, I believe that this is a plea from concerned adults who would like to connect their sons, students, grandsons, nephews, brothers, cousins, and so on, to credible, supportive, and sustainable programs that are assisting young Black males academically, socially, emotionally, or culturally. Given many of the challenges that are apparent in Black communities across the country, many caregivers are seeking positive male role models for young men, some are looking to connect them with other positive and ambitious young men, while still others are looking for ways to steer their loved ones to a more positive pathway. In an attempt to respond to this request, I have assembled a number of programs that I have come to learn about across the country that are dedicated to improving social outcomes, academic success, and overall life chances of Black males. Needless to say, what I present here is not an exhaustive list, or the best programs available, but it is an effort to share with parents, school personnel, and concerned community members the types of resources that are available and could be present in their own communities or cities. Furthermore, it is my hope that as individuals learn about these programs, they may be moved to participate in them or look into the creation of similar programs at their schools, districts, or communities. My recommendation would be to learn as much about these programs as possible to see how they were formed, where their support comes from, and what their core goals and mission are, and to document their effectiveness. It also should be noted that not all of these programs target Black males exclusively. Some target students from low-income communities, some target exclusively Black student populations, while others target males of color in particular. Nonetheless, what is clear is that young Black males from across the country are beneficiaries of these programs in ways that are contributing to success in the classroom, at home, and in their communities. I know that there are countless other efforts under way across the country that have long track records of proven effectiveness, which may not be included in this list; their exclusion is not deliberate. The programs discussed below are ones that I have firsthand knowledge of or have worked with, or that have been spoken highly of by individuals I have talked to. I list these programs as follows:

Alliance for Boys and Men of Color. California-based PolicyLink developed its Alliance for Boys and Men of Color as an alliance of change agents committed to improving the life chances of California's boys and young men of color. The Alliance includes youth, community organizations, foundations, and systems leaders such as education, public health, and law enforcement officials.

The work is active at the local and state levels, with a particular focus on Oakland, Los Angeles, and Fresno. The Alliance is actively pursuing reforms that do the following:

- Increase access to health services that recognize the strengths and assets of boys and young men of color while also responding to the trauma and chronic adversity that many face
- Achieve 100% high school graduation rates among boys and young men of color by strengthening the performance of public schools and reducing expulsion rates
- Ensure boys and young men of color live in safe neighborhoods and can attend safe schools
- Reduce the numbers of youth who enter the juvenile justice system and ensure that those who leave the system have the skills needed to succeed

Alliance members worked in 2013 to build support for state policy proposals to fix school discipline; namely, the willful defiance policy that disproportionately affects boys of color throughout the state. This effort included mobilizing letters of support for the slate of bills that school discipline advocates and educators moved through the legislature. The Alliance's Change.org petition to Governor Brown generated over 10,000 signatures. Meanwhile, through partnership with the Assembly Select Committee on the Status of Boys and Men of Color, Alliance members provided a platform for more than 2,000 youth, community, and system leaders to voice their concerns in the six hearings and six policy working groups that were held across the state. Alliance members' advice about promising solutions and policy and system reforms on which the state could act were included among the 67 recommendations in the Select Committee's Action Plan.

Black Male Leadership Development Institute. The Black Male Leadership Development Institute (BMLDI) is in its 6th year and has significantly impacted the lives of nearly 400 African American young men in the Pittsburgh area. Each year, the program inducts a cohort of no more than 75 males from 13 different regional high schools. Significant outreach is focused on youth in high-risk neighborhoods or who attend schools deemed "dropout factories." According to data compiled by the Commonwealth of Pennsylvania, 14,000 African Americans between the ages of 14 and 18 live in Allegheny County. Only 22% are projected to be living in a family with two parents, and 75% are estimated to live in a female-headed household, many of which are poor. BMLDI recognizes that many young African American males are growing up in impoverished families without a male presence and how that affects school and social outcomes.

The BMLDI appears to be well positioned for growth, as indicated by continued funding support from the Heinz Endowments and the Buhl Foundation. In addition, the demand for the services provided the BMLDI has increased significantly, as evidenced by the nearly 30% increase in applicants since its inception in 2007. Pilot programs using the leadership development model also have been tested for regional and potentially national replication. Numeretics, an evaluation consultant, noted in their annual study that participants consistently rated their experience well above average, with focus-group reports from parents and participants asserting that the program had ignited a sense of excitement about learning, service, and success. A parent shared that it was not until after the BMLDI that she even realized that her son had aspirations to attend college. Most telling is an account shared by a participant after a community service experience at a city elementary school; he told the cohort that "it was the first time that he ever felt like a role model." In less than 6 years, the BMLDI has grown from a 1-day summit into a year-round leadership experience.

Black Male Youth Academy. Founded at Morningside High School in Inglewood, CA, this Urban Scholars Program is called the Black Male Youth Academy (BMYA). Created in response to the disproportionate numbers of African American male youth who face high imprisonment, recidivism, and death rates, BMYA is centered on empowerment. The organization operates from a standpoint that challenges the manner in which schools contribute to a negative cycle of social reproduction through consistent deculturalization, reduced financial resources, and the lack of a culturally relevant teaching/learning style. In order to reverse this cycle, BMYA contends that African American male youth must be immersed in a schooling experience that is humanizing, values their cultural heritage, and creates strong opportunities for academic achievement. In this program, youth build knowledge of self for personal and social transformation. By the end of the program, youth are confident enough to demonstrate their knowledge of their ancestors, community, history, and the Diaspora. They discuss topics focused on their identity, issues of manhood and race, as well as their social condition. Finally, youth strategize specific ways to transform society and themselves in order to create a more just and human world. Using the Urban Scholars Program model as the foundation, the Black Male Youth Academy works with approximately 20–25 African American youth 4–5 days a week over the academic school year. Academy specific goals are:

- To help youth maintain a minimum 3.0 GPA by the end of the year
- To help youth achieve a proficient score (or higher) on the California Standards Test (CST)
- To help youth become a community of leaders

- To help youth develop "critical consciousness"
- To help youth become change agents in their community

Black Star Project. Founded in 1996, the Black Star Project is committed to improving the quality of life in Black and Latino communities of Chicago and nationwide by eliminating the racial academic achievement gap. The project's mission is to provide educational services that help preschool through college students succeed academically and become knowledgeable and productive citizens with the support of their parents, families, schools, and communities. One of their more pointed programs is the Black Men of Honor Mentor Program, whose goal is to provide mentorship for young Black males between the ages of 6 and 18. The program meets four times a month; has a one mentor to four youth ratio; works on the issues of respecting elders; teaches youth to value education, and honor parents, young women, and girls; teaches youth to be leaders and not followers; connects youth to positive male role models; travels to other parts of the city on field trips; brings in guest speakers; and practices self-discipline.

Building a Lifetime of Options and Opportunities for Men. In April 2012, the California Community Foundation (CCF), a public, charitable organization serving Los Angeles County, funded seven community-based organizations to carry out a new initiative focused on serving Black male youth involved in the juvenile delinquency system. Building a Lifetime of Options and Opportunities for Men (BLOOM), a 5-year initiative, was launched with the goal of redirecting Black male youth ages 14–18 involved with the Los Angeles County probation system toward improved education and employment opportunities and outcomes. This work is based on the premise that system-involved Black male youth can follow such a pathway with positive outcomes if: (1) policies that lead to chronic system involvement are altered or mitigated; (2) there is more positive messaging about redemption of youth and success stories are highlighted; and (3) Black male youth are exposed to new vocational and academic opportunities. CCF identifies key strategies as necessary to achieve its goal of a 10% decrease in the number of Black male youth under Los Angeles County probation supervision over the next 5 years (approximately 480 youth). To achieve this goal, the BLOOM initiative currently is funding ten community-based organizations providing activities in at least one of the key strategy areas. One year into the program, the BLOOM initiative had serviced 174 youth and reported a 45% decrease in school suspensions among its program participants; moreover, 93% of the young men had not re-offended, and approximately 98% had re-engaged with their schools, families, and communities. The year two goal is to service approximately 600 system-involved youth to empower them with knowledge, skills, and supports necessary for re-engagement. BLOOM is the only project of its type in the country that is focused solely on system-involved Black male youth ages 14–18.

Concerned Black Men Inc. Concerned Black Men (CBM) seeks to enhance the academic and social development of children by providing homework assistance, reading and math instruction, test-taking skills, and enrichment activities that center on improving student achievement and standardized test scores, and encouraging the pursuit of higher education. A key component of CBM's outreach is its Saving Lives and Minds (SLAM) project. SLAM's model is an all-day enrichment program for approximately 8 weeks during the months of July and August, where youth and preteens receive intense instruction in the arts, sciences, and sports. The program also includes field trips to broaden students' horizons and peer leadership training for older youth that focuses on life skills, education, conflict resolution, anger management, and leadership development. The program is currently operating in Washington, DC; Richmond, Virginia; Philadelphia, Pennsylvania; Columbia, South Carolina; and Prince George's County, Maryland. Sites to be opened in 2014 include Cape Cod and the Islands, Dallas, and Los Angeles. Details of the program include the following:

- It presently serves more than 600 boys.
- Mentee average length in the program is 2 years.
- Average mentoring time is 2.8 hours per week.
- It has conducted over 350 life skills and enrichment activities.
- Mentor average length in the program is 18 months.
- Mentor retention rate is 80%.

Children's Defense Fund—Freedom Schools. Created by the Children's Defense Fund, CDF Freedom Schools program engages children in grades K–12 in a 6- or 7-week summer program designed to prevent the "learning loss" that students (known as Scholars in the program) typically experience over the months when school is not in session, as well as to have a positive impact on children's character development, leadership, and community involvement. The CDF Freedom Schools program provides enrichment with the stated goals of "helping children fall in love with reading, increase their self-esteem, and generate more positive attitudes toward learning." CDF reports that more than 80,000 children have participated in the Freedom Schools program since its inception in 1995. Scholars are taught using a model curriculum that supports children and families around five essential components: high-quality academic enrichment; parent and family involvement; civic engagement and social action; intergenerational leadership development; and nutrition, health, and mental health. In the summer of 2012, CDF Freedom Schools served more than 11,500 children in 83 cities and 25 states (including Washington, DC). CDF Freedom Schools sites work to ensure that each child is equipped with the necessary skills to succeed in life. The program boosts student motivation to read and generates a more positive attitude toward learning; it also connects the needs of children and families to the resources of their communities. Results at sites across the country have shown that students have maintained or increased their levels of reading proficiency and fluency, as well as their overall interest in literature.

The CDF Freedom Schools program uses a literature-based reading curriculum called the Integrated Reading Curriculum (IRC). About 80 books are on the IRC booklist and feature the work of many well-known authors. CDF has developed 6 weeks of lesson plans for approximately half of the books to help staff and Scholars reflect on culturally and community relevant themes, topics, and issues. CDF requires that CDF Freedom Schools programs be offered at no charge to participating families and that no fewer than 50 children receive service at each site. Freedom Schools have been recognized nationally for their innovative approaches to boosting literacy outcomes for underserved youth in many of the nation's most challenging urban and rural communities.

Cleveland Municipal School District: Closing the Achievement Gap Program. In an effort to stem the tide of increasing negative data affecting minority males in its district, the Closing the Achievement Gap (CTAG) program has a particular focus on Black males, which includes the following components:

- Targeted intervention for a targeted population (minority males)
- Connections to agencies and resources that students and families may need
- Attendance and discipline intervention
- Role models and life coaches through the Linkage Coordinators
- Exposure trips to colleges and cultural sites
- Connections to book clubs

The key to the CTAG program has been the effectiveness of the Linkage Coordinators. These men act as mentors, life coaches, motivators, and advocates, ensuring that students' social, academic, and emotional needs are addressed so that they can achieve academically and graduate on time. Over the past 4 years, CTAG has witnessed an increase in minority males graduating and a direct correlation between minority male participants and a decrease in dropout rates.

Coalition of Schools Educating Boys of Color. The mission of the Coalition of Schools Educating Boys of Color (COSEBOC) is to connect, inspire, support, and strengthen school leaders dedicated to the social, emotional, and academic development of boys and young men of color. COSEBOC is the only national education organization of practitioners focused solely on promoting the educational success of boys and young men of color. COSEBOC works with all schools—pre-K–12th grade; public, charter, and private; coed and single gender. COSEBOC connects research, policy, and practice, and is a learning community for school leaders. COSEBOC's growing menu of programs and services is rooted in its Standards and Promising Practices for Educating Boys and Young Men of Color, a framework for what a school should offer and do if it intends for its male students of color to succeed. COSEBOC's mission is tied to three key goals:

1. Build a network of school leaders who are able to increase their schools' success with boys and young men of color
2. Provide professional development, promising practices, and other resources to support and strengthen its network of school leaders as a learning community
3. Promote the concept of schools that are intentionally designed to ensure educational success for their male students of color and the reality of COSEBOC Award Schools that have met this goal and whose male students of color demonstrate success

Don Bosco Hall Inc. Don Bosco Hall is a private nonprofit agency that provides supportive human services to enhance the quality of life for youth and their families in the Metropolitan Detroit–Wayne County community. The Don Bosco Hall Male Leadership Academy provides youth with a variety of educational and support services. The youth attend an intensive educational program during school days. The school operates between the hours of 8:00 A.M. and 3:30 P.M. At the completion of the school day, the youth participate in a variety of after-school recreational, cultural arts, career development, leadership training, and tutorial services. Students are transported to and from the site Monday through Saturday. The Academy also provides community monitoring services for the youth during the evening hours and on Sunday. Listed below are the types of services that are provided.

- Educational instruction
- Crisis management
- After-school services
- Group counseling
- Family counseling
- Career planning
- Community service projects
- Psychotherapeutic services
- Community monitoring
- Random drug screening/counseling
- Pre-employment training
- Meals
- Reintegration/follow-up services
- Referral services

The Don Bosco Hall Eagle Program is an intensive, short-term intervention program for adjudicated male youth. The goal of the program is to assist young men and their families in successfully returning the youth home, if possible, or securing the most appropriate setting upon program completion. Residents of the program progress through a four-level system (Freshman to Senior) by demonstrating appropriate behavior, participating in therapy, and progressing through their Care Pathway. The level system in the Eagle Program is designed to assist residents in improving positive behavior, leadership skills, and responsibility.

Eagle Academy. Founded in 2005, the New York City–based Eagle Academy Foundation (EAF) is nationally recognized for increasing the academic achievement of inner-city young men. The all-male public schools outperform national averages for Black male high school graduation and college persistence. Based on the premise that increasing educational attainment is the most fundamental way to change the life trajectory of a young Black male, they seek to increase the number of Black and Latino men who graduate from high school and succeed in college. When at full capacity in 2015, seven Eagle Academies will serve 4,200 young men of color and their parents. Eagle Academies prove that the Eagle Model, emphasizing parental engagement, extended learning, mentorship, moral character, and high expectations, can help Black males achieve academic and social success. The Foundation states that it achieves mission impact by shaping education across the country to address the educational needs of urban males through leadership and professional development.

East Oakland Step to College Program—The Urban Hope Project Program. The East Oakland Step to College (STC) Program is a direct-service educational program dedicated to racial justice for Oakland youth. The program takes the position that a core component of racial justice is the provision of a high-quality and critical education that prepares youth of color to confront and change the course of racial justice in their community and the nation. To meet this challenge, STC provides two university professors as instructors for the cohort's high school English class for 4 consecutive years (9th–12th grades). These professors are also veteran urban high school English teachers with a combined experience of 25 years in the classroom. In addition to these core instructors, the program also brings in undergraduate and graduate students of color from the university to act as urban teacher apprentices and tutors.

The support provided to students to engage in this work includes afterschool tutoring (study table) in all subjects 3 days a week for 2.5 hours per session. Study table draws from university students to provide a nearly one student to one tutor ratio. These university students work with the high school students over multiple years in the cohort, building strong social bonds that allow for mentorship and social development. Additionally, the Colleges of

Ethnic Studies and Education at San Francisco State University (SFSU) act as partnering university. In this capacity, the institution provides supports for the program, allowing students to participate in dual enrollment during their 11th- and 12th-grade years, so that they receive transferrable university credit during their last 2 years in STC.

ExpandED Schools. In 2011, encouraged by a 3-year pilot program and building from the evidence base of high-quality, after-school and summer programming, TASC launched ExpandED Schools. Working in 11 K–8 public schools in Baltimore, New Orleans, and New York City, the ExpandED model gives students 35% more learning time for 10% of the cost. ExpandED Schools re-engineer the use of time, staff, and money to expand time and opportunity for every child. Each ExpandED School commits to four core elements: (1) more learning time for a balanced curriculum; (2) school–community partnership; (3) engaging and personalized instruction; and (4) sustainable cost model. Schools and community educators work together to re-engineer their staffing, schedule, and curriculum to make learning more engaging for low-income, Black male students. The goal of ExpandED Schools is to improve academic and life outcomes for students by preparing them to be on track to graduate from high school, college- and career-ready. Of the approximately 1 million New York City K–8 public school students, slightly more than one-quarter are Black, half are male, and two-thirds qualify for free or reduced lunch (FRPL). Baltimore City public schools serve about 85,000 K–8 students, of whom more than 85% are Black and qualify for FRPL, and slightly more than half are male. New Orleans public schools serve roughly 42,000 K–8 students, and more than 85% are Black and qualify for FRPL (Baltimore City Public Schools, NYC Department of Education and Cowen Institute for Public Education Initiatives, 2012). In New York City, five different ExpandED Schools serve 2,140 students; 21% are Black, 52% are male, and 75% qualify for FRPL. In Baltimore, ExpandED Schools serve 1,186 students; nearly 100% are Black, slightly more than half are male, and 94% qualify for FRPL. In New Orleans, ExpandED Schools serve 1,656 students; 93% are Black, 53% are male, and 92% qualify for FRPL.

Oakland (CA) Unified School District African American Male Achievement. In the fall of 2010, concerned about the increased disenfranchisement of its African American male population, the Oakland Unified School District (OUSD) created the Office of African American Male Achievement (AAMA) to make explicit and systemic attempts to improve the fortunes of African American males who historically had been underserved academically and consequently got absorbed in the school–prison pipeline. The mission of the AAMA is to stop the epidemic failure of African American male (AAM) students in OUSD. The AAMA attempts to disrupt the school failure of its

African American males by creating the systems, structures, and spaces that guarantee success for all AAM students across the district. By using data, the AAMA has sought to identify entry points into schools and systems to increase equity, improve cultural competency, and implement practices that support AAM students. The bold step of having a districtwide program specifically targeted to Black male youth is unprecedented for a school district on the west coast. The efforts put forth by the AAMA are expected to result in notable increases in literacy proficiency and attendance rates, and decreases in school suspensions and incarceration rates.

Los Angeles Brotherhood Crusade—ONYX Black Male Achievement Initiative. The Los Angeles Brotherhood Crusade offers a comprehensive set of programs dedicated to holistic development of youth in the greater Los Angeles area. The programs have had a direct impact on Black male youth through a cadre of programs such as the following:

Mentor and Me: Housed at Horace Mann Junior High School, Mentor and Me provides mentorship opportunities to 6th-, 7th-, and 8th-grade students. Academic, sociobehavioral, and prosocial mentoring are featured.

Brother to Brother Program: This program focuses on using various mentoring experiences to teach young men and boys of color how to be men and effectively perform their role in society. The Family Violence Prevention Fund's Coaching Boys into Men curriculum, which teaches youth about domestic violence and respect for women, is featured in this program.

SES: The Supplemental Educational Services initiative is available to all South Los Angeles students attending Title 1 schools. The initiative specifically focuses on improving academic proficiency in math, English language arts, and science.

Junior Executive Leadership Program: Through hands-on experiences, volunteerism, and career-based mentoring, this innovative program prepares 14- to 17-year-olds for work readiness, career development, and entrepreneurship. Participants learn the dynamics of leadership, responsibility, social justice, and accountability, while developing skills to succeed in college and/or the real-world marketplace.

The programs offer the following evidence of their direct influence on academic and social outcomes for youth:

Academic achievement results: After one program year, the 132 youth tested realized a median improvement in content standard–specific learning gap academic performance scores of 135%, 105%, and 261% in English language arts (ELA), math, and science, respectively. Median general knowledge academic performance scores also increased by 98% and 45% in ELA and math, respectively.

Social behavioral results: The 117 youth tested showed the following improvements after 1 year: youth relationships—350%; aggressive and externalizing behaviors—600%; delinquent beliefs—1,000%; negative life events—266%; prosocial relationships (delinquent peers)—200%; and prosocial relationships (commitment to peers)—350%. Additionally, supervision and parenting skills of the youth's parents/guardians improved 211%.

Qualitative assessments: At the end of the program year, parent/guardians, teachers (regular school day instructors, mentors, coaches, pastors, etc.), other individuals with whom the youth maintain close relationships, and the youth themselves reported observing significant improvements with respect to social relationships, personal relationships, attitude about school, commitment to school, civic and community engagement, school attendance, incidents of aggression, incidents of violence, drug use, inappropriate behaviors, tardiness, and truancy.

Reaching Back Male Mentoring Program. Reaching Back Male Mentoring is a Pittsburgh-based program that was developed to address the need for African American male youth to connect with African American men in ways that facilitate their growth as leaders of their own lives and change agents in society. As an outgrowth of a large-scale initiative to effect better outcomes among this population, they attempt to fuse the best elements of Manhood Training and Male Mentoring in their model. After almost 2 years running, this program has seen a full evolution from being principally a mentoring program to a full-fledged Rites of Passage model that enlists the support of almost 20 dynamic mentors who facilitate both the personal growth and social development of adolescent Black males in the areas of health/wellness, cultural development, academic achievement, social/interpersonal responsibility, and core growth. The regular program schedule incorporates exercise, nutrition, academic support, mentoring, workshops, and retreats. Organizational progress is measured by the impact that the program has had on its target population and, by extension, the impact that participants have had socially as a result. The program measures progress in several areas:

- Physical fitness and wellness
- Academic progress and indicators
- College and work readiness

- Participation in leadership and social projects
- Attainment of specific behavioral objectives

Because the program is principally a school-based educational program, participants have made strides with regard to school indicators, as follows:

- Nine out of 36 (25%) program participants have proven eligible for the Pittsburgh Promise Scholarship Honor Roll.
- Sixteen of 36 (44%) have made honor roll during their time in the Academic Improvement program.
- Five of the 16 (31%) honor roll participants made honor roll for the first time while in the program.
- Ninety-five percent of program participants had an at least an 80% attendance rate.
- Grades overall improved from an overall 2.3 collective GPA to a 2.88 collective GPA.

United Negro College Fund. The United Negro College Fund (UNCF) has implemented a few different initiatives to improve the life outcomes of Black males. The most notable effort is the Male Initiative within the Gates Millennium Scholars (GMS) Program. The goal of the GMS Male Initiative is to increase college readiness in general, and competitiveness for the GMS Program in particular, among males of color. The GMS Program uses data to understand how to engage male Scholars once they have been selected. The number of Black males who have applied to, and have been selected for, the GMS Program has increased over a 5-year period. Black males represent 17.5% of Gates Millennium Scholars and they graduate at rates similar to Gates Millennium Scholars across all race and gender lines. The 6-year undergraduate degree completion rate of Gates Millennium Scholars is 88%, and the overall rate of students is 90%. Additionally, UNCF Patterson Research Institute—the premier research institute focusing on African American education—conducted a study with Manpower Demonstration Research Corporation (well known for its work in randomized assignment testing) about whether performance-based scholarships influenced African American male student outcomes.

Urban Prep Academies. Urban Prep Academies is a Chicago-based 501(c)(3) nonprofit organization that operates a network of all-boys public schools, including the country's first charter high school for boys. Urban Prep's mission is to provide a high-quality and comprehensive college-preparatory educational experience to young men that will result in its graduates succeeding in college. The schools are a direct response to the urgent need to reverse abysmal graduation and college completion rates among boys in urban centers. While most of Urban Prep students come to the schools from economically disadvantaged households and behind in many subject areas, Urban Prep remains committed to preparing all of its students for college and life. Urban Prep Academies currently operates three open enrollment public charter high schools in high-need communities in the city of Chicago. At capacity, these three schools enroll approximately 2,000 students. Over 85% of the students qualify for free and reduced lunch, and many come to Urban Prep several grade levels behind in the core subject areas.

Students are admitted to the schools via a random lottery, with no evaluation of test scores or special needs. Distinctive elements of the school program include:

- A rigorous college-prep curriculum
- Extended school day and year
- Focus on language arts and math
- Extracurricular activities
- Community service requirements
- Parental engagement expectations
- Positive school culture
- Regular professional development for teachers

Through its first 2 graduation cohorts, Urban Prep has reported a 100% graduation rate, along with all of its graduates pursuing postsecondary education upon completing high school.

As previously noted, there are countless other programs in cities across the nation. Many of the Black fraternities and sororities offer programs specific to Black males and have had notable results in changing lives. Many churches have innovative programs in place that target young men of color in general and Black males specifically, and the same can be said for various chapters of the National Urban League and the NAACP. Finally, there are a growing number of 100 Black Men of America organizations that offer mentorship programs for young Black males that have had success.

CHAPTER 7

The Obama Paradox

Cautions, Concerns, and
Considerations for Researchers
and Practitioners Working
with Black Males

The 2008 election of President Barack Obama initiated a growing amount of discussion about the United States entering its first ever post-racial era. Some viewed the purported post-racial era as the beginning of a new and progressive era in U.S. life, law, and politics, where race no longer would be relevant: an era where America's history of racial strife and discrimination could be considered issues of the past, with little to no contemporary meaning in how an increasingly racially diverse society experienced life in the 21st century (Pierre & Jeter, 2009). The election of an African American man, who ran for president as a race-neutral candidate, signaled a major paradigm shift about how the United States deals, or chooses not to deal, with the explosive issue that is race. Although race has played out in a multitude of ways with different groups over the course of U.S. history, arguably the group that has been most vilified by racial animosity, angst, and hatred has been Black males. From the inception of slavery and the role that Black males played in that horrific institution (not to discount or dismiss the terrible experiences endured by Black females), to the tens of thousands of Black men who were brutally lynched during the 18th, 19th, and 20th centuries (Allen et al., 2000), racial stigmatization has plagued Black males for well over 3 centuries (Madhubuti, 1990). These atrocities continue even in the 21st century, with such tragic deaths as those of Oscar Grant, Jordan Davis, Sean Bell, and Trayvon Martin being prime cases where the value of life for Black males is frequently minimized. The roles of race and racism are part of a larger historical legacy that undoubtedly continues to shape many of the challenges facing Black males in schools and the wider society. The irony of a Black man becoming the most powerful and influential leader of the free world provides perfect fodder for the call for a post-racial society in America. How could such an event occur if racial discrimination still exists? Would Obama have been elected twice if not for the millions of White voters who supported his candidacy? These are only a few of the questions that could be, and have been, posed by the post-racial advocates. However, what cannot be lost in the discussion of a post-racial society are the dismal realities that still confront many people of color in the United States.

An examination of labor, justice, and education data reveals a grim reality faced by growing numbers of Black males in the United States. According the Bureau of Labor Statistics (2010), the median Black worker earns just over $621 a week, about 80% of what the median White worker earns. The U.S. Department of Justice (2009) reports that Black men are incarcerated at six times the rate of White men, with almost one in 20 Black men spending some time in jail or prison at some point in their life. Approximately 37% of all male inmates in 2007 were Black, down 41% from 2000, despite the fact that Black males make up only 7% of the nation's population (U.S. Department of Justice, 2009). Black males also continue to drop out of schools at an alarming rate and attend college at disproportionately lower rates; moreover, the likelihood that Black males will suffer from a multitude of mental health or substance abuse challenges has been well documented (Poussaint & Alexander, 2000).

This final chapter of the book examines research on Black males in what some are attempting to label the first U.S. "post-racial era." I take strong exception to the term *post-racial* and any suggestion that we are beyond race and that race no longer matters in U.S. life, law, policy, and life chances. A conversation with many young Black males would provide painful insight into the manner in which they frequently are questioned, followed, suspected, feared, and loathed on a regular basis, and they would contend this happens due to their race. I also challenge the notion of being post-racial when it comes to analyzing the issues that affect life for Black males across the United States. Cornel West (2009) writes that "we must not confuse the empty media category of 'post-racial' with the reality of America becoming less racist. The former is an empty illusion, the latter is a grand achievement" (p. 240). More specifically, I challenge this notion when it comes to research on the educational experiences of Black males. Moreover, I contend that post-racial and color-blind approaches have greater potential than post-racial advocates may recognize to do lasting harm to Black males, other males of color, and students of color. In examining the educational experiences and outcomes of Black males, I maintain that race has always mattered, and continues to matter even with the election of a Black man as president. Issues affecting Black males in schools remain highly racialized and require ongoing examination from equity-minded researchers and practitioners who are concerned with improving conditions for this population. The current state of educational affairs for Black males in a "post-racial" society poses significant risks for them that researchers and practitioners must be aware of as they engage in scholarly inquiry.

The goal of this chapter is to offer researchers and practitioners *cautions, concerns, and considerations* that should be adhered to in work on, about, or with Black males. I raise these issues because failure to pay special attention to the manner in which Black males and their experiences are described and analyzed can lead to grossly misguided results. I will discuss three primary charges in this chapter that I argue researchers should be mindful of before participating in work with or about Black males: (1) do not ignore race as a variable in examining their school experiences; (2) acknowledge the complex historical context of Black males and research in the United States; and (3) put forward considerations for future research on Black males that is informed by new paradigms, transformative frameworks and methods, and an overall mode of inquiry and approach to teaching that are concerned with transforming the life experiences of Black males.

In addition to research cautions, concerns, and considerations, I offer similar implications for individuals who teach Black males. I provide these in attempt to create a theory-to-practice alignment, wherein scholars and individuals working firsthand with young men can begin to operate within an asset-based paradigm that is informed by racial realities, historical context, and social, emotional, and economic considerations of Black males in schools.

A RATIONALE FOR RESEARCH WITH BLACK MALES: THE CONSIDERATIONS

The significance of a Black male president cannot be overstated when evaluating the state of affairs for Black males in schools and society. The paradox could not be greater, and in many ways it presents a conundrum for those working with Black males: How can an individual be the most powerful person in the country (and the free world), yet individuals who look like him are among the most marginalized and criminalized members in the United States? Obama's elections represent monumental and historical feats, the clearing of significant social and political hurdles by citizens of the United States, and do provide tangible evidence that racial animosity has decreased compared with a generation ago. They also provide convincing evidence that race relations have improved and that on some level people's angst and fears about Black people and Black males in particular, and their intelligence—negative ideas that were deeply entrenched in previous generations—are being transformed by authentic personal experiences and positive cross-racial interactions. Yet, what cannot be lost amid the euphoria of the Obama elections, are the realities still faced by countless numbers of young Black males in the 21st century. A basic question that must be asked is: "What has fundamentally changed about the experience of Black males in American society over the past 6 years?" Over the past 6 years, the number of Black men in poverty and under the supervision of the penal system has increased. Obama himself has cautioned against those who sought to deem him as a messiah who would cure all the country's ills. He also has stated that the quality of conditions for the urban poor (which includes many Black males) remains a huge challenge for the nation. While many are heartened by the fact that Obama became president, how long can the reality of his presidency compete with the dismal reality that schools and society are still unjust and uncaring spaces for many Black males?

One of the purposes of social science research is to examine society through individuals' relationships in and to various social, political, and cultural contexts. Social science research, at least in theory, should provide a much-needed method of inquiry into various challenges faced by populations in the quest for a more harmonious and just nation-state, and should work toward attainment of the goals and aims best suited for the public interest (Tate, 2006). To that end, our role as social scientists should be to identify problems that exist, raise important questions about them, identify reliable modes of inquiry into them, and offer plausible interventions for disrupting the problems faced by the larger society. The challenges faced by the social sciences are that issues of race, class, and gender add layers of complexity to the arduous situations that increasing members of the society find themselves in (Crenshaw, 1989). Prompting scholars to contend that research is done for the good of the public interest, what public interest are we talking about? And whose interest are we serving (Grant, 2006)? Perhaps more than any other nation in the world, the United States has been beset by its inability to deal with a past that has been steeped in racial inequities and discord that have created a different reality for countless numbers of its non-White citizens (Wilson, 2008). These racial inequities have manifested themselves in a multitude of areas from economic opportunities, political viability, healthcare disparities, as well as educational experiences and overall life chances (Omi & Winant, 1994). Before we advance to a post-racial society, I would contend that we need to become *racial.* By this I mean that racial considerations need to be an integral part of the questions that are asked, the frameworks that are used, and the analyses that we engage in. I also would contend that becoming racial means a national acknowledgment of what slavery and Jim Crow have done over the course of the past 3 centuries to create a caste system in American life. I would contend that these racial considerations should be present in all research, but in particular when engaging in research with people of color, and in the instance of this work, Black males. In short, before becoming post-racial, we need to shed an intense spotlight on the legacy that race has left on the United States, and what it means for individuals whose interests have not been well served by the racial hierarchies and race-based policies that have been created.

Previous research on Black males has helped to provide useful insight into examining and understanding factors contributing to their educational and social disenfranchisement (Madhubuti, 1990; Martin, 2007, 2009; Noguera, 2008; Polite, 1994; Polite & Davis, 1999). What is most obvious in each of these works is the salience of race. Each of these works explicitly identifies the history and complexity of racialized experiences that Black males encounter in U.S. schools and society. I share similar concerns of previous scholars in problematizing the importance of race in the schooling experiences of Black males and offer cautions about what the failure to recognize race can do, and what it may mean for Black males, as well as other non-White populations. It is important for researchers to seek divergent paths in working with Black males by calling for thoughtful research paradigms and alternative theoretical frameworks that can help to identify methods for developing more nurturing schooling environments that cater to African American males in U.S. schools. Moreover, I argue that scholars should seek paradigms that give more credence to the significance of race and ethnicity and all of their manifestations in education (Ladson-Billings, 1998; C. D. Lee, 1995; Solorzano & Delgado Bernal, 2001). Race, in particular, has been and remains undertheorized in education (Ladson-Billings & Tate, 1995); therefore, any efforts to move beyond race should seek to extract a core variable in explaining why we see disparate educational experiences and outcomes.

The need for carefully conducted, race-based research on Black males is critical, because much of the inquiry on this population has centered on deficit-based, pathological accounts (Polite, 1994). These works in the social and biological sciences have contributed to distorted constructions of Black males and have led to what Earl Ofari Hutchinson (1997) refers to as the "assassination of the Black male image." Memories of the Tuskegee experiment and the complete absence of moral and ethical standards in the name of medicine and science provide an important cautionary tale about how Black males have been objectified in the name of science and research. Rendered subhuman without any regard to their health, well-being, family, and friends, Black males often have been reduced to America's guinea pigs whose lives possessed so little value that they could be sacrificed for medical experimentation, or any other reason deemed appropriate by the powers that be of the time. Steven Selden's (1999) work on the Eugenics movement offers yet another cautionary tale of how ideologies of racial inferiority of Blacks were constructed and "proven" in the name of scientific inquiry. Washington (2006) chronicles the long, disturbing history of Blacks and illegal medical testing, and contends that "dangerous, involuntary and non-therapeutic experimentation upon African Americans has been practiced widely and documented extensively at least since the eighteenth century" (p. 7). She pays particular attention to the manner in which Black males were often the primary targets of these efforts, and how in many ways this historical account continues to keep many Black males from being participants in scientific research because of an ongoing skepticism as to how they may be misrepresented or outright harmed through the process. A plethora of works have documented the long and sordid accounts that have demonized Black males as intellectually inferior, prone to violence, and unworthy of being fit for society, and have used research to justify these outcomes (Gould, 1981; Horsman, 1981). This book has sought to put forward a framework that disrupts problematic frameworks and methodologies that appear innocuous on the surface but may still reify distorted accounts of Black males. Recently, a number of works have begun to allow Black males to offer their own accounts of these experiences. These works have been important because they have sought to shift the paradigm on Black males from one that renders them as subjects, to a more nuanced and rigorous one that seeks to have Black males author their own stories and experiences (Dimitriadis, 2001; Duncan, 2002; Howard, 2008; Kirkland, 2013; Noguera, 2008; Price, 2000).

Considerations of race-based research are not new and continue to take on a more prevalent place in educational research and theory (Lynn, 1999). Stanfield (1993) has written about the reluctance historically of social scientists to explicitly examine sensitive issues such as race, ethnicity, and discrimination in their work. He called for researchers to be willing to talk about the particular challenges and unique stances that are essential to doing research on racialized populations. Banks (1993) has raised the question about the epistemological stance of researchers as they engage in work with diverse populations, and called for researchers to reflect on, and identify, their own positionality and to examine what this means for their research in a multicultural society. Tillman (2002) has called for culturally sensitive research approaches for African Americans, which she asserts are critical for understanding the cultural and racial nuances involved in the examining of African American experiences. She states that "it is important to consider whether the researcher has the cultural knowledge to accurately interpret and validate the experiences" of a particular group (p. 4). Milner (2007a) makes a similar call when he refers to the *seen, unseen,* and *unforeseen* approaches for thinking about race, culture, and equity in research. His research outlines an important framework for researcher racial and cultural positionality that should inform social scientists working with diverse populations. What these researchers remind us is that research is never neutral, it is never apolitical, and for researchers whose work examines diverse populations, a number of key considerations should be given serious thought and failure to do so only creates further racial hierarchies and disrupts the quest for racial justice and equity. More important, these scholars suggest not that racial or cultural outsiders cannot effectively do quality research on diverse populations, but that it is crucial to be armed with a cultural and racial knowledge base that does not demonize diverse populations, yet recognizes the contextual nature of race, class, culture, and gender.

BLACK MALES AND A POST-RACIAL SOCIETY?

The Cautions

The very nature of the term *caution* suggests pausing and giving careful fore-thought while being attentive to the possible dangers that may lie ahead. The term also suggests counsel against danger or evil: a warning. I assert that this is vitally important given the historical manner in which Black men have been portrayed, misrepresented, and distorted in the name of research. One of the initial questions concerning researchers interested in Black males is *who* can do this work? A number of researchers have raised questions about the reliability of members outside of particular groups and the manner in which they can and cannot conduct research with a given population (Banks, 1993; Scheurich & Young, 1997). I maintain that culturally sensitive and humanistic research with, on, or about Black males can be conducted by members of any ethnic, racial, or gender group, but particular attention should be given to the historical contexts, social realities, diverse identities, and complexities that are part of the Black male experience. The process requires researchers to engage in their own process of self-reflection about their own positionality as they do this work. This would be critical even for members who are Black and male.

Another note of caution is for researchers to recognize the multifaceted nature of Black male identity, which I have spoken of in several previous chapters. Research on the educational experiences of Black males has to recognize the complexity that is Black male identity within the context of learning institutions. For well over a century, the fields of education and psychology have struggled to adequately address the significant challenges Black males face in constructing identities that function in academic achievement settings. Du Bois (1903) paid particular attention to the internal conflict that Black men faced in a United States that, on one hand, promoted individual freedoms, while, on the other hand, it limited the rights of communities of color. His notion of double-consciousness recognized the psychological and sociohistorical realities of American oppression and sought to shed light on the complex ways Black men develop a sense of self in the United States. In the time since then, we have seen the manifestation of this conflict in soaring dropout rates, high levels of in-carceration, and the deterioration of health in the Black community, particularly among young Black men. Conversely, we have seen countless numbers of Black males overcome challenging environments, succeed in the face of dysfunctional schools and communities, and become notable contributors to society across a wide spectrum of disciplines. In short, Black male diversity represents opposite ends of the spectrum and represents unparalleled progress coinciding with persistent peril. How can these two realities coexist?

A number of works have documented how the complexity of identity, race, and schooling intersect to shape the experiences of young people. Fordham (1988) sought to explore the process by which African American students achieve academic success. Her findings suggest that in order to succeed academically, African American students must disassociate themselves from the African American community. Believing that this process happens consciously or unconsciously, Fordham asserts that these students must leave behind values, beliefs, and customs of their own community in order to embrace the culture of school. Fordham and Ogbu (1986) describe this phenomenon as "the burden of acting White," which they contend has to do with the prevailing notion that academic success is a White characteristic. The resulting effect is the development of African American oppositional identities in schools. Their work has received a great deal of attention and acceptance in the academic community over the past 2 decades. However, as I noted in Chapter 6, the issue of race now must be coupled with notions of masculinity and gender identity in order to capture the breadth and depth of Black male experiences.

Ward (1990) proposed an alternative explanation for high-achieving African American high school students. She found that racial identity, personal commitment, and academic achievement successfully converged during the high school years. Ward reported that students felt good about their race and were personally strengthened by their racial status. She concluded that African American students must reject society's negative assessment of Blackness and construct identities that value African American culture. Furthermore, Ainsworth-Darnell and Downey (1998) state:

> [The oppositional identity] argument is misplaced. If anything, African Americans maintain *more* pro-school values and are *more* likely to esteem their high-achieving peers than are Whites. What African Americans lack, however, are the material conditions that foster the development of skills, habits, and styles rewarded by teachers. (p. 551, emphasis in original)

Consequently, scholars have been forced to rethink the factors that are believed to influence African American identity in the context of schools.

An additional caution that I would offer is to recognize the contextual nature of behavior. In other words, much of the work on Black males centers on observed behavior; however, much of this work is done without critical analysis of factors that contribute to such behavior. For example, research that examines the experiences of people living in poverty must be aware that conditions tend to influence the manner in which people interpret and respond to the harsh realities that poverty can bring. A careful understanding of history is warranted to make authentic meaning of how and why young Black males respond to their home, school, and community environments in the way they do. In many instances, young Black males are responding negatively to what they perceive to be dehumanizing and apathetic schooling and social conditions. In some cases, behavior may be a result of less than flattering home and life circumstances, which several of the young men mentioned in Chapter 5 of this work. The work of researchers cannot operate from a frame of reference that further patholo-gizes young Black males or renders them as the root cause of their disenfran-chisement. Noguera (2008) suggests that "Black males often adopt behaviors that make them complicit in their own failure" (p. 23). Solorzano and Delgado Bernal (2001) state that resistance theories offer researchers a lot to ponder when analyzing student behavior. They contend:

> Theories of resistance draw on an understanding of the complexities of culture to explain the relationship between schools and the dominant society. . . . Resistance theories are different than social and cultural reproduction theories because the con-cept of resistance emphasizes that individuals are not simply acted on by structures. In contrast, resistance theories demonstrate how individuals negotiate and struggle with structures and create meanings of their own from these interactions. (p. 315)

Recognition of the social, economic, and political contexts that shape stu-dents' behaviors is rarely included in the analysis of young Black men. One example is the criticism of hip-hop and rap music. A more careful, critical, and culturally informed analysis of hip-hop culture and music reveals a more com-plex and creative manner of self-expression for many urban youth. The failure to engage in more comprehensive analysis of behaviors and the factors that in-fluence them only contributes to blaming the victim. These frames of reference will only reinforce problematic paradigms about Black males. What researchers need to consider are questions about how they have developed their viewpoints of Black males. What experiences have constructed the images? And how au-thentic are the portrayals?

The fourth and final caution that I would offer is to pay attention to the intersectionality of race, class, and gender. This intersectionality is vital in re-search concerned with young Black males, because each marker in its own ways profoundly influences their identity construction and meaning-making. Black males, like any other population of students, possess multiple identities that are profoundly shaped by race, socioeconomic status, and gender in all of their complex manifestations. Patricia Hill Collins (2004) refers to the intersectional paradigm as an analytical framework that explains the interrelationships of po-litical and social systems of race, class, gender, and other social divisions that may capture more accurately the complex realities of oppression and marginalization for nondominant groups. The social and political arrangements and intersection of these identities play out in unique ways that have critical implications for racial and gender minorities, and in particular for young Black males.

A conceptual framework with an explicit examination of the ways that race and racism manifest themselves, and their juxtaposition with gender, in education may offer new analyses of the underachievement of African American males and provide new insight and direction for reversing their underachievement.

From a practitioner standpoint, identity must be recognized and understood as a conduit to better outcomes for Black males. Each young Black man (like all other students) enters a classroom with a set of experiences that shape the way he views learning, teaching, classrooms, schools, and his role in them. It is the task of practitioners to engage in carefully crafted scientific inquiry on a daily basis in order to best understand the multitude of students' experiences. In teaching young Black males, trust can be an important factor for engagement. The teacher's merely being an adult is not enough for most students to develop respect and trust. These are now qualities that must be earned. So teachers must work persistently to build authentic relationships with Black males that are built on reciprocity, trust, honesty, respect, and a sensitivity to students' multiple identities. Thus, the caution is to not paint a generalized approach to interacting with Black males. Identity is so complicated that each and every student must be viewed as a separate case study that can be 180 degrees different from a young man sitting in the next seat. All too often the one-size-fits-all approach is taken with Black males, and the results can be less than ideal.

An additional factor to be considered for young Black males is the importance of care. Other researchers have spoken to the salience of care in education (Noddings, 1999; Valenzuela, 1999). For many youth, learning is a social and cultural process before it becomes a cognitive one. A big part of that social and cultural context is the degree to which teachers do or do not care about the students they teach. And from our conversations with young men, we learned that they are able to detect caring or uncaring teachers quite efficiently, and then make deliberate choices about their levels of participation, engagement, and learning in those classrooms. According to many young men, this care is shown through high expectations, accountability, connection of content to out-of-school experiences, displays of empathy, and being demanding, yet nurturing. There are excellent sources that unpack many of these accounts of teaching for Black students (and Black males) in more detail that can be instrumental for practitioners concerned with engagement, learning, and fostering high achievement (Ford, 2011; Foster, 1997; Irvine, 1990; Ladson-Billings, 1994; Milner, 2007a; Noguera, 1996, 2001).

The Concerns

The primary concern I would offer when it comes to Black males as a research community is that we have fallen terribly short in examining the wide range of complexities associated with the perennial underperformance of Black males in U.S. schools. Some researchers have raised the question as to whether we as a research community really care about the plight of young Black males (Howard, 2008), others have suggested that not enough has occurred because young Black males have been rendered as being "beyond love" (Duncan, 2002), and still others posit that Black males are the miner's canary in our nation's schools (Noguera, 2008). One of the pressing concerns is that at a time when race, gender, and poverty continue to shape the experiences of countless numbers of young Black males, some are suggesting that we give greater attention to the "post-racial" society that we currently are experiencing (Metzler, 2008). The failure to recognize race can omit a critical variable in understanding the schooling experiences of Black males. A number of scholars have examined the manner in which young Black males disengage from schools and the traditional ways schooling has been arranged (Fordham & Ogbu, 1986; Ogbu, 1987a). Prudence Carter (2005) outlines a framework of why some Black students succeed, and why some do not. One of her contentions is that many Black students who do not succeed in schools are what she refers to as *noncompliant believers*: students who exert minimal to no effort to acquiesce to the norms and codes of mainstream schooling. The disconnect between school culture and norms with those that students have is directly tied to students' cultural knowledge, which is typically a by-product of race and racial socialization (C. D. Lee, 2007). The concern about omitting race and the influence that race may have on Black males is that it has the potential to overlook, devalue, or misunderstand the complex types of cultural knowledge that Black males possess based on their experiences in their homes, neighborhoods, and communities. The race–culture connection has been explored in a number of scholars' works (C. D. Lee, 2007; Nasir, 2002, 2012) and should be thoroughly understood when engaging in this work.

A second pressing concern about research on Black males in a post-racial context is the problematic nature of adopting a color-blind context for educational research and practice. I continue to be disappointed by the widespread presence of color-blind realities in urban and suburban schools. I talk with many classroom teachers about how they engage their students of color about issues of race and racism when they come up in classroom discourse, and I consistently hear the typical reply, "I don't see color or talk about color," or, "I see all my students as the same; they are all human." Such responses represent an unwillingness or inability to think, talk, and teach about racial realities and differences in a racially diverse society, despite the manner in which many young people see their lives primarily through a racial lens. Such approaches by White teachers in particular speak to privileges that many are unwilling to interrogate. Ullucci and Beatty (2011) contend:

> That blindness to skin color and race remains a "privilege" available exclusively to White people. It is the refusal to acknowledge the costs and benefits associated with one's racial and cultural identity. It provides cover for many Whites, who by claiming color blindness are able to dismiss their complicity in racial hierarchies. (p. 1196)

Bonilla-Silva (2003) outlines four central frames around the potential dangers of color-blind ideology in the work we do as practitioners and researchers. These four frames, *abstract liberalism, naturalization, cultural racism,* and the *minimization of racism,* each elaborate on the problems with the egalitarian, "racism is behind us" approach that can become acceptable if we believe that we have entered a post-racial society. The mere mention of a color-blind approach to our work poses a set of problematic contradictions. Crenshaw (1995) suggests that a color-blind approach seeks to conceal the power and ugliness of race, but at the same time highlights its very significance by claiming that to acknowledge it would lead to troublesome outcomes. A careful analysis of the school outcomes and experiences of Black males would uncover ugly realities that researchers and practitioners should be willing to examine in an open, straightforward, and critical manner. Undoubtedly, the centrality of race is a part of this examination, and color-blind approaches would dismiss such accounts. Gotanda (1991) reiterates the shortcomings with color-blindness, stating that it serves to maintain racial subordination. A legitimate concern becomes that omitting race negates perhaps the primary part of students' identity that shapes their schooling experiences. Students are asked to learn without being who they are, or they are told implicitly and explicitly that their experiences do not matter in the classroom and do not relate to learning. And we wonder why so many students of color disengage from schools. Nasir, McLaughlin, and Jones (2009) call for "the need for a nuanced conception of African American racial identity that considers both the strength of the identity and the local meaning of the identity" (p. 107). To better understand this identity, race is vital. The call for a color-blind approach frequently seeks to cover the past indignities that have afflicted people of color and Black people in particular. For many researchers race becomes the paradigmatic paradox, the variable that many least want to engage in, yet it may very well be the one that offers the most valuable insight into how people see the world around them. When it comes to gaining a comprehensive picture of the way in which many Black males experience schools, the accounts of how they are treated by adults in schools may be damning, indicting, hostile, and in many ways overtly critical of the types of learning environments they encounter on a daily basis. As noted in the voices quoted in this book, many young men struggle to succeed in schools because of apathetic, uncaring, and dismissive teachers, many of whom do not recognize their important identities.

A growing number of works have begun to unpack the ways that Black males understand their learning environments from an identity standpoint. For example, Stinson's (2010) study of Black males and how they negotiate sociocultural discourses around race and mathematics provides a cogent example of how researchers can situate race as a central component of young people's educational experiences. Incorporating a critical postmodern theoretical analysis, Stinson discovered that the highly successful students in his study found their realities to be extremely racialized, despite the fact that each of them was a high-performing student. Several of the participants talked about the ongoing efforts they had to put forth to combat the stereotypical images of Black males, which characterize them as genetically inferior and academically incapable. Their stories illustrate the sophisticated steps that they had to take to disarm the fear and alter the low expectations that many of their teachers had for them. Studies such as Stinson's underscore how interrogating race and racism with young Black males has the potential to provide important understanding of how they experience school; how they navigate such structures, ideologies, and practices; and how schooling environments can be racially affirming and culturally supportive. The opening up of Black male discourses about how these students experience schools can be illuminating, but researchers and practitioners also must be prepared for the harsh critiques that such approaches can produce. Some Black males may provide stinging condemnations of schools and schooling practices, social and economic conditions, White people, White supremacy, and the ideological frames that support its maintenance.

One of the most pressing concerns about individuals conducting research with Black males is a refusal to acknowledge the pernicious effects that the legacy of racism had, and continues to have, on Black males. For example, Oliver (2006) talks about how Black males feel the sting of racism in a manner that marginalizes them from the larger society, and how as a result the streets, which honor their racial and cultural integrity, become a primary socializing influence in their development. Moreover, Smith, Hung, and Franklin (2011) contend that Black males on college campuses confront mixed messages in pursuit of education. Their study of 661 Black men discovered that while the ideal of the American dream is promoted, and the young men are encouraged to pursue postsecondary education, racial climates in predominately White institutions are quite stifling. The young men reported that racial climates are replete with racism, blocked opportunities, and *mundane, extreme, and environmental stress* brought on by racism. The authors concluded that the young men seem to experience racial battle fatigue from both racial micro-aggressions and societal problems, which hinder their academic pursuits. One can only wonder to what degree, if any, similar types of experiences afflict males of color in elementary and secondary classrooms as well.

An additional concern that can occur when examining Black males is the gross generalization of them. One of the mistakes that can be made is to assume that all Black males are at risk. As I have pointed out previously in this book, not all young Black males are failing in schools (although I recognize the disturbing numbers that are); not all Black males reside in large, urban centers; and most Black males are not aggressive, hostile, and prone to violence, despite repeated media and social portrayals of them as such. Most of them are not persistently in trouble, law breakers, or menaces to society. Many of them are sensitive, caring, loving sons, siblings, nephews, and caretakers of family and friends, yet this does not become part of the narrative. Not all of them are athletes and into rap music. Many enjoy science, history, dance, the arts, and explorations of the environment. Future research on Black males should seek to identify high-achieving Black males, or document the experiences of Black males in urban, suburban, or rural communities, which may provide more insight into the realities of this population. I also would argue that not enough work has looked at the experiences of biracial or multiracial Black males, who often have a differing account of how they experience race. An increasing body of research is emerging on the spike in mixed-race individuals (Lopez, 2003); the manner in which these individuals make racial meaning is understudied and undertheorized, and may have lots to offer to our knowledge of race, identity, and education. The concern also should recognize that while race continues to matter for many young Black males, others may contend that it is less of a factor, or perhaps a non-factor, in their lives. The latter opinions and viewpoints are equally valid as those that consider race to be salient, and they need to be part of the larger narrative on Black males. Giving attention to such viewpoints may prove useful in developing a more nuanced, comprehensive, yet complex characterization of Black males—a characterization that can depict them as thoughtful, caring, sensitive, high-achieving, nurturing sons, siblings, friends, fathers, brothers, and uncles.

The Considerations

There are a number of considerations that I offer as a framework for inquiry and teaching of Black males. These considerations are informed by the important work that has been done by scholars over the past 3 decades (Brown & Davis, 2000; J. E. Davis, 2003; Duncan, 2002; C. W. Franklin, 1991; Gibbs, 1988; Hopkins, 1997; Howard, 2008; Kirkland, 2013; Madhubuti, 1990; Milner, 2007a; Noguera, 2008; Nasir et al., 2009; Polite, 1994; Polite & Davis, 1999; Price, 2000). This body of work serves as an important starting point on the experience of Black males, racial identity, and the need to rethink existing research, policy, and practice in order to create optimum schooling experiences and life chances for Black males. One of the considerations is to allow Black males to be the author of their own experiences. As I have stated throughout this work, Black male voices are poignant, insightful, and diverse. The reality is that Black males have been picked, prodded, analyzed, studied, dissected, spoken to, spoken for, and spoken about for over 3 centuries. The salience of allowing young Black males to name, describe, analyze, and interpret their experiences cannot be stated enough. bell hooks (2004) says that "every black male in the United States has been forced at some point in his life to hold back the self he wants to express, to repress and contain for fear of being attacked, slaughtered, destroyed." (p. xii). Each life has its own unique trajectory, set of experiences, triumphs, tragedies, conflicts, and contradictions that represent human beings fighting and striving for self-actualization. Who better to report these accounts than the actors who have endured these realities? Allowing young Black males to probe into the intricacies of, and ponder the possibilities of hope for, school reform and individual uplift can prove to be liberating. Unfortunately, for too long the accounts of Black males have been told by others who are neither Black nor male, and the inaccuracies of such depictions has contributed to the distorted image of Black men. Research that allows Black males to be the authors of their own experiences is not only liberating for the individual, in the name of self-actualization, self-critique, and self-authorship, but can be radically enlightening in the pursuit of social equity. Ayers (2006) writes that the purpose of "social justice research [is] to resist harm and redress grievances, research with the explicit goal of promoting a more balanced, fair, and equitable social order" (p. 88).

A second consideration is to incorporate nontraditional frameworks to be used in research. Narrative theory, for example, can offer critical insight into how Black males understand and describe their realities. Coulter and Smith (2009) contend that narrative research "strives to portray experience, to question common understandings" (p. 577). Denzin (1992) lauds the value of narrative research because it introduces the centrality of emotion that is frequently lacking in traditional research, and Barone (2001) describes narrative research as a framework that offers "a degree of interpretive space" (p. 150). One of the advantages of nontraditional frameworks would be to recognize the ways in which race, language, culture, literacy, lived experiences, and historical context influence how knowledge is constructed and maintained over time. Yosso's (2005) work on cultural capital presents an illuminating framework of the unique, yet diverse, ways that communities of color respond to their social environments, and of how cultural practices can be interpreted in deficit or transformative ways, and she makes a strong call for the latter. Milner (2007b) argues that transformative frameworks "can be useful to researchers serious about interpreting and representing people and communities of color in ways that honor those communities and in ways that maintain their integrity" (p. 397). Terry and Howard (2013) make the call for *critical race phenomenology* wherein youth of color are allowed to talk about their experiences with and around race in a manner that speaks to their emotions, feelings, and detailed experiences, where they can be their authentic selves, unedited, and unapologetic. What I would suggest is for researchers to be thoughtful, reflective, nonjudgmental, and illuminating in their work on African American males.

It is also important to take note of the delicate manner in which identity is constructed, maintained, and transformed over time for Black males. Flennaugh (2011) used identity mapping with Black males in his research, wherein his participants were able to identify all the salient parts of their lived experiences that made them who they were in their totality. What is important about Flennaugh's work is the manner in which these maps allowed participants to speak to the significance of certain people, activities, and circumstances in their lives. The take-away from this work highlights the multilayered complexity of Black male identity, how diverse and similar these realities are for young men, and how they change over time. All of these areas are tightly connected to race and would disrupt the call for post-racial examinations of schooling experiences. Schools in the United States are experiencing unprecedented racial and ethnic diversity, and outcome data on student performance consistently show the disparate outcomes that fall along racial and class lines. It should be noted that in the Obama age of post-racialism, a number of men, all of whom went on to successful political careers, including the presidency, were White and came from impoverished conditions (e.g., Lincoln, Clinton, Reagan). Yet none of their elections resulted in a call for recognition of a "post-poverty era." These calls were not heeded because even though individuals overcame the obstacles of poverty, it did not negate the widespread poverty that affected millions of people, then and now. I would contend that similar consideration is warranted when it comes to race in the era of the nation's first non-White president.

An example of one of the more probing and penetrating frameworks that could be helpful for work on Black males would be critical race theory. Critical race theory in education seeks to give much-needed attention to the role of race in educational research, scholarship, and practice (Dixson & Rousseau, 2006; Ladson-Billings, 2000; Parker et al., 1999; Solorzano & Yosso, 2002). The inclusion of a critical race framework in education is essential when one considers the perennial underachievement of African American, Latino/Latina, Native American, and certain Asian American students in U.S. schools. Educators can ill afford to subscribe to the notion that mere coincidence explains the perpetual school failure of students of color. At some point, the question must be posed: What's race got to do with it? (Parker & Lynn, 2002). A similar question can be posed when it comes to the educational disenfranchisement of Black males: What does race have to do with the perennial underachievement and exclusion of Black males? Critical race theory in education is an evolving methodological, conceptual, and theoretical construct that attempts to dismantle racism in education. It provides scholars with unique ways to ask the important question of what racism has to do with inequities in education by centering the discussion on racism. From a practitioner standpoint, Ladson-Billings (2004) raises thoughtful questions, within a CRT framework, about the inclusion of non-White narratives, histories, and experiences in school curriculum. Huber, Johnson, and Kohli (2006) make a similar claim when they challenge school personnel to rethink curricular content to be sensitive to, and supportive of, non-White populations. They assert:

> It is imperative that curriculum be evaluated to assure that content does not per-
> petuate the ever present face of racism in our society. Unfortunately, in the vast
> majority of schools in the U.S. this is not the case. Curriculum often reinforces the
> hierarchical status quo of White supremacy and renders the race and culture of
> non-whites inferior. (p. 193)

Calls such as Huber et al.'s and Ladson-Billings's are centered on practitioners, asking them to examine state standards and the content that is given premium status and the knowledge that consequently is omitted. Scholars such as Banks (1993, 1997), Gay (1994, 2010), and others have long made the call for more inclusive curriculum that represents the experiences of racially and culturally diverse groups. Thus, an important consideration must be to ensure that students of all backgrounds have access to content that is reflective of the entire racial and cultural spectrum.

The final consideration is that this work should be done in a manner that is authentically concerned with transforming the schooling experiences and life chances of Black males. Unfortunately, many see work about Black males as just another publication on a vita, or as studying the "in" topic of the day. I contend that this work is controversial at heart and should be transformative in nature because it seeks to humanize a dehumanized population. It works to reconstruct an image that has been terribly distorted over time. I strongly suggest that those who are faint of heart, and unwilling to listen to and think long and hard about the criticisms of school structures, racial ideologies, and historical remnants of race and racism, reconsider whether this work is for them. As a Black male who has encountered the terrain that is public education in the United States, I know all too well that this is the road less traveled. This work should not just be reduced to theory, but should become part of a much larger effort and movement to reconstruct how society, and consequently educator researchers and practitioner, see Black males. Robin Kelly (2002) reminds us that "social movements do not simply produce statistics and narratives of oppression; rather the best ones do what great poetry does: transport us to another place, compel us to relive horrors and, more importantly, enable us to imagine a new society" (p. 9).

To consider the magnitude of the type of research that is needed to produce new knowledge about Black males, I pose a critical question: What is the researchers' response to the extended misery, suffering, and educational malpractice that far too many Black males endure in America's schools and society? How will you act? How will we all act? What steps are we as a research and practitioner community willing to take to end exclusion and injustice? Cornel West (2009) states that

> your life becomes your response. Your response doesn't take the form of a written-down, reasoned-out argument. Your response becomes the quality of your day-to-day behavior. The question doesn't go away. It remains powerful and daunting. . . . do what you can to help the least among us. (p. 101)

I offer these cautions, concerns, and considerations to conclude this book with the hope that they remain ever present in the work that we all do with Black males, as well as other racially marginalized populations. The questions remain as poignant as ever about how we construct a knowledge base to transform the schooling experiences of the least among us. Let us hope that our work becomes a vital component in significantly changing the schooling experiences of racially diverse populations so that the day arrives when we are truly a post-racial America.

CONCLUDING THOUGHTS

The final consideration is that real moral consideration should be given to the plight of young Black males in this moment. At a time when opportunity for young people is increasingly limitless, the frustration that many Black males feel in their denied efforts to participate in the wider society is palpable. So while I have raised concerns, cautions, and considerations about race where Black males are concerned, I also do not want human connectedness and human agency to be absent from the conversation. As a society that purports to care about all of its citizens, we find ourselves in the unfortunate time and place where many young Black males do not subscribe to that narrative. All it takes is a drive down a block or two in southeast Washington, DC, the south side of Chicago, Rochester, New York, Gary, Indiana, Los Angeles, or New Orleans, and the story seems to be the same: Black men are often homeless, hopeless, on the margins of mainstream society more than any other group of people. The questions that we need to consider are: "How did this happen?" and more important, "How can we prevent this from happening over and over again with another generation of young men?" I would contend that our families, communities, and nation cannot stand by idly and witness the dramatic loss of human potential never realized. I would offer a plea that all educators and concerned citizens play a role, whether big or small, in addressing the state of affairs, educational experiences and opportunity, and overall life chances for Black males. I offer this plea because if the conditions for Black males improve, everyone wins. I am often reminded of the following by a mentor of mine who has been in public education for over 50 years: When those at the very bottom of the educational ladder do better, have more opportunity, and feel better about themselves and their life chances, everyone else has a better experience in schools and society. Therefore, one of the major efforts that we must be successful in accomplishing is getting school personnel to see that their fate is tied to that of all students, but especially young Black males. When there is a real sense of deep-seated and persistent care, support, and love that adults have for students, the possibilities for young people are endless. The call to support those who often have been overlooked, ignored, or dismissed in schools and society needs to be loud and persistent. As citizens in a democratic society, we live by ideals such as fairness, justice, inclusiveness, equality, and the pursuit of happiness. Unfortunately, those ideals are just that—ideals—for far too many Black males. It is imperative that all educators work toward making these ideals realistic life chances and practical pathways where young men can feel valued and respected, and see all schools as places for thinking, learning, teaching, and human fulfillment and transformation.

As I conclude this work, I cannot help but think about the recent events surrounding the Trayvon Martin case. Segments of the nation recently showed outrage, disappointment, and disbelief upon the acquittal of George Zimmerman in the tragic shooting of Trayvon Martin. Much of this outrage was centered on the lack of value that seems to be placed on the lives of young Black males. Sadly, many were not shocked by these events because there has been a narrative in the U.S. which has consistently stated that the intersection of being Black and male is often fraught with a different set of rules, a different reality, and the experiencing of a different America. Trayvon, unfortunately, was one of countless numbers of young Black males who lost his life all too soon, and will not be able to live another day or see a better tomorrow. While the spotlight shone on the Martin case, it is imperative to note that there are millions of young Black males across this country that are hoping for and wanting a better tomorrow. Yet, for many of them it seems fleeting at best. Many young Black males are in schools and communities that are contributing to a slow, painful, and predictable emotional and academic death. Many of these young men are asking for help, demonstrating resilience, showing resistance, or deliberately disengaging from schools. There must be a concerted response to this state of affairs. As many young Black males hope for a better tomorrow, today's challenges are full of pitfalls and problems, yet for many there is some hope and possibility. The narrative has to be changed so that more of them see, feel, and experience hope and possibility. The state of affairs for Black males can and will get better when we as a nation do not view these challenges as Black problems, male problems, urban problems, or poor people's problems, but when we see them as American problems; problems that can be solved when we use our collective wills and infinite knowledge to do what is right to support individuals who are often in the greatest need of our time and talents.

References

Action for Healthy Kids. (2004). *The learning connection: The value of improving nutrition and physical activity in our schools.* Executive summary. Available at http://www.action-forhealthykids.org/special_exclusive.php

Ainsworth-Darnell, J., & Downey, D. (1998). Assessing the oppositional culture explanation for racial/ethnic differences in school performance. *American Sociological Review, 63,* 536–553.

Alexander, K. L., Entwisle, D. R., Dauber, S. L., & Kabbani, N. (2004). Dropout in relation to grade retention: An accounting from the beginning school study. In H.J. Walberg, A.J. Reynolds, & M.C. Wang (Eds.), *Can unlike students learn together? Grade retention, tracking, and grouping* (pp. 5–34). Greenwich, CT: Information Age.

Alexander, M. (2010). *The new Jim Crow.* New York, NY: New Press.

Alim, S. (2006). *Roc the mic right: The language of hip hop culture.* New York, NY: Routledge.

Allen, B. J. (1996). Feminist standpoint theory: A Black woman's review of organizational socialization. *Communication Studies, 47*(4), 257–271.

Allen, J., Lewis, J., Litwack, L. F., & Als, H. (2000). *Without sanctuary: Lynching photography in America.* Santa Fe, NM: Twin Palms.

Allen, R., & Nee, V. (2003). *Contemporary Asian American communities. Remaking the American mainstream: Assimilation and contemporary immigration.* Cambridge, MA: Harvard University Press.

Allensworth, E. M., & Easton, J. (2001). *Calculating a cohort dropout for the Chicago public schools.* Chicago, IL: University of Chicago, Consortium on Chicago Schools Research.

Anderson, E. (2008). *Against the wall: Poor, young, Black, and male.* Philadelphia: University of Pennsylvania Press.

Anderson, J. A. (1988). *The education of Blacks in the south, 1860–1935.* Chapel Hill: University of North Carolina Press.

Anyon, J. (2005). *Radical possibilities: Public policy, urban education, and a new social movement.* New York, NY: Routledge.

Arthur, G. (1936). A study of the achievement of sixty grade I repeaters as compared with that of non-repeaters of the same mental age. *The Journal of Experimental Education, 5,* 203–205.

Artiles, A. J., Trent, S. C., & Palmer, J. (2004). Culturally diverse students in special education: Legacies and prospects. In J. A. Banks & C.A.M. Banks (Eds.), *Handbook of research on multicultural education* (2nd ed., pp. 716–735). San Francisco, CA: Jossey-Bass.

Aud, S., Fox, M., & KewalRamani, A. (2010). *Status and trends in the education of racial and ethnic groups* (NCES 2010-015). Washington, DC: U.S. Government Printing Office.

Ayers, W. (2006). Trudge toward freedom: Educational research in the public interest. In G. Ladson-Billings & W.F. Tate (Eds.), *Education research in the public interest: Social justice, action, and policy* (pp. 81–97). New York, NY: Teachers College Press.

Baldridge, B. J., Hill, M. L., & Davis, J. E. (2011). New possibilities: (Re)engaging Black male youth within community-based educational spaces. *Race, Education, and Education, 14*(1), 121–136.

Balfanz, R., & Legters, N. (2004). *Locating the dropout crisis. Which high schools produce the nation's dropouts? Where are they located? Who attends them?* Report 70. Baltimore, MD: Johns Hopkins University.

Balfour, L. (2001). *The evidence of things not said: James Baldwin and the promise of American democracy.* Ithaca, New York: Cornell University Press.

Banks, J. A. (1992). African American scholarship and the evolution of multicultural education. *Journal of Negro Education, 61*(3), 273–286.

Banks, J. A. (1993). Multicultural education: Historical development, dimensions, and practices. *Review of Research in Education, 19,* 3–49.

Banks, J. A. (1997). Multicultural education: Characteristics and goals. In J.A. Banks & C.A.M. Banks (Eds.), *Multicultural education: Issues and perspectives* (3rd ed., pp. 3–31). Boston, MA: Allyn & Bacon.

Barone, T. (2001). *Teaching eternity: The enduring outcomes of teaching.* New York, NY: Teachers College Press.

Barron, J. M., Ewing, B. T., & Waddell, G. R. (2000). The effects of high school athletic participation on education and labor market outcomes. *The Review of Economics and Statistics, 82*(3), 409–421.

Beamon, K. K. (2009). Are sports overemphasized in the socialization process of African American males? A qualitative analysis of former collegiate athletes' perception of sport socialization. *Journal of Black Studies, 41*(2), 281–300.

Beamon, K., & Bell, P. (2006). Academics versus athletics: An examination of the effects of background and socialization on African-American male student athletes. *Social Science Journal, 43,* 393–403.

Beets, M. W., & Pitetti, K. H. (2005). Contribution of physical education and sport to health-related fitness in high school students. *Journal of School Health, 75*(1), 25–30.

Bell, D. A. (1992). *Faces at the bottom of the well.* New York, NY: Basic Books.

Bell, D. A. (1995). Racial realism-After we're gone: Prudent speculations on America in a post racial epoch. In R. Delgado (Ed.), *Critical race theory: The cutting edge* (pp. 2–8). Philadelphia, PA: Temple University Press.

Benson, K. F. (2000). Constructing academic inadequacy: African American athletes' stories of schooling. *Journal of Higher Education, 71*(2), 223–246.

Berlin, I., Favreau, M., & Miller, S. F. (1998). *Remembering slavery.* New York, NY: The New Press.

Bogle, D. (2002). *Toms, coons, mulattoes, mammies, & bucks.* NewYork, NY: Continuum.

Bonilla-Silva, E. (2003). *Racism without racists: Colorblind racism and the persistence of racial inequality in the United States.* Lanham, MD: Rowman & Littlefield.

Booker, C. (2000). *"I will wear no chain!" A social history of African American males.* Westport, CT: Praeger.

Boskin, J. (1986). *Sambo: The rise and demise of an American jester.* New York, NY: Oxford University Press.

Brand, M. (2008). *President's report: An update from NCAA President Myles Brand.* Available at http://web1.ncaa.org/web_files/president_reports/2008%20Reports/4.08%20Report.pdf

Brandt, G. L. (1986). *The realization of anti-racist teaching.* Lewes, UK: Falmer Press.

Brennan, R. T., Kim, J. S., Wenz-Gross, M., & Siperstein, G. N. (2001). The relative equitability of high-stakes testing versus teacher-assigned grades: An analysis of the Massachusetts Comprehensive Assessment System (MCAS). *Harvard Educational Review, 71*(2), 173–216.

Brookings Institute. (2011). *The recession's ongoing impact on America's children: Indicators of children's economic well-being through 2011.* Available at http://brookings.edu/research/papers/2011/12/20-children well-being-isaacs

Brown, A. (2011). Racialised subjectivities: A critical examination of ethnography on Black males in the USA, 1960s to early 2000s. *Ethnography and Education, 6*(1), 45–60.

Brown, E. (2005). We wear the mask: African American contemporary gay male identities. *Journal of African American Studies, 9*(2), 29–38.

Brown, L. (2009). "Brothers gonna work it out": Understanding the pedagogic performance of African American male teachers working with African American male students. *Urban Review, 41,* 416–435.

Brown, M. C., & Davis, J. E. (2000). *Black sons to mothers: Compliments, critiques, and challenges for cultural workers in education.* New York, NY: Peter Lang.

Brown, R. N. (2009). *Black girlhood celebration: Toward a hip-hop feminist pedagogy.* New York, NY: Peter Lang.

Browser, B. P. (1994). African American male sexuality through the early life course. In A. S. Rossi (Ed.), *Sexuality across the life course* (pp. 127–150). Chicago, IL: University of Chicago Press.

Burden, J. W., Jr., Hodge, S. R., & Harrison, L., Jr. (2004). African-American and White American students' beliefs about ethnic groups' aspirations: A paradoxical dilemma of academic versus athletic pursues. *E-Journal of Teaching and Learning in Diverse Settings, 2,* 54–77.

Butchart, R. E. (2010). *Schooling the freed people; Teaching, learning, and the struggle for Black freedom, 1861–1976.* Chapel Hill: University of North Carolina Press.

Butler, P. (2007). Academics vs. athletics: Black parents dilemma. *PBS Communications.* Available at http://searchwarp.com/swa231491.htm

Camangian, P. (2010). Starting with self: Teaching autoethnography to foster critically caring literacies. *Research in the Teaching of English, 45*(2), 179–204.

Carter, P. L. (2005). *Keepin' it real: School success beyond Black and White*. New York, NY: Oxford University Press.

Castagno, A. E., & Brayboy, B., McK. J. (2008). Culturally responsive schooling for Indigenous youth: A review of the literature. *Review of Educational Research, 78*(4), 941–993.

Centers for Disease Control & Prevention. (2011). *Leading causes of death in males United States*. Atlanta, GA. Available at http://www.cdc.gov/men/lcod/index.htm

Children's Defense Fund. (2011). *Black children: A portrait of inequality*. Washington, DC.

Childs-Davis, F. (2013). *A case study of collaboration between a culturally responsive urban high school teacher and a Haitian teaching artist* (Unpublished dissertation). University of California, Los Angeles.

Clandinin, D. J., & Connelly, F. M. (2000). *Narrative inquiry: Experience and story in qualitative research*. San Francisco, CA: Jossey-Bass.

Cleaver, E. (1968). *Soul on ice*. New York, NY: Dell.

Coakley, J. (2004). *Sports in society: Issues and controversies* (8th ed.). New York, NY: Mc-Graw-Hill.

Coley, R. J. (2011). *A strong start: Positioning young Black boys for educational success: A statistical profile*. Princeton, NJ: Educational Testing Service/Children's Defense Fund.

College Board. (2012). *8th annual AP report to the nation*. Available at http://media.collegeboard.com/digitalServices/public/pdf/ap/rtn/AP-Report-to-the-Nation.pdf

Collins, P. H. (2004). *Black sexual politics: African Americans, gender, and the new racism*. New York, NY: Routledge.

Collins, P. H. (2006). New commodities, new consumers: Selling Blackness in a global marketplace. *Ethnicities, 6*(30), 297–317.

Comeaux, E., & Harrison, C. K. (2011). A conceptual model of student-athlete academic success for student-athletes. *Educational Researcher, 40*(5), 235–245.

Conchas, G. Q., & Noguera, P. A. (2004). Understanding the exceptions: How small schools support the achievement of academically successful Black boys. In N. Way & J. Chu (Eds.), *Adolescent boys in context* (pp. 317–337). New York, NY: New York University Press.

Conchas, G. Q., & Vigil, J. D. (2012). *Streetsmart, school smart: Urban poverty and the education of adolescent boys*. New York, NY: Teachers College Press.

Conover, T. (2000). *Newjack: Guarding Sing Sing*. New York, NY: Knopf.

Coulter, C. A., & Smith, M. L. (2009). The construction zone: Literary elements in narrative research. *Educational Researcher, 38*(8), 577–590.

Cowen Institute for Public Education Initiatives. (2012). *State of public education in New Orleans 2012 Report*. Tulane University. Available at http://www.coweninstitute.com/wp-content/uploads/2012/07/SPENO-20121.pdf

Crenshaw, K. (1989). Demarginalizing the intersection of race and sex: A black feminist critique of antidiscrimination doctrine, feminist theory, and antiracist politics. *University of Chicago Legal Files, 139*, 139–168.

Crenshaw, K. (1995). Mapping the margins: Intersectionality, identity politics, and violence against women of colour. In K. Crenshaw, N. Gotanda, G. Peller, & K.

Thomas (Eds.), *Critical race theory: The key writings that formed the movement* (pp. 357–383). New York, NY: New Press.

Crenshaw, K. (2009). Mapping the margins: Intersectionality, identity politics, and violence against women of color. In E. Taylor, D. Gilborn, & G. Ladson-Billings (Eds.), *Foundations of critical race theory in education.* (pp. 213–258). New York, NY: Routledge.

Crenshaw, K., Gotanda, N., Peller, G., & Thomas, K. (Eds.). (1995). *Critical race theory: The key writings that formed the movement.* New York, NY: New Press.

Dance, L. J. (2008). Black male students and reflections on learning and teaching. In. E. Anderson (Ed.), *Against the wall: Poor, young, Black, and male* (pp. 138–146). Philadelphia: University of Pennsylvania Press.

Darling-Hammond, L. (2006). The flat earth and education: How America's commitment to equity will determine our future. *Educational Researcher, 36*(6), 318–334.

Darling-Hammond, L. (2010). *The flat world and education: How America's commitment to equity will determine our future.* New York, NY: Teachers College Press.

Davis, J. E. (1994). College in black and white: Campus environment and academic achievement of African American males. *Journal of Negro Education, 63*(4), 620–633.

Davis, J. E. (2003). Early schooling and academic achievement of African American males. *Urban Education, 38*(5), 515–537.

Davis, J. E., & Jordan, W. J. (1994). The effects of school context, structure, and experiences on African American males in middle and high school. *Journal of Negro Education, 63*, 570–587.

Davis, P. (1989). Law as microaggression. *Yale Law Journal, 98*, 1559–1577.

DeCuir, J. T., & Dixson, A. D. (2004). So when it comes out, they aren't that surprised that it is there: Using critical race theory as a tool of analysis of race and racism in education. *Educational Researcher, 33*(5), 26–31.

Dee, T. S., & Jacob, B. (2006, April). *Do high school exit exams influence educational attainment or labor market performance?* (NBER Working Paper No. W12199). Available at http://ssrn.com/abstract=900985

Delgado, R. (Ed.). (1995). *Critical race theory: The cutting edge.* Philadelphia, PA: Temple University Press.

Delgado, R. (1999). *When equality ends: Stories about race and resistance.* Boulder, CO: Westview Press.

Delgado, R., & Stefancic, J. (2000). *Critical race theory: The cutting edge* (2nd ed.). Philadelphia, PA: Temple University Press.

Delgado, R., & Stefancic, J. (2001). *Critical race theory. An introduction.* New York, NY: New York University Press.

Delpit, L. (1995). *Other people's children: Cultural conflict in the classroom.* New York, NY: New Press.

Delpit, L. (2012). *Multiplication is for White people: Raising expectations for other people's children.* New York, NY: New Press.

Delpit, L., & Dowdy, J. K. (Eds.). (2002). *The skin that we speak.* New York, NY: New Press.

Denzin, N. (1992). The many faces of emotionality: Reading persona. In C. Ellis & M. G. Flaherty (Eds.), *Investigating subjectivity: Research on lived experience* (pp. 17–30). Newbury Park, CA: Sage.

Dimitriadis, G. (2001). *Performing identity/performing culture: Hip hop as text, pedagogy, and lived practice.* New York, NY: Peter Lang.

Dixson, A. D., & Rousseau, C. K. (2006). *Critical race theory in education.* New York, NY: Routledge.

Dohrmann, G. (2010). *Play their hearts out: A coach, his star recruit, and the youth basketball machine.* New York, NY: Random House.

Donnor, J. K. (2005). Towards an interest-convergence in the education of African-American football student athletes in major college sports. *Race Ethnicity and Education, 8*(1), 45–67.

Du Bois, W.E.B. (1903). *The souls of Black folk.* Chicago, IL: A. C. McClurg. Available at www.bartleby.com/114/

Duncan, G., & Jackson, R. (2004). The language we cry in: Black language practice at a post desegregated urban high school. *GSE Perspectives on Urban Education, 3*(1).

Duncan, G. A. (2002). Beyond love: A critical race ethnography of the schooling of adolescent Black males. *Equity & Excellence in Education, 35*(2), 131–143.

Duncan-Andrade, J. A. (2010). *What a coach can teach a teacher: Lessons Urban Schools Can Learn from a Successful Sports Program.* Washington, DC: Peter Lang.

Duncan-Andrade, J., & Morrell, E. (2008). *The art of critical pedagogy possibilities for moving from theory to practice in urban schools.* Washington, DC: Peter Lang.

Duursma, E., Pan, B. A., & Raikes, H. (2008). Predictors and outcomes of low-income fathers' reading with their toddlers. *Early Childhood Research Quarterly, 23,* 351–365.

Eccles, J. S., Barber, B. L., Stone, M., & Hunt, J. (2003). Extracurricular activities and adolescent development. *Journal of Social Issues, 59*(4), 865–889.

Edwards, H. (1983). The exploitation of Black athletes. *AGB Reports, XX,* 37–46.

Edwards, H. (1998). An end of the golden age of Black participation in sport? *Civil Rights Journal, 3,* 18–24.

Edwards, H. (2000, March/April). Crisis of Black athletes on the eve of the 21st century. *Society, 37*(3), 9–13.

Eide, E. R., & Showalter, M. H. (2001). The effect of grade retention on educational and labor market outcomes. *Economics of Education Review, 20,* 563–576.

Eitle, T., & Eitle, D. (2002). Race, cultural capital, and the educational effects of participation in sports. *Sociology of Education, 75,* 123–146.

Elkins, S. (1968). *Slavery: A problem in American institutions and intellectual life.* Chicago, IL: University of Chicago Press.

Elsner, A. (2004). *Gates of injustice: The crisis in America's prisons.* Upper Saddle River, NJ: Prentice Hall.

Entine, J. (2000). *Taboo: Why Black athletes dominate sports and why we're afraid to talk about it.* New York, NY: Perseus Books.

Escott, P. D (2009). *What shall we do with the Negro: Lincoln, White racism, and Civil War America.* Charlottesville, VA: University of Virginia Press.

Evans-Winters, V. (2005). *Teaching Black girls: Resiliency in urban classrooms.* New York, NY: Peter Lang.

Farber, D., & Sherry, S. (1997). *Beyond all reason: The radical assault on truth in American law.* New York, NY: Oxford University Press.

Fashola, O. S. (2003). Developing the talents of African American male students during the non-school hours. *Urban Education, 38*(4), 398–430.

Fergus, E., & Noguera, P. (2010). *Theories of change among single-sex schools for Black and Latino boys: An intervention in search of theory.* New York, NY: New York University, Metropolitan Center for Urban Education.

Ferguson, A. A. (2003). *Bad boys: Public schools in the making of Black masculinity.* Ann Arbor, MI: University of Michigan Press.

Fine, J. G., & Davis, J. M. (2003). Grade retention and enrollment in post-secondary education. *Journal of School Psychology, 41,* 401–411.

Flennaugh, T. (2011). *Mapping me: A mixed-method approach to understanding academic self-concept among Black males in today's urban schools* (Unpublished dissertation). University of California, Los Angeles.

Flores, G., Tomany-Korman, S. C., & Olson, L. (2005). Does disadvantage start at home? Racial and ethnic disparities in health-related early childhood home routines and safety practices. *Archives of Pediatric Adolescence, 159,* 158–165.

Ford, D. Y. (2011). *Multicultural gifted education: Rationale, models, strategies, and resources* (2nd ed.). Waco, TX: Prufrock Press.

Fordham, S. (1988). Racelessness as a factor in Black students' school success: Pragmatic strategy or pyrrhic victory? *Harvard Educational Review, 58*(1), 54–85

Fordham, S., & Ogbu, J. U. (1986). Black students' school success: Coping with the "burden of 'acting White.'" *The Urban Review, 18,* 178–206.

Foster, M. (1997). *Black teachers on teaching.* New York, NY: New Press.

Foster, M., & Peele, T. B. (1999). Teaching Black males: Lessons from the experts. In V. C. Polite & J.E. Davis (Eds.), *African American males in school and society* (pp. 8–19). New York, NY: Teachers College Press.

Franklin, C. W. (1991). The men's movement and the survival of African American men in the 90's. *Changing Men, 21,* 20–21.

Franklin, J. H. (1995). *The free Negro in North Carolina, 1790–1860.* Chapel Hill, NC: University of North Carolina Press.

Fullilove, M., Fullilove, R., Haynes, K., & Gross, S. (1990). Black women and AIDS prevention: A view towards understanding the gender rules. *The Journal of Sex Research, 27,* 47–64.

Garibaldi, A. M. (1992). Educating and motivating African American males to succeed. *Journal of Negro Education, 61*(1), 12–18.

Gates, H. L. (1997). *Thirteen ways of looking at a Black man.* New York, NY: Random House.

Gay, G. (1994). *At the essence of learning: Multicultural education.* Lafayette, IN: Kappa Delta Pi.

Gay, G. (2010). *Culturally responsive teaching: Theory, research, and practice* (2nd ed.). New York, NY: Teachers College Press.

Gay, G., & Howard, T. C. (2001). Multicultural education for the 21st century. *The Teacher Educator, 36*(1), 1–16.

Gibbs, J. T. (1988). *Young, Black, and male in America.* New York, NY: Auburn House.

Gill, W. (1992). Helping African American males: The cure. *The Negro Educational Review, 63,* 31–36.

Gilmore, A. (1973, January). Jack Johnson and White women: The national impact. *Journal of Negro History,* pp. 18–38.

Gladwell, M. (2000). *The tipping point: How little things can make a big difference.* New York, NY: Little, Brown.

Gladwell, M. (2008). *Outliers.* New York, NY: Little, Brown.

Gonzalez, A. (2009). *NBA gets high marks for diversity in new study.* Available at http://www.nba.com/2009/news/06/10/NBA.diversity.ap/index.html?rss=true

Gordon, B. (2012). "Give a brotha a break!": The experiences and dilemmas of middle-class African American male students in white suburban schools. *Teachers College Record,114*(5) 1–26.

Gordon, E. T., Gordon, E. W., & Gordon-Nembhard, J. G. (1994). Social science literature concerning African American men. *Journal of Negro Education, 63*(4), 508–531.

Gordon, E. W. (1996). *Fostering wholesome development and enabling rehabilitation in African American males* (Tech. Rep.). Kalamazoo, MI: Kellogg Foundation.

Gordon, E. W. (1997). African American males and the second Reconstruction. In *Proceedings of the Kenneth B. Clarke Colloquium Series* (Vol. 2). New York, NY: IRADAC, City University of New York.

Gordon, L. M., & Graham, S. (2006). Attribution theory. In N.J. Salkind (Ed.), *The encyclopedia of human development* (Vol. 1, pp. 142–144). Thousand Oaks, CA: Sage.

Gotanda, N. (1991). A critique of "our constitution is color-blind." *Stanford Law Review, 44,* 1–68.

Gould, S. J. (1981). *The mismeasure of man.* New York, NY: Norton.

Grant, C. A. (2006). Multiculturalism, race, and the public interest: Hanging on to great-great-granddaddy's legacy. In G. Ladson-Billings & W. F. Tate (Eds.), *Education research in the public interest: Social justice, action, and policy* (pp. 158–172). New York, NY: Teachers College Press.

Grant, C. A., & Sleeter, C. E. (1986). Race, class, and gender in education research: An argument for integrative analysis. *Review of Educational Research, 56*(2), 195–211.

Gregory, A., Skiba, R. J., & Noguera, P. A. (2010). The achievement gap and the discipline gap: Two sides of the same coin? *Educational Researcher, 39,* 59–68.

Guinier, L., & Torres, G. (2003). *The miner's canary: Enlisting race, resisting power, transforming democracy.* Cambridge, MA: Harvard University Press.

Gurian, M. (2001). *Boys and girls learn differently! A guide for teachers and parents.* San Francisco, CA: Jossey-Bass.

Gutman, H. G. (1976). *The Black family in slavery and freedom, 1750–1925.* New York, NY: Pantheon Books.

Haberman, M. (1991, December). The pedagogy of poverty versus good teaching. *Phi Delta Kappan,* pp. 290–294.

Hale, L., & Canter, A. (1998). *School dropout prevention: Information and strategies for educators.* Bethesda, MD: National Association of School Psychologists (NASP). Available at http://www.naspcenter.org/adol_sdpe.html

Hall, R. E. (2001). The ball curve: Calculated racism and the stereotype of African American men. *Journal of Black Studies, 32*(1), 104–119.

Hargrove, B. H., & Seay, S. E. (2011). School teacher perceptions of barriers that limit the participation of African American males in public school gifted programs. *Journal for the Education of the Gifted, 34*(3), 434–467.

Harper, S. R. (2012) *Black male student success in higher education: A report from the National Black Male College Achievement Study.* Philadelphia, PA: University of Pennsylvania Center for the Study of Race and Equity in Education. Available at www.works-bepress.com/sharper/43

Harper, S. R., & Davis, C.H.F. (2012, Winter–Spring). They (don't) care about education: A counternarrative on Black male students' responses to inequitable schooling. *Educational Foundations,* pp. 103–120.

Harper, S. R., & Harris, F. (2010). *College men and masculinities: Theory, research, and implications for practice.* San Francisco, CA: Jossey-Bass.

Harper, S. R., & Nichols, A. H. (2008). Are they not all the same? Racial heterogeneity among Black male undergraduates. *Journal of College Student Development, 49*(3), 199–214.

Harris, O. (1994). Race, sport, and social support. *Sociology of Sport Journal, 11,* 40–50.

Harris, P. C. (2012). The sports participation effect on educational attainment of Black males. *Education and Urban Society,* 1–15. doi: 10.1177/0013124512446219

Harrison, C. K. (2000, March/April). Black athletes at the millennium. *Journal of Negro Education, 37*(3), 35–39.

Harrison, C. K. (2007). *There is more to life than sports: Getting brothers to take the road less traveled.* Available at http://diverseeducation.com/article/8143/1.php

Harrison, C. K., & Lawrence, S. M. (2003). African-American student athletes' perception of career transition in sport: A qualitative and visual elicitation. *Race Ethnicity and Education, 6*(4), 373–394.

Harrison, C. K., & Lawrence, S. M. (2004). College students' perceptions, myths, and stereotypes about African American athleticism: A qualitative investigation. *Sport, Education and Society, 9*(1), 33–52.

Harrison, L., Jr. (2001). Understanding the influence of stereotypes: Implications for the African American in sport and physical activity. *Quest, 53,* 97–114.

Harrison, L., Jr., Azzarito, L., & Burden, J., Jr. (2004). Perceptions of athletic superiority: A view from the other side. *Race Ethnicity and Education,7,* 149–166.

Harrison, L., Jr., & Belcher, D. (2006). Race and ethnicity in physical education. In D. Kirk, D. Macdonald, & M. O'Sullivan (Eds.), *The handbook of physical education* (pp. 740–751). Thousand Oaks, CA: Sage.

Harrison, L., Jr., Harrison, C. K., & Moore, L. N. (2002). African American racial identity and sport. *Sport, Education and Society, 7*(2), 121–133.

Harry, B., & Klingner, J. (2006). *Why are so many minority students in special education? Understanding race and disability in schools.* New York, NY: Teachers College Press.

Hartmann, D. (2000). Rethinking the relationships between sport and race in American culture: Golden ghettos and contested terrain. *Sociology of Sport Journal, 17,* 229–253.

Hartmann, D. (2008). *High school participation and educational attainment: Recognizing, assessing, and utilizing the relationship.* Report to the LA84 Foundation. Minneapolis, MN: University of Minnesota.

Hilfiker, D. (2002). *Urban injustice. How ghettoes happen.* New York: Seven Stories Press.

Hill, M. L. (2009). *Beats, rhymes, and classroom life: Hip-hop pedagogy and the politics of identity.* New York, NY: Teachers College Press.

Hoberman, J. (1997). *Darwin's athletes: How sport has damaged Black America and preserved the myth of race.* New York, NY: Houghton Mifflin.

Hoberman, J. (2000, March/April). The price of "Black dominance." *Journal of Negro Education,* pp. 49–56.

Hodge, S. R., Burden, J. W., Robinson, L. E., & Bennett, R. A., III. (2008). Theorizing on the stereotyping of Black male student-athletes: Issues and implications. *Journal for the Study of Sports and Athletes in Education, 2*(2), 203–226.

Hoffman, F. L. (1896). *Race traits and tendencies of the American Negro.* New York, NY: American Economic Association.

Hong, G., & Yu, B. (2007). Early-grade retention and children's reading and math learning in elementary years. *Educational Evaluation and Policy Analysis, 29,* 239–261.

hooks, b. (1990). *Yearning: Race, gender, and cultural politics.* Boston, MA: South End Press.

hooks, b. (2004). *We real cool: Black men and masculinity.* San Francisco, CA: Routledge.

Hopkins, R. (1997). *Educating Black males: Critical lesson in schooling, community, and power.* New York: State University of New York Press.

Horsman, R. (1981). *Race and manifest destiny: Origins of American racial Anglo-Saxonism.* Cambridge, MA: Harvard University Press.

Howard, T. C. (2001). Powerful pedagogy for African American students: Conceptions of culturally relevant pedagogy. *Journal of Urban Education, 36*(2), 179–202.

Howard, T. C. (2008). "Who really cares?" The disenfranchisement of African American males in preK–12 schools: A critical race theory perspective. *Teachers College Record, 110*(5), 954–985.

Howard, T. C. (2010). *Why race and culture matters in schools: Closing the achievement gap in America's classrooms.* New York, NY: Teachers College Press.

Howard, T. C. (2013, March). How does it feel to be a problem? Black male students, schools, and learning in enhancing the knowledge base to disrupt deficit frameworks. *Review of Research in Education, 37*(1), 66–98.

Howard, T. C., Flennaugh, T., & Terry, C. L. (2011). Black males and the disruption of pathological identities: Implications for research and teaching. *Educational Foundations,* pp. 85–102.

Howard, T. C., & Reynolds, R. E. (2012). Examining Black male identity through a raced, classed, and gendered lens: Critical race theory and the intersectionality of the Black male experience. In M. Lynn & A.D. Dixson, (Eds.), *Handbook of research on critical race theory* (pp. 232–259). New York, NY: Routledge Press.

Huber, L. P., Johnson, R. N., & Kohli, R. (2006). Naming racism: A conceptual look at internalized racism in US schools. *Chicano-Latino Review, 26,* 183–206.

Hutchinson, E. O. (1994). *Assassination of the Black male image.* Los Angeles, CA: Middle Passage Press.

Hutchinson, E. O. (1997). *The assassination of the Black male image* (2nd ed): New York, NY: Touchstone.

Hutchinson, E. O. (1999). My gay problem, your Black problem. In D. Constantine-Simms & H. L. Gates (Eds.), *The greatest taboo: Homosexuality in Black communities* (pp. 2–6). Los Angeles, CA: Alyson.

Irvine, J. (1990). *Black students and school failure.* New York, NY: Praeger.

Jackson, J. F. L. (2007). *Strengthening the African American educational pipeline: Informing research, policy, and practice.* New York, NY: State University of New York Press.

Jimerson, S. R. (2001). Meta-analysis of grade retention research: Implications for practice in the 21st century. *School Psychology Review, 30,* 420–437.

Jimerson, S. R., Anderson, G. E., & Whipple, A. D. (2002).Winning the battle and losing the war: Examining the relation between grade retention and dropping out of high school. *Psychology in the Schools,* 39, 441–457.

Jimerson, S. R., & Ferguson, P. (2007). A longitudinal study of grade retention: Academic and behavioral outcomes of retained students through adolescence. *School Psychology Quarterly, 22,* 314–339.

Jordan, W. (1968). *White over Black: American attitudes toward the Negro 1550–1812.* Chapel Hill, NC: University of North Carolina Press.

Kane, M. (1971, January 18). An assessment of "Black is best." *Sports Illustrated,* pp. 72–83.

Kellner, D., & Share, J. (2009). Critical media education and radical democracy. In M.W. Apple, W. Au, & L.A. Gandin (Eds.), *The Routledge international handbook of critical education.* (pp. 281–295). New York, NY: Routledge.

Kelly, R.D.G. (2002). *Freedom dreams: The Black radical imagination.* Boston, MA: Beacon Press.

King, J. E. (1991). Dysconscious racism: Ideology, identity, and the miseducation of teachers. *Journal of Negro Education, 60*(2), 133–146.

Kirkland, D. E. (2013). *A search past silence: The literacy of young Black males.* New York, NY: Teachers College Press.

Kitwana, B. (2002). *The hip hop generation: Young Blacks and the crisis in African American culture.* New York, NY: Basic Civitas Books.

Kleinfeld, J. (1975). Effective teachers of Eskimo and Indian students. *School Review, 83,* 301–344.

Kohl, H. R. (1994). *"I won't learn from you": And other thoughts on creative maladjustment.* New York, NY: The New Press.

Kuhn, T. S. (1970). *The structure of scientific revolution.* (2nd ed.). Chicago, IL: University of Chicago Press.

Kushman, C. (2003). *Fires in the bathroom: Advice for teachers from high school students.* New York, NY: New Press.

Lacy, D. (2008). The most endangered title VII plaintiff: Exponential discrimination against African American males. *Nebraska Law Review, 86*(3), 552.

Ladson-Billings, G. (1994). *The dreamkeepers: Successful teachers of African American children.* San Francisco, CA: Jossey-Bass.

Ladson-Billings, G. (1998). Just what is critical race theory and what's it doing in a nice field like education? *International Journal of Qualitative Studies in Education, 11*(1), 7–24.

Ladson-Billings, G. (2000). Racialized discourses and ethnic epistemologies. In N. Denzin & Y. Lincoln (Eds.), *Handbook of qualitative research* (2nd ed., pp. 257–277). Thousand Oaks, CA: Sage.

Ladson-Billings, G. (2004). New directions in multicultural education: Complexities, boundaries, and critical race theory. In J.A. Banks & C.A.M. Banks (Eds.), *Handbook of research on multicultural education* (2nd ed., pp. 50–65). San Francisco, CA: Jossey-Bass.

Ladson-Billings, G. (2006). From the achievement gap to the education debt: Understanding achievement in U.S. schools. *Educational Researcher, 35*(7), 3–12.

Ladson-Billings, G. (2011). Boyz to men? Teaching to restore Black boys' childhood. *Race Ethnicity and Education, 1,* 7–15.

Ladson-Billings, G., & Tate, W. F. (1995). Toward a critical race theory. *Teachers College Record, 97*(1), 47–68.

Larabee, D. F. (2003). The peculiar problems of preparing educational researchers. *Educational Researcher, 32*(4), 13–22.

Lee, C. D. (1995). Signifying as a scaffold for literary interpretation. *Journal of Black Psychology, 21*(4), 357–381.

Lee, C. D. (2007). *Culture, literacy, and learning: Taking bloom in the midst of the whirlwind.* New York, NY: Teachers College Press.

Lee, P. W. (1999). In their own voices: An ethnographic study of low-achieving students within the context of school reform. *Urban Education, 34*(2), 214–244.

Lee, S. (1996). *Unraveling the "model minority" stereotype: Listening to Asian American youth.* New York, NY: Teachers College Press.

Leonard, D. L., & King, C. R. (2011). *Commodified and criminalized: New racism and African Americans in contemporary sports.* New York, NY: Rowman & Littlefield.

Lesnick, J., Goerge, R., Smithgall, C., & Gwynne, J. (2010). *Reading on third grade level in third grade: How it is related to high school performance and college enrollment?* Chicago, IL: Chapin Hall at the University of Chicago Press.

Lewis, C. W., Butler, B. R., Bonner, F. A., & Jourber, M. (2010, February/March). African American male discipline patterns and school district responses resulting impact on academic achievement: Implications for urban educators and policy makers. *Journal of African American Males in Education, 1*(1), 8–25.

Lopez, A. M. (2003). Collecting and tabulating race/ethnicity data with diverse and mixed heritage populations: A case-study with US high school students. *Ethnic and Racial Studies, 26*(5), 931–961.

Losen, D., & Orfield, G. (Eds.). (2002). *Racial inequity in special education.* Cambridge, MA: Harvard Education Press.

Losen, D. J., & Skiba, R. J. (2010). *Suspended education: Urban middle schools in crisis.* Montgomery, AL: Southern Poverty Law Center.

Lynn, M. (1999). Toward a critical race pedagogy: A research note. *Urban Education, 33*(5), 606–626.

Lynn, M. (2002). Critical race theory and the perspectives of Black men teachers in the Los Angeles public schools. *Equity & Excellence in Education, 35*(2), 87–92.

Lynn, M., Bacon, J. N., Totten, T. L., Bridges, T. L., & Jennings, M. E. (2010). Examining teachers' beliefs about African American male students in a low performing high school in an African American school district. *Teachers College Record, 112*(1), 289–330.

Madhubuti, H. (1990). *Black men: Obsolete, single, dangerous?* Chicago, IL: Third World Press.

Madyun, N., & Lee, M. S. (2010). The influence of female-headed households on Black achievement. *Urban Education, 45*(4), 424–447.

Majors, R., & Billson, J. M. (1992). *Cool pose: The dilemmas of Black manhood in America.* New York, NY: Simon & Schuster.

Malle, B. F. (2004). *How the mind explains behavior: Folk explanations, meaning, and social interaction.* Boston, MA: MIT Press.

Martin, D. B. (2007). Mathematics learning and participation in the African American context: The co-construction of identity in two intersecting realms of experiences. In N.S. Nasir & P. Cobb (Eds.), *Improving access to mathematics* (pp. 146–158). New York, NY: Teachers College Press.

Martin, D. B. (2009). Does race matter? *Teaching Children Mathematics, 16*(3), 134–139.

Massey, D. S., & Denton, N. A. (1993). *American apartheid.* Cambridge, MA: Harvard University Press.

Matsuda, M. (1989). Public response to racist speech: Considering the victim's story. *Michigan Law Review, 87*, 2320–2381.

Matsuda, M. J. (1993). Public response to racist speech: Considering the victim's story. In M. J. Matsuda, C. R. Lawrence III, R. Delgado, & K. Crenshaw. *Words that wound: Critical race theory, assaultive speech, and the first amendment* (pp. 17–52). San Francisco, CA: Westview Press.

Matsuda, M. J., Lawrence, C. R., III, Delgado, R., & Crenshaw, K. (1993). *Words that wound: Critical race theory, assaultive speech, and the first amendment.* San Francisco, CA: Westview Press.

McCall, L. (2005, Spring). The complexity of intersectionality. *urnal of Women in Culture and Society, 30*(3), 1771–1800.

McCready, L. (2004). Understanding the marginalization of gay and gender non-conforming Black male students. *Theory into Practice, 43*(2), 136–143.

McCready, L. T. (2009). Troubles of Black boys in urban schools in the United States: Black feminist and gay men's perspectives. In W. Martino, M. B. Weaver-Hightower, & M. Kehler (Eds.), *The problem with boys' education: Beyond the backlash* (pp. 124–148). New York, NY: Routledge.

McCready, L. T. (2010a). Black queer bodies, Afrocentric reform and masculine anxiety in an African dance program. *International Journal of Critical Pedagogy 3*(1), 52–67.

McCready, L. T. (2010b). *Making space for diverse masculinities: Identity, intersectionality, and engagement in an urban high school.* New York, NY: Peter Lang.

McKown, C., & Weinstein, R. S. (2008). Teacher expectations, classroom context, and the achievement gap. *Journal of School Psychology, 46*(3), 235–261.

McLaren, P. (1994). White terror and oppositional agency: Towards a critical multiculturalism. In D. T. Goldberg (Ed.), *Multiculturalism: A critical reader* (pp. 45–74). Cambridge, MA: Blackwell.

McLaren, P. (2006). *Rage + hope.* New York, NY: Peter Lang.

McWhorter, J. H. (2000, Summer). Explaining the Black education gap. *The Wilson Quarterly, 24*(3), 72–92.

Melnick, M., Sabo, D., & Vanfossen, B. (1992). Educational effects of interscholastic athletic participation on African American and Hispanic youth. *Adolescence, 27,* 295–308.

Merriam, S. B. (1998). *Qualitative research and case study application in education.* San Francisco, CA: Jossey-Bass.

Metzler, C. J. (2008). *The construction and rearticulation of race in a post racial America.* Bloomington, IN: Authorhouse.

Mickelson, R. A. (1990). The attitude–achievement paradox among Black adolescents. *Sociology of Education. 63*(1), 44–61.

Miller, P. B. (1998). The anatomy of scientific racism: Racialist responses to Black athletic achievement. *Journal of Sport History, 25*(1), 119–151.

Milner, H. R. (2007a). African American males in urban schools: No excuses–teach and empower. *Theory into Practice 46*(3), 239–246.

Milner, H. R. (2007b). Race, culture, and researcher positionality: Working through dangers seen, unseen, and unforeseen. *Educational Researcher, 36*(7), 388–400.

Milner, H. R. (2008). Disrupting deficit notions of difference: Counter-narratives of teachers and community in urban education. *Teaching and Teacher Education 24*(6), 1573–1598.

Milner, H. R. (2010). *Start where you are, but don't stay there.* Cambridge, MA: Harvard Education Press.

Milner, H. R. (2013). A talk to teachers about Black male students. In M. C. Brown, T. E. Dancy, & J. E. Davis (Eds.), *Educating African American males: Contexts for consideration, possibilities for practice* (pp. 67–85). New York, NY: Peter Lang.

Mincy, H. R. (2006). *Black males left behind.* Washington, DC: Urban Institute.

Moll, L. (1996). Educating Latino students. *Language Arts, 64,* 315–324.

Morgan, P. D. (1998). *Slave counterpoint: Black culture in the eighteenth-century Chesapeake and lowcountry* (published for the Omohundro Institute of Early American History and Culture, Williamsburg, VA). Chapel Hill, NC: University of North Carolina Press.

Muhammad, K. G. (2010). *The condemnation of Blackness: Race, crime, and the making of modern urban America.* Cambridge, MA: Harvard University Press.

Murphy S. L., Xu, J. Q., & Kochanek, K. D. (2012). Deaths: Preliminary data for 2010. *National vital statistics reports* (Vol. 60, no. 4). Hyattsville, MD: National Center for Health Statistics.

Murrell, P. (1999). Responsive teaching for African American male adolescents. In V. C. Polite & J. E. Davis (Eds.), *African American males in school and society: Practices and policies for effective education* (pp. 82–96). New York, NY: Teachers College Press.

Myrdal, G. (1944). *The American dilemma: The Negro problem and modern democracy.* London, UK: Harper & Brothers.

Nagin, D. S., Pagani, L., Tremblay, R. E., & Vitaro, F. (2003). Life course turning points: The effect of grade retention on physical aggression. *Development and Psychopathology, 15,* 343–361.

Nasir, N. S. (2002). Identity, goals, and learning: Mathematics in cultural practice. *Mathematical Thinking and Learning, 4*(2 & 3), 213–247.

Nasir, N. S. (2012). *Racialized identities: Race and achievement among African American youth.* Redwood City, CA: Stanford University Press.

Nasir, N., McLaughlin, M., & Jones, A. (2009). What does it mean to be African American? Constructions of race and academic identity in an urban public high school. *American Educational Research Journal, 46*(1), 73–114.

National Center for Education Statistics. (2009). *Latino achievement in America.* Prepared by the Education Trust. Available at http://nces.ed.gov/nationsreportcard/nde

Noddings, N. (1999). *Justice and caring: The search for common ground in education.* New York, NY: Teachers College Press.

Noguera, P. (1996). Responding to the crisis of Black youth: Providing support without further marginalization. *Journal of Negro Education, 65*(1), 37–60.

Noguera, P. (2001). The role and influence of environmental and cultural factors on the academic performance of African American males. *In Motion Magazine.* Available at http://www.inmotionmagazine.com

Noguera, P. (2003). The trouble with Black boys: The role and influence of environmental and cultural factors on the academic performance of African American males. *Urban Education, 38*(4), 431–459.

Noguera, P. (2008). *The trouble with Black boys . . . and other reflections on race, equity, and the future of public education.* San Francisco, CA: Jossey-Bass.

Office for Civil Rights. (2000). *Elementary and secondary school civil rights compliance report.* Washington, DC: U.S. Department of Education.

Ogbu, J. (1987a). Opportunity structure, cultural boundaries, and literacy. In J. Langer (Ed.), *Language, literacy, and culture: Issues of society and schooling* (pp.149–177). Norwood, NJ: Ablex Press.

Ogbu, J. (1987b). Variability in minority school performance: A problem in search of an explanation. *Anthropology and Education Quarterly, 18*(4), 312–334.

Ogbu, J. (2003). *Black American students in an affluent suburb: A study of academic disengagement.* Mahwah, NJ: Erlbaum.

Oliver, W. (2006). "The streets": An alternative Black male socialization institution. *Journal of Black Studies, 36,* 918–938.

Omi, M., & Winant, H. (1994). *Racial formation in the United States: From the 1960s to the 1990s.* New York, NY: Routledge.

Orfield, G. (2004). *Dropouts in America.* Cambridge, MA: Harvard University Press.

Osborne, J. (1997). Race and academic misidentification. *Journal of Educational Psychology, 89*(4), 728–735.

Ou, S., & Reynolds, A. J. (2010). Grade retention, postsecondary education, and public aid receipt. *Educational Evaluation and Policy Analysis, 32*(1), 118–139.

Ou, S., & Reynolds, A. J. (2013). Timing for first childbirth and young women's postsecondary education in an inner-city minority cohort. *Urban Education, 48*(2), 289–313.

Page, T. N. (1904). *The Negro: The southerners' problem.* New York, NY: Scribner.

Pang, V. O., & Cheng, L. L. (1998). *Struggling to be heard: The unmet needs of Asian Pacific American children.* Albany, NY: State University of New York Press.

Parker, L. (1998). Race is . . . race ain't: An exploration of the utility of critical race theory in qualitative research in education. *International Journal of Qualitative Studies in Education, 11*(1), 7–24.

Parker, L., Deyhle, D., & Villenas, D. (Eds.). (1999). *Race is . . . race isn't: Critical race theory and qualitative studies in education.* Boulder, CO: Westview Press.

Parker, L., & Lynn, M. (2002). What's race got to do with it? Critical race theory's conflicts with and connections to qualitative research methodology and epistemology. *Qualitative Inquiry, 8*(1), 7–22.

Patterson, O. (1967). *The sociology of slavery.* London, UK: Granada.

Patterson, O. (1995). The crisis of gender relations among African-Americans. In A. Hill & E. C. Coleman (Eds.), *Race, gender, and power in America: The legacy of the Hill–Thomas Hearings* (pp. 56–104). New York, NY: Oxford University Press.

Paul, D. G. (2003). *Talkin' back: Raising and educating resilient Black girls.* Westport, CT: Praeger.

Petit, B. (2012). *Invisible men: Mass incarceration and the myth of Black progress.* New York, NY: Russell Sage Foundation.

Pew Research Center. (2013). Social networking use. Available at http://www.pewresearch.org/data-trend/media-and-technology/social-networking-use/

Pew Research Center's Internet & American Life Project. (2012). The demographics of social media users. Available at http://pewinternet.org/Reports/2013/Social-media-users.aspx

Phillips, U. (1918). *American Negro slavery*. Baton Rouge, LA: Louisiana State University Press.

Pickett, W. P. (1969). *The Negro problem: Abraham Lincoln's solution*. New York, NY: Negro Universities Press.

Pierce, C. (1974). Psychiatric problems of the Black minority. In S. Arieti (Ed.), *American handbook of psychiatry* (pp. 512–523). New York, NY: Basic Books.

Pierre, R. E., & Jeter, J. (2009). *A day late and a dollar short: High hopes and deferred dreams in Obama's "Post-Racial" America*. Hoboken, NJ: Wiley.

Polite, V. C. (1993a). African American males and academic failure. *Secondary Education Today, 35*(2), 32–49.

Polite, V. C. (1993b). If only we knew then what we know now: Foiled opportunities to learn in surburbia. *Journal of Negro Education, 62,* 337–354.

Polite, V. C. (1994). The method in the madness: African American males, avoidance, schooling, and chaos theory. *Journal of Negro Education, 60*(30), 345–359.

Polite, V. C., & Davis, J. E. (1999). *African American males in school and society: Practices and policies for effective education*. New York, NY: Teachers College Press.

Posner, R. A. (1997). Narrative and narratology in classroom and courtroom. *Philosophy and Literature, 21*(2), 292–305.

Poussaint, A. F., & Alexander, A. (2000). *Lay my burden down: Suicide and the mental health crisis among African Americans*. Boston, MA: Beacon Press.

Powell, S. (2008). *Souled out? How Blacks are winning and losing in sports*. Champaign, IL: Human Kinetics.

Price, J. N. (2000). *Against the odds: The meaning of school and relationships in the lives of six African American men*. Stamford, CT: Ablex.

Purdie-Vaughns, V., & Eibach, R. P. (2008). Intersectional invisibility: The distinctive advantages and disadvantages of multiple subordinate-group identities. *Sex Roles*. doi: 10.1007/s11199-008-9424-4

Reynolds, R. (2010, April/May). "They think you're lazy," and other messages Black parents send their Black sons: An exploration of critical race theory in the examination of educational outcomes for Black males. *Journal of African American Males in Education, 1*(2), 143–165.

Rhoden, W. (2006). *Forty million dollar slaves: The rise, fall, and redemption of the Black slave*. New York, NY: Random House.

Riess, S. (1980). Sport and the American dream: A review essay. *Journal of Social History, 14,* 295–303.

Riley, B. F. (1910). *The White man's burden: A discussion of the interracial question with special reference to the responsibility of the White race to the Negro problem*. Birmingham, AL: Kessinger Publisher.

Rios, V. (2011). *Punished: Policing the lives of Black and Latino boys.* New York, NY: New York University Press.

Rist, R. (1970). Student social class and teacher expectations: The self-fulfilling prophecy in ghetto education. *Harvard Educational Review, 40*(3), 411–451.

Rogoff, B. (1990). *Apprenticeship in thinking.* New York, NY: Oxford University Press.

Ronfeldt, M., Loeb, S., & Wyckoff, J. (2013). How teacher turnover harms student achievement. *American Educational Research Journal, 50*(1), 4–36.

Rong, X. L. (1996). Effects of race and gender on teachers' perceptions of the social behavior of elementary students. *Urban Education, 31*(3), 261–290.

Rose, M. (2012). *Back to school: Why everyone deserves a second chance at education.* New York, NY: New Press.

Rosen, J. (1996, December 9). The bloods and the crits. *The New Republic,* p. 27.

Rosenthal, R., & Jacobson, L. (1968). *Pygmalion effect in the classroom: Teacher expectations and pupils' intellectual development.* New York, NY: Holt, Rinehart & Winston.

Rumberger, R.W. & Larson, K.A. (1998). Student mobility and the increased risk of high school drop out. *American Journal of Education, 107,* 1–35.

Russell-Brown, K. (1998). *The color of crime: Racial hoaxes, White fear, Black protectionism, police harassment and other macroaggressions.* New York, NY: New York University Press.

Ryan, J. P., Testa, M. F., & Zhai, F. (2008). African American males in foster care and the risk of delinquency: The value of social bonds and permanence. *Child Welfare, 87,* 115–140.

Ryan, W. (1976). *Blaming the victim.* New York, NY: Vintage Books.

Sabo, D., Melnick, M., & Vanfossen, B. (1993). High school athletic participation and post-secondary educational and occupational mobility: A focus on race and gender. *Sociology of Sport Journal, 10,* 44–56.

Sailes, G. A. (1991). The myth of Black sports supremacy. *Journal of Black Studies, 21*(4), 480–487.

Sailes, G. A. (1993). An investigation of campus stereotypes: The myth of Black athletic superiority and the dumb jock stereotype. *Sociology of Sport Journal, 10,* 88–97.

Sailes, G. A. (1996). A comparison of professional sports career aspirations among college athletes. *Academic Athletic Journal, 11,* 20–28.

Sailes, G. A. (1998). The African-American athlete: Social myths and stereotypes. In G. A. Sailes (Ed.), *African-Americans in sport: Contemporary themes* (pp. 183–198). New Brunswick, NJ: Transaction.

Sammons, J. (1988). *Beyond the big ring: The role of boxing in American society.* Urbana, IL: University Illinois Press.

Scheurich, J. J., & Young, M. D. (1997). Coloring epistemologies: Are our research epistemologies racially biased? *Educational Researcher, 26*(4), 4–16.

Schott Foundation for Public Education. (2006). *Public education and Black male students: The 2006 state report card.* Cambridge, MA: Author. Available at http://www.schott-foundation.org

Schott Foundation for Public Education. (2010). *Yes we can: The Schott 50 state report on public education and Black males.* Cambridge, MA: Author.

Schott Foundation for Public Education. (2012). *The urgency of now: Schott 50 state report on public education and Black males.* Available at www.blackboysreport.org

Selden, S. (1999). *Inheriting shame: The story of eugenics and racism in America.* New York, NY: Teachers College Press.

Shaler, N. S. (1884). The Negro problem. *Atlantic Monthly, 54,* 696–709.

Silberglitt, B., Appleton, J. J., Burns, M. K., & Jimerson, S. R. (2006). Examining the effects of grade retention on student reading performance: A longitudinal study. *Journal of School Psychology, 44,* 255–270.

Skelton, C. (2001). *Schooling the boys: Masculinities and primary education.* Buckingham, UK: Open University Press.

Skiba, R. J., & Noam, G. (2001). *Zero tolerance: Can suspensions and expulsions keep schools safe?* San Francisco, CA: Jossey-Bass.

Skiba, R. J., Simmons, A. B., Ritter, S., Gibbs, A. C., Rausch, M. K., Cuadrado, J., & Chung, C. G. (2008). Achieving equity in special education: History, status, and current challenges. *Exceptional Children, 74,* 264–288.

Skiba, R. J., Simmons, A., Staudinger, L., Rausch, M., Dow, G., & Feggins, R. (2003, May). *Consistent removal: Contributions of school discipline to the school–prison pipeline.* Paper presented at the School to Prison Pipeline Conference, Boston, MA.

Sleeter, C. E., & Delgado Bernal, D. (2004). Critical pedagogy, critical race theory, and antiracist education: Implications for multicultural education. In J. A. Banks & C.A.M. Banks (Eds.), *Handbook of research on multicultural education* (2nd ed., pp. 240–258). San Francisco, CA: Jossey-Bass.

Smith, W. A. (2010). Toward an understanding of Black misandric microaggressions and racial battle fatigue in historically White institutions. In V.C. Polite (Ed.), *The state of the African American male in Michigan: A courageous conversation* (pp. 265–277). East Lansing: Michigan State University Press.

Smith, W. A., Hung, M., & Franklin, J. D. (2011). Racial battle fatigue and the miseducation of Black men: Racial microaggression, societal problems, and environmental stress. *The Journal of Negro Education, 80*(1), 63–82.

Smith, W. A., Allen, W. R., & Dantley, L. L. (2007). "Assume the position . . . you fit the description": Psychosocial experiences and racial battle fatigue among African American male college students. *American Behavioral Scientist, 51,* 551–578.

Smith-Maddox, R., & Solorzano, D. G. (2002). Using critical race theory, Paulo Freire's problem-posing method, and case study research to confront race and racism in education. *Qualitative Inquiry, 8*(1), 66–84.

Solorzano, D. G. (1998). Critical race theory, race and gender microaggressions, and the experience of Chicana and Chicano scholars. *International Journal of Qualitative Studies in Education, 11*(1), 121–136.

Solorzano, D., Allen, W., & Carroll, G. (2002). Keeping race in place: A case study of racial microaggressions and campus racial climate at the University of California, Berkeley. *UCLA Chicano/Latino Law Review, 23,* 15–111.

Solorzano, D., & Delgado Bernal, D. (2001). Examining transformational resistance through a critical race and LatCrit theory framework: Chicana and Chicano students in an urban context. *Urban Education, 36*(3), 308–342.

Solorzano, D., & Yosso, T. (2001). Critical race and LatCrit theory and method: Counterstorytelling, Chicana and Chicano graduate school experiences. *International Journal of Qualitative Studies in Education, 14*(4), 471–495.

Solorzano, D., & Yosso, T. (2002). Critical race methodology: Counterstorytelling as an analytical framework for educational research. *Qualitative Inquiry, 8*(1), 23–44.

Spence, C. (2000). *The skin I'm in: Racism, sports, and education.* Nova Scotia, Canada: Fernwood.

Spigner, C. (1993). African American student-athletes: Academic support of institutionalized racism? *Education, 114*(1), 144–150.

Stanfield, J. (1993). *A history of race relations research: First-generation recollections.* Newbury Park, CA: Sage.

Staples, R. (1978), Masculinity and race: The dual dilemma of Black men. *Journal of Social Issues, 34,* 169–183.

Staples, R. (1982). *Black masculinity: The Black man's role in American society.* Washington, DC: Black Scholar Press.

Steele, C. M. (1992, April). Race and the schooling of Black Americans. *Atlantic Monthly, 269,* 68–78.

Stinson, D. W. (2010). When the "burden of acting White" is not a burden: School success and African American male students. *Urban Review, 43,* 43–65.

Stovall, D. O. (2013). Fightin' the devil 24/7: Context, community and critical race praxis in education. In M. Lynn & A. D. Dixson (Eds.), *Handbook of critical race theory in education* (pp. 289–301). New York, NY: Routledge.

Swanson, D. P., Cunningham, M., & Spencer, M. B. (2003). Black males' structural conditions, achievement patterns, normative needs, and "opportunities.". *Urban Education, 38*(5), 608–633.

Tate, W. F. (2006). In the public interest. In G. Ladson-Billings & W. F. Tate (Eds.), *Education research in the public interest: Social justice, action, and policy* (pp. 247–260). New York, NY: Teachers College Press.

Tatum, B. (1997). *"Why are all the Black kids sitting together in the cafeteria?" And other conversations about race.* New York, NY: Basic Books.

Taylor, E. (1999, April). Bring in "da noise": Race, sports, and the role of schools. *Educational Leadership, 56*(7), 75–78.

Terry, C. L. (2010). Prisons, pipelines, and the president: Developing critical math literacy through participatory action research. *Journal of African American Males in Education, 1*(2), 1–33.

Terry, C. L., Flennaugh, T. K., Blackmon, S., & Howard, T. C. (in press). Does the "Negro" *still* need separate schools? Single-sex educational settings as critical race counterspaces. *Urban Education.*

Terry, C. L., & Howard, T. C. (2013). The power of counterstories: The complexity of Black male experiences in pursuit of academic success. In J.A. Donnor & A.D. Dixson (Eds.), *The resegregation of schools: Education and race in the 21st century* (pp. 44–62). New York, NY: Routledge.

Tillman, L. C. (2002). Culturally sensitive research approaches: An African American perspective. *Educational Researcher, 31*(9), 3–12.

Toldson, I. A. (2008). *Breaking barriers: Plotting the path to academic success for school age African American males.* Washington, DC: Congressional Black Caucus Foundation.

Truman, J. L., & Rand, M. R. (2010, October). *Criminal victimization* (2009 Bureau of Justice Statistics Bulletin, NCJ231327).

Tucker, L. G. (2007). *Lockstep and dance: Images of Black men in popular culture.* Oxford: University of Mississippi Press.

U.S. Census Bureau. (2011). CPS 2011 annual social and economic supplement. Available at http://www.census.gov/cps/data/cpstablecreator.html

U.S. Department of Commerce, Census Bureau, American Community Survey. (2009). *Bureau of Justice Statistics, Prison inmates at midyear,* Current Population Survey, 2009.

U.S. Department of Education, Institute of Education Sciences, National Center for Education Statistics. (2009). *National Assessment of Educational Progress (NAEP) and mathematics.* Washington, DC: U.S. Government Printing Office.

U.S. Department of Education, National Center for Education Statistics. (1998). *Digest of Education Statistics.* Washington, DC: National Center for Education Statistics.

U.S. Department of Education, National Center for Education Statistics. (2000). *Digest of Education Statistics.* Washington, DC: National Center for Education Statistics. Available at http://nces.ed.gov/nationsreportcard/nrc/reading_math_2005/s0011.asp?subtab_id=Tab_2 &tab_id=tab1&printver=Y

U.S. Department of Education, National Center for Education Statistics. (2010). Early childhood longitudinal study. Birth cohort, longitudinal 9 month–preschool. In S. Aud, M. Fox, & A. KewalRamani (Eds.), *Status and trends in the education of racial and ethnic groups.* Washington, DC: U.S. Government Printing Office.

U.S. Department of Education, National Center for Education Statistics. (2011). *Digest of Education Statistics, 2010* (NCES 2011-015), Chapter 1, College Board 8th annual AP report to the nation. Available at http://apreport.collegeboard.org/

U.S. Department of Education. National Center for Education Statistics. (2012a). Reading proficiency scores. *Table E-17-1. Percentage distribution of students at National Assessment of Education Progress reading achievement levels by grade, sex, race/ethnicity: Various years, 2005–2011.* Available at http://nces.ed.gov/pubs2012/2012046/tables/e-17-1.asp

U.S. Department of Education. National Center for Education Statistics. (2012b). Math proficiency scores. *Table E-18-1. Percentage distribution of students at National Assessment of Education Progress mathematics achievement levels by grade, sex, race/ethnicity: Various years, 2005–2011.* Available at http://nces.ed.gov/pubs2012/2012046/tables/e-18-1.asp

U.S. Department of Education. National Center for Education Statistics. (2012c). *Table E-5-1. Percentage of students receiving special education services in 9th grade, by race/ethnicity and sex.* Available at http://nces.ed.gov/pubs2012/2012046/tables/e-5-1.asp

U.S. Department of Education. National Center for Education Statistics. (2012d). Table E-24-2. Average SAT scores for students who took the SAT during high school, by subject, sex, and race/ethnicity: Selected years, 2008–2011 Available at http://nces.ed.gov/pubs2012/2012046/tables/e-24-2.asp

U.S. Department of Education, National Center for Education Statistics. (2012e). *Parent and Family Involvement in Education Survey of the 2012 National Household Education Surveys Program* (PFI-NHES:2012).

U.S. Department of Justice. (2009). Office of justice programs. Available at www.ojp.usdoj.gov/bjs on November 25, 2009.

U.S. Department of Labor. Bureau of Labor Statistics. (2010). *Highlights of Women's Earnings in 2009* Report 1025. Available at http://www.bls.gov/cps/cpswom2009.pdf

Ullucci, K., & Beatty, D. (2011). Exposing color blindness/grounding color consciousness: Challenges for teacher education. *Urban Education, 46*(6), 1195–1225.

Valencia, R. R. (1997). *The evolution of deficit thinking: Educational thought and practice.* San Francisco, CA: Routledge Falmer Press.

Valenzuela, A. (1999). *Subtractive schooling: U.S.-Mexican youth and the politics of caring.* Albany: State University of New York Press.

Ward, J. (1990). Racial identity formation and transformation. In C. Gilligan, N. Lyons, & T. Hanmer (Eds.), *Making connections: The relational worlds and adolescent girls at Emma Willard School* (pp. 215 –232). Cambridge, MA: Harvard University Press.

Washington, H. A. (2006). *Medical apartheid: The dark history of medical experimentation on Black Americans from colonial times to the present.* New York, NY: Random House.

Watkins, B. (2013). How sports marginalizes Black men from society. Available at http://newsone.com/875945/dr-boyce-how-sports-marginalizes-black-men-from-society/Dr.Boyce

Watts, I. E., & Erevelles, N. (2004). These deadly times: Reconceptualizing school violence by using critical race theory and disability studies. *American Educational Research Journal, 41*(2), 271–299.

Waxman, H. C., & Huang, S. (1997). Classroom instruction and learning environment differences between effective and ineffective urban elementary schools for African American students. *Urban Education, 32*(4), 7–44.

Weatherspoon, F. (2007). *Black male student-athletes owe themselves, forefathers more.* Available at http://diverseeducation.com/article/6912/black-male-studentathletes-owe-themselves-forefathers-more.html

Weaver-Hightower, M. (2003, Winter). The "boy turn" in research on gender and education. *Review of Educational Research, 73*(4), 471–498.

Weiner, B. (1992). *Human motivation: Metaphors, theories and research.* Newbury Park, CA: Sage.

West, C. (2004). *Democracy matters: Winning the fight against imperialism.* London, England: Penguin Books.

West, C. (2009). *Brother West: Living & loving out loud.* New York, NY: Smiley Books.

West, J., Denton, K., & Germino Hausken, E. (2000). *America's kindergartners* (NCES 2000-070). Washington, DC: National Center for Education Statistics.

West, J., Denton, K., & Reaney, L. (2001). *The kindergarten year* (NCES 2001-023). Washington, DC: National Center for Education Statistics.

White, J. L., & Cones, J. H., III. (1999). *Black man emerging: Facing the past and seizing a future in America.* New York, NY: Freeman.

Wiggins, D. K. (1989). "Great speed but little stamina": The historical debate over Black athletic superiority. *Journal of Sport History, 16*(2), 158–185.

Wilson, W. J. (1978). *The declining significance of race.* Chicago, IL: University of Chicago Press.

Wilson, W. J. (1987). *The truly disadvantaged.* Chicago, IL: University of Chicago Press.

Wilson, W. J. (2008). *More than just race: Being Black and poor in the inner city.* New York, NY: Norton & Simon.

Winbush, R. A. (1987). The furious passage of the African American intercollegiate athlete. *Journal of Sport and Social Issues, 11,* 97–103.

Winn, M. T. (2011). *Girl time: Literacy, justice, and the school-to-prison pipeline.* New York, NY: Teachers College Press.

Wood, D., Kaplan, R., & McLoyd, V. C. (2007). Gender differences in the educational expectation of urban, low-income African American youth: The role of parents and the school. *Journal of Youth and Adolescence, 36,* 417–427.

Yates, J. R. (1998, April). *The state of practices in the education of CLD students.* Paper presented at the annual meeting of the Council for Exceptional Children, Minneapolis, MN.

Yep, G. A. (2003). The violence of heteronormativity in communication studies: Notes on injury, healing, and queer world-making. *Queer Theory and Communication, 45*(2/3/4), 11.

Yosso. T. (2005). Whose culture has capital? A critical race theory discussion of community cultural wealth. *Race Ethnicity and Education, 8*(1), 69–91.

Zeiser, K. L. (2011). Examining racial differences in the effect of popular sports participation on academic achievement. *Social Science Research, 40,* 1142–1169.

Index

Note: Page numbers followed by *f* indicate a figure.

About the Author

Tyrone C. Howard is a professor of education at UCLA in the Urban Schooling Division of the Graduate School of Education and Information Studies. He is also the director of Center X, a consortium of urban school professionals working toward social justice and educational equity in transforming Los Angeles schools. In addition, he is the director and founder of the Black Male Institute at UCLA, an interdisciplinary cadre of scholars, practitioners, community members, and policymakers dedicated to improving the educational experiences and life chances of Black males. Professor Howard's research is concerned primarily with academic achievement of youth in urban schools. His work has centered on the achievement gap facing African American and other culturally diverse students, and the importance of providing teachers the skills and knowledge to assist them in reversing persistent underachievement. Before entering higher education, Dr. Howard was a classroom teacher in the Compton Unified School District. A native of Compton, California, Dr. Howard is one of the foremost experts on race, culture, teaching, and learning in urban schools. His book *Race, Culture, and the Achievement Gap* is a Teachers College Press bestseller that examines the roles that race and culture play in educational outcomes. Professor Howard has been a frequent contributor on National Public Radio and is also a contributor to *The New York Times* Educational Issues Forum. Dr. Howard has published more than 50 peer review journal articles, book chapters, and technical reports. In 2007 he was awarded an Early Career Award by the American Educational Research Association.

5/24